# THE NEW MARKETING

# The New Marketing

**Richard Brookes**

Gower

Published by
Gower Publishing Company Limited,
Gower House,
Croft Road,
Aldershot,
Hants GU11 3HR,
England

**British Library Cataloguing in Publication Data**
Brookes, Richard
  The new marketing
  1. Marketing
  I. Title
  658.8      HF5415

ISBN-0-566-02677-5

Printed and bound in Great Britain by
Anchor Brendon Ltd, Tiptree, Essex

# Contents

# Preface

So.ne time in the early 1980s the practice of marketing, in America especially, began to change. The change is still going on; in fact it has spread to other countries, especially in the UK and the rest of Europe. This has been no cohesive, concerted movement across the spectrum of companies that make up America's industrial base. Rather, individual firms of all sizes, and from a variety of industries, have been in the vanguard. What united them was the realization that past – and hitherto successful – marketing practices were no longer sufficient. Simply, they were no longer working as expected. A new way of marketing, of competing even, had to be found. To a large extent, it became a do-it-yourself approach. There were no textbooks to provide guidance and there were few experts to propose immediate solutions. Instead, companies began by developing their own rules, as they struggled with the demands and constraints of the time: the deregulation of many industries; intense competition from all sides; an on-rush of new product and production technologies; the need for innovative R & D approaches; the importance of flexible manufacturing; the growing power of retail groups; the splintering of mass markets and mass media; the necessity for improved customer servicing; and the realization that grand strategic designs were failing for the lack of committed tactical support.

It has taken some time for American companies to recover their initiative, but recovering it they are. They are now coming on – leaner, stronger, and faster than ever before. They are being led by a new breed of top executives: smart, well-trained, and tough. These executives are also very realistic – they know that their personal success is determined by what they contribute to their company's trading success. There are few spear carriers in the corporate armies of America today.

In their efforts to establish modern marketing methods these companies have fundamentally altered the traditional processes involved in moving goods and services from producer to consumer. This book attempts to synthesize the various ways in which this new marketing is being applied by a host of companies that reads like a Who's Who: Apple, IBM, Chrysler, Ford, General Motors, Coca-Cola, Pepsi-Cola, McDonald's, Campbell Soup, Procter and Gamble. There are many other companies that could be added to this list, and some of them are mentioned in the book. However, these are the firms that dominate the pages of the business press, and they are the principal examples I have used. They also reflect my own working background and research interests.

The organizations examined in the following pages are not necessarily being held up as examples of how the new marketing is best practised. Some of them (like General Motors, for instance) are struggling with their new-found practices, and if it is difficult to identify all the rules of this new marketing, it is virtually impossible to predict their outcomes as well.

I have found this a challenging book to write. It has also been frustrating, in the same way that it is both challenging and frustrating to take a snapshot of a rapidly passing object. Even as the photograph is taken the object has moved on, and when the print has finally been developed and viewed, the object is no longer quite as it originally appeared to be.

Despite these problems and limitations, I have attempted to describe the main features of this new marketing, to examine the actions of some of the companies who are both caught up in, and contributing to, the events that are shaping this new era, and to suggest some of the changes to traditional marketing practices that are necessary if other firms are to survive in it.

There are no quick-fix solutions on offer in this book, no shiny new concepts to be quickly grasped and put into practice. Rather, I am proposing that every firm needs to re-evaluate and rework almost every element in the four main processes to do with moving goods and services from producer to consumer – *innovation* and *R & D*; *production* and *operations*; *trade marketing*; and *consumer marketing* – if they are to achieve leveraging advantages. 'Leveraging' is not a new buzzword; as will be shown, it has been used in several ways in the past. What is new is that the companies examined in this book, whether they know the term or not, are seeking new leveraging advantages and in doing so they are rewriting the rules of marketing.

This book has been written for two main audiences. Firstly, the busy executive grappling with the problems of today's high-speed markets. While this book assumes that the reader has some grasp of the fundamentals of marketing, it has not been written exclusively for marketing and planning executives hoping to find some new insights. Those of you who are in production or technical operations, in particular, should find it both worthwhile and encouraging. Never before has marketing so needed your ideas, your expertise, and your willingness to create change. Secondly, it has been written for the senior marketing student who is trying to make sense of the complexities and confusion out there in the marketplace. This is not a textbook for you, but it will challenge many of the assumptions to be found in the textbooks currently being prescribed to you. The marketing described in these texts is not the marketing that you will shortly encounter in the 'real world' of the late 1980s.

This book was written over a period of some two years. During that time the many suggestions and other forms of encouragement received, both directly and indirectly, from the following are gratefully acknowledged: Professors David Cullwick and Ron Stiff, and Bob Bilton. The support of Malcolm Stern of Gower Publishing is also recognized. Without it, this book would still be a collection of ideas whizzing around inside my head. Finally, this book is dedicated to: Colin James, for his initial impetus; my wife, Susan, for her continued understanding; and my personal computer, for just about everything else.

Richard Brookes

# 1     Breaking with the past

The classical approach to marketing, as taught for so many years by leading academics, such as Philip Kotler, and successfully practised by marketing-oriented giants, such as Procter & Gamble, now appears to be coming to an end. We are entering a new era in marketing.

The chief evidence for this claim is that so many leading corporations in the United States, in particular, have recently revised at least one key aspect of their traditional approach to the marketing of their goods or services. In many instances they have totally abandoned practices which worked perfectly well only a few years ago.

Incidents which initially appeared to be isolated, when viewed collectively and cumulatively, indicate that some time during the early 1980s a fundamental shift in the approach to marketing began to take place in the US. The adoption of this new approach is not the result of a new general theory promulgated by academics or promoted by consultants. Rather, it appears to be happening as the result of a series of quite separate decisions made by executives in many firms in a variety of industries. For example, how many readers would have suggested that any of the following news items concerning some of the largest US corporations, as reported at various times over the past few years, may have been harbingers of a new trend?:

- *General Electric Corporation*, a pioneer in strategic planning, with a portfolio model that has been memorized by every MBA student, not so long ago cut from 58 to 33 the number of strategic planning positions at the corporate level, and drastically slashed the number of planners in its operating sections, even though the US economy had entered a new expansionary phase. In a 1984 cover story on strategic planning *Business Week* remarked: 'After more than a decade of near dictatorial sway over the future of US corporations, the reign of the strategic planner may be at an end.'

- *General Motors Corporation*, which dominates the United States automobile industry, began in 1984 the most radical internal corporate restructuring since Alfred Sloan controlled the company back in the 1920s, and first introduced the GM segmentation strategy based on its five competing car divisions: Chevrolet, Pontiac, Oldsmobile, Buick and Cadillac – a strategy which helped GM to overtake Ford, and which has been successful for more than half a century. On top of this wholesale restructuring, GM then announced in 1985 that it was also investing some $5 billion to create the new Saturn Corporation, an undertaking that *Business Week* termed 'GM's bold bid to reinvent the wheel'.

There is no guarantee that GM's 'bold bid' will succeed. By the end of 1986 the Saturn project was being scaled down, and the launch date pushed back. GM is now under seige from the combined efforts of the Japanese, Koreans and Europeans from without – with many of them now setting up their own factories in the US – and Ford and Chrysler from within. Roger Smith, GM's chairman, believes the chances of their succeeding will be lessened if they have to compete on GM's terms. As he explained in *Advertising Age* in 1985, GM's two guiding principles are:

1  'Use your weight to your advantage – and shed any weight that is a disadvantage.'
2  'Always set the rules.'

General Motors – plus Ford and Chrysler – is now setting the rules in another industry: banking. As *Time* asked in 1986, 'When is a bank not a bank? One answer: when it is a car company.' *Time* reported that GM's financial arm, General Motors Acceptance Corp., with over $75 billion in assets, is one of the US's largest financial institutions, offering not just car loans, but also 'they are lending to other businesses, giving out mortgages and helping consumers finance everything from washing machines to vacations.' In the process Detroit's car companies are rewriting the rules of banking and, not surprisingly, traditional bankers are alarmed at this foray into their territory, and angry at laws which restrict their interstate activities but which do not affect car companies in the same way. The president of the American Bankers Association told *Time* that the way to eliminate the hobbling of banking is to speed up deregulation. Should this happen, then the US banking industry will probably see a shake-out similar to that now occurring in the airline, trucking and railroad industries.

- *Ford Motor Co.*, staggering under losses of $3.3 billion between 1980 and 1982, was not so long ago being written off as a has-been – the perennial, plodding follower of GM, and the company that once gave us the Edsel. That's all forgotten now for, as Anne Fisher wrote in a *Fortune* article: 'Ford is back on the track. . . . A glance at the results in 1985 shows not a has-been but a here-again.' By 1986 Ford was truly here. It reported record profits of $3.3 billion, more than its larger rival, GM, whose profits fell by 25 per cent to less than $3 billion. It was the first time Ford had overtaken GM since 1924. How had Ford managed to do so well?

A revival in the US auto market, continued restraints on Japanese imports, and sheer hard work to reduce costs and its break-even level may help explain some of Ford's current prosperity, but not its recent climb in market share. That appears to be the result of Ford's new determination to fight *any* competitor on quality and 'drivability' terms, and its bold new styling strategy that is setting market trends – something that hasn't happened at Ford since Lee Iacocca introduced the Mustang back in 1964. One GM designer, who asked not to be identified, admitted: 'Ford's new cars look just like what we were going to be putting out two years from now.'

Ford's newest models, the Taurus and its twin, the Mercury Sable, are especially proving to be winners in the marketplace, and drawing rave reviews from the once critical motoring press. While this success deserved praise, *Business Week* in a 1986 editorial explained: 'the real reason for cheer about Ford's good fortune is what it says about the carmaker's willingness to learn from its mistakes and from what the Japanese and Germans could teach. By displaying an open-mindedness once rare in Detroit, Ford has demonstrated that product quality and price competitiveness can still flourish in the industry.' In the process, Ford has shown other beleaguered 'smoke-stack' manufacturing companies what can be achieved.

- *Procter & Gamble*, the great packaged-goods firm which made the 'slice of life' formula a way of life for its advertising agencies for more than twenty-five years, recently won a rare distinction for one of its TV commercials. Its Ivory Liquid *'Our Song'* won an

*Advertising Age* 'Best TV Commercial for 1983' award for an advertisement that the panel of judges described as 'involving, convincing, different'. Even the length, 45 seconds, was seen as unusual. And in the same year, another P & G commercial, for top-selling Head and Shoulders shampoo, also broke away from standard P & G approaches – such as efficacy claims, product comparisons, demonstrations and testimonials. A rather incredulous *Advertising Age* in 1983 commented: 'This is image advertising, pure and simple.' By 1985 P & G was running an ad for a bathroom tissue that featured talking clouds, and one for a fabric softener that was set to the bouncing tune of a Pointer Sisters' pop hit.

• *Colgate-Palmolive Co.* showed that when it comes to image advertising, it too could jive with the times. Not only did it beat P & G to the market with its toothpaste pump, by 1986 it had also changed its Colgate pump advertising in two significant ways. It was directed at children, that is, the users of toothpaste, not the traditional American 'mom' – who is now an endangered species anyway – and it was creative. As Bob Garfield exclaimed in *Advertising Age*:

> Clip and save. What follows is a favourable appraisal of a Ted Bates/New York toothpaste commercial. In fact, this is about *two* Ted Bates commercials for the Colgate pump, and – pinch me so I'm sure I'm awake – both are very good.

The applause had hardly died away when Colgate announced that it was withdrawing its account – worth about $100 million in total billings in 1986 – over a conflict of interest issue. In mid-1986 Ted Bates was taken over by Saatchi & Saatchi Co., which also worked for P & G. The move was just one more example of what has been dubbed 'merger mania' among the world's major advertising agencies. Even though there was talk that the various agencies in the vast Saatchi network could service competing accounts, Colgate for one, decided that the move was not in its best interest. Its withdrawal from a partnership with Bates that had lasted for nearly half a century foreshadowed a changing agency-client relationship.

P & G served notice it too was not impressed, by withdrawing some $65 million in billings from Saatchi agencies. One of P & G's top people revealed to *Advertising Age*:

In essence, when an agency creates separate networks and argues that these will be kept totally separate, there will be no communication, there will be no transfer of personnel or knowledge... they are basically saying that the companies we own are bigger, but the parts aren't going to work together. If the parts aren't going to work together, how can the clients be served?

That is the question many clients are now asking, as they look for ways to maintain profitability, and find they are spending a growing proportion of their budgets on sales promotions to prop up sales volumes. Total ad expenditures grew by about 8 per cent in 1985, less than half the 1984 rate, and companies are now crying halt to the ever-increasing costs of television time, in particular – the very basis of an agency's existance. 'As a result', observed Christine Dugas, in a 1986 *Business Week* article:

Madison Avenue is undergoing an unprecedented upheaval. Many agencies have attempted to keep growing by gobbling each other up. Others have opted to expand into related services, such as public relations and direct marketing. And everyone is scrambling to cut costs.

One top agency executive told Dugas: 'You're going to see agencies under a lot of pressure – clients wanting more for less. Agencies have to be more productive for less money.' This last statement simply reflects the reality that marketers have lived with for some time now.

- *Campbell Soup Co's* ubiquitous red-and-white soup label has long symbolized mass-marketing: standardized products, massive production and a 'one-sight one-sound' national brand image created through blanket advertising coverage. That approach is now changing. Campbell is starting to tailor some of its products, advertising, sales and merchandising efforts to suit not just different regions of the country, but even individual neighbourhoods within a city. As *Business Week* predicted in 1987: 'These are the first rumblings of a seismic change at Campbell that could eventually redefine mass marketing in the US.'
  *Business Week* noted that twenty-five years ago Campbell could reach half of all US households by sponsoring *Lassie* on TV, and added: 'That may have been the last time things were so simple.'

Things are much more complex now. A combination of factors are forcing companies such as Campbell to shift their marketing focus to the grass-roots level: the American mass market is breaking up into a constellation of fragmented segments, and firms need to take much more care when aiming at their scattered targets; while national television advertising rates continue to rise, their cost-effectiveness in reaching specific target markets is now in doubt, and so firms are looking for more efficient local media alternatives; the increased buying power of supermarket chains is forcing companies to switch from national advertising 'pull' strategies to more localized promotion and trade-related 'push' strategies. Moreover, sophisticated market research techniques that link in-store consumer purchasing – via bar code scanners – with in-home media usage – via 'people meters' – now mean that marketers can measure the impact of all their activities, right down to the individual store level. To be 'street wise' has now taken on a new meaning.

- *McDonald's Corporation*, already No. 1 in hamburger outlets – plus sales and profits – has recently rewritten its distribution policy by opening new outlets in such diverse places as a high school, a university, a navy base, a childrens' hospital, a zoo, a museum, a bus depot, a river boat and a state tollway. By 1986 McDonald's had even opened a restaurant in a Los Angeles office building, in an attempt to provide 'power-lunches' for the new executive set who, after all, had grown up on Big Macs. In 1984 it had also rewritten its successful menu. And in only one month after nationally intro-ducing chicken McNuggets – chicken finger-food, without the bones – McDonald's became the second-largest chicken retailer after Kentucky Fried Chicken. Where's the beef, indeed!

- *Coca-Cola Corporation*, after 99 years, changed the formula of the most popular soft drink in the world. *Fortune* initially called the move 'one of the boldest gambles in marketing history'. Then, three months later, when Coke's original formula – renamed Coca-Cola *Classic* – was brought back after a storm of protest from Coke partisans, *Fortune* reported: 'In what will go down as one of the classic marketing retreats in the annals of business, Coca-Cola admitted it had goofed by taking old Coke off the market.' Yet, no matter what the critics may say about the capacity of research to predict consumer behaviour, or the ability of management to understand what constitutes the essence of brand image and loyalty, Coca-Cola's new chairman, Roberto Goizueta, in 1985, confirmed that in today's market-place nothing should be considered sacred and that anything can be changed, including the formula for the real thing.

- *PepsiCo Inc.*, unfizzed by Coca-Cola's actions, showed that in the battle for market share the best defence is to counter-attack. In one of its biggest moves yet it announced it was buying up a struggling competitor – Seven-Up Co., the un-cola pop maker that even mighty Philip Morris Inc. couldn't turn around. By this move Pepsi sought to gain a few more market share points on its arch rival, and in the process make it the leading soft drink marketer in food stores.

  Stung by this move, Coca-Cola quickly announced it too was buying one of the few remaining competitors left – Dr Pepper Co., the No. 4 soft-drink company, already reduced to a largely regional role. This would boost Coke's share of the beverage market to about 45 per cent vs. PepsiCo's anticipated 34 per cent. In the end, neither side snared its prey. By mid-1986 the Federal Trade Commission had voted to block PepsiCo's $380 million bid for Seven-Up, and Coca-Cola's proposed $480 million acquisition of Dr Pepper, arguing that a combined 80 per cent share would decrease competition.

  Undaunted, PepsiCo soon afterwards announced it was offering $850 million to buy Kentucky Fried Chicken, the world's second-biggest restaurant chain. The benefit of such a takeover was immediately obvious. Worldwide, KFC had more than 6500 outlets; no doubt they would convert to Pepsi, thereby denying Coke a major pipeline to thirsty consumers. PepsiCo already owned two franchise chains: Taco Bell Mexican outlets and Pizza Hut pizza outlets. The KFC move would give PepsiCo leading positions in three fast-food segments, and industry observers were speculating that the company would next attempt to round out its food business with a burger chain. Though such a move would bring PepsiCo into a showdown with the mighty McDonald's, it would take a brave analyst to predict the outcome. If nothing else, PepsiCo is showing that when it comes to waging marketing warfare today, only the strong, fast and totally committed will survive.

- *International Business Machines Corp.*, the 'Big Blue' computer maker, despite its late entry into the personal computer market, grabbed the leadership position from Apple Computer Inc. by changing a few rules of marketing warfare. These included using basic software that any company could license, thereby establishing a new industry standard – and dramatically reducing the PC's development time and costs. In the process IBM also demonstrated the advantages of setting up teams of 'intrapreneurs' in a large, conservative corporation.

Five years later IBM was fighting a new PC battle – not with the Japanese, as everyone originally expected, but with low-wage companies in Taiwan and South Korea. By 1986 IBM's PC had become a commodity product, and was being copied by more than two hundred firms. In order to drive down its own production costs IBM has not gone offshore, as so many US companies have done. Rather, it has embarked on a bolder strategy, and one that will change the rules of marketing once again. In 1986 IBM announced that it would build personal computers entirely by robots in America, starting with its lap-top model, the PC Convertable. Bill Saporito in *Fortune* called it IBM's 'no-hands assembly line', and said it could cut the cost of making a PC by as much as 50 per cent. That was not the only reason IBM opted for state-of-the-art 'flexible manufacturing' technology. 'Equally important', said Saporito, 'it puts IBM in a strong position to respond with unprecedented alacrity to the almost monthly shifts in the computer market. There's no evidence that the Japanese – or anyone else – have anything as advanced'. It was not very long ago that US manufacturing was being written off. Now, it has become a key marketing weapon.

• *Apple Computer Inc.*, the *prima technicala* of personal computer makers, though battered by IBM's success, refused to retire from the battle like so many other hapless US competitors, and instead began its counter-attack by hiring a top marketing whiz from Pepsi-Cola USA, the beverage subsidiary of PepsiCo.

And, keeping within the norms of Pepsi's competitive behaviour, but departing radically from Apple's, one of John Scully's first moves was to launch the new Macintosh with the futuristic '1984' commercial, which cost $500000 and ran only once, during the 1984 Super Bowl. *Advertising Age* described it as 'the bold, bizarre TV spot that made Apple a household word during a dull Super Bowl XVIII'. In the first ten days 70000 units, worth about $100 million, were sold, and the commercial – not to mention the machine – is still receiving acclaim. One of Scully's next moves was to launch the Apple IIc with a one-day dealer conference that cost

$2 million, thereby introducing the personal computer industry to
'event marketing' – corporate extravaganzas that reap lavish press
coverage. The gimmick worked. *The Wall Street Journal* featured
the launch on the front page of its business section, describing it as a
'blend of pep rally, rock concert and revival meeting'.

Faced with a faltering market in 1985, some later moves by Scully
were not so extravagant, though they attracted as much media
attention. *Fortune* reported that, from the end of May to the middle
of June, 1985: 'Apple reorganized in a rush, fired 20 per cent of its
work force, announced that it would record its first-ever quarterly
loss, saw its stock hit a three-year low of $14.25 a share, and stripped
Steven P. Jobs, Apple's 30-year old co-founder and chairman, of all
operating authority.' Within two months Jobs had left, and Scully
too had shown that, in order to survive in today's business world,
nothing is sacred, not even someone *Time* called 'the prototype of a
new American hero – the irreverent and charismatic young entrepreneur'.

## Fundamental changes

Events such as these demonstrate that even those firms which may be
leaders in their respective markets are neither immune nor immutable.
Like every other competitor they too can be buffeted by changing
market forces, and eventually they too have to respond if they want to
hold on to their position – and perhaps even survive.

And when indomitable corporations such as Campbell, GM, IBM
and P & G respond in ways – and often with a speed – that seem quite
contrary to previous, and successful, patterns of competitive behaviour, then there is a strong possibility that fundamental changes are
taking place in the ways that market-share battles are being fought in
the increasing number of mature and over-crowded markets that now
exist in the United States.

Even though the actions of the above and many other leading
companies have been extensively reported, the full implications of
these seemingly isolated events were not readily apparent, probably
not even to those directly involved.

Perhaps with the advantages of some hindsight, it now appears that
changes such as these, plus many others not directly connected, were

signifying that the process of marketing goods and services was entering a new phase by the early 1980s.

The evidence which demonstrates that a new era in marketing is now underway comes mostly from the United States, mainly because American firms came charging out of the last recession much earlier – and, more important, more aggressively – than leading companies in other industrial nations. Consequently, American corporations seem to be in the vanguard of this movement, though there is now evidence that leading firms in other countries are also beginning to rethink their approach to marketing.

There can be no single, or simple, explanation to account for the changes that are now taking place. Nor can it be argued that the practice of marketing alone is changing. Rather, the whole process of doing business, of being more competitive, appears to be undergoing a transformation. The resulting new marketing is but one manifestation of this.

In a special report on corporate restructuring, *Time* commented in 1987 that, faced with intense global competition, an upsurge of corporate mergers and acquisitions, and the related fears of a takeover:

> American companies have started the huge task of rebuilding themselves from the ground up, erecting a sleek new operating architecture to replace the unwieldy processes of the past. At corporate headquarters and on factory floors from New York City to Los Angeles, newly cost conscious executives are on a relentless examination of the efficiency and effectiveness of everything they do. They are tearing up organization charts, selling off unsatisfactory product lines and closing down unprofitable plants at a rate never seen before. Their aim: to produce streamlined, combative concerns that can withstand the frenetic, competitive pace of the late '80s.

As the chairman of Eastman Kodak which, in 1986, abandoned its policy of job security and eliminated 13000 people from its 129000 workforce, explained to *Time*: 'The principal objective is to make the company more agile, more competitive and more flexible.' While those American managers who still have their jobs may now find they are working harder, many have also found something else as compensation – the room to make more decisions, more quickly.

# New realizations

There are many underlying forces that, together account for much of this change. Collectively these forces have turned a great many stable and secure domestic markets into veritable war zones. In the process they have dramatically reshaped the ways even the market leaders compete, for eventually, they too have come to certain realizations about their markets and marketing processes. The following points are worth noting:

## * *The practice of marketing has reached 'maturity'*

The initial acceptance of marketing rested largely on the finding that reliance on a production – and/or selling – orientation to business was inadequate. What was needed, instead, was a new, marketing approach – an approach based on anticipating and then satisfying customer needs and wants at a profit. For many US firms this acceptance came in the 1950s or 1960s.

However, once many companies began to apply a marketing philosophy, the efforts of any one marketing-oriented firm to gain a competitive advantage quickly became negated by its equally marketing-oriented rivals. Eventually, the more astute firms came to realize that a new approach was needed in order to break out of this impasse. P & G, for one, showed that it was prepared to take an unheard-of profit decline, in 1985, in order to prepare for its new approach.

## * *Even market leaders cannot count on a long-term competitive edge*

There are many reasons for this. New technologies and production techniques now get quickly equalized, thereby eliminating what may have once been a competitive advantage. At the same time, so-called patent protection rights are now quickly challenged and, in the case of some imported goods, ignored altogether. Legal redress may take years to achieve, if ever. A case in point is P & G which always places the achievement of a technological edge as a pre-condition for entry into a new market. In 1983 P & G began test-marketing a new soft-centred cookie, yet even before its testing programme was completed, two competitors, Nabisco and Keebler, had introduced similar products.

Firms are also finding that product life-cycles are shortening. In the computer industry, product cycles now last six to eight quarters, about half the time than at the beginning of the 1980s. A similar situation is beginning to emerge in the car industry. This means companies need more than one generation of product in the development pipeline. It is also forcing them to pump out a continuous stream of new products – yet launch costs are climbing inexorably and, even though new product research and forecasting procedures continue to improve, new product failure rates remain as high as they were twenty years ago.

New competitors, local and foreign, are threatening the existence of established firms. Much has been written of the influx of cheaper and frequently better-quality imported goods, from cars to videos, and their impact on 'smoke-stack' America. Another transformation is also taking place as a result of deregulation in the banking, financial services, telecommunications, transportation and airline sectors, and this is forcing companies in those industries to turn to marketing techniques. In some of these industries new competitors – such as People Express Airlines – rewrote the rules of competitive behaviour, thereby making the prevailing marketing practices obsolete. The spectacular rise and fall of People Express also shows what can happen when existing competitors quickly learn the new rules, and the interloper fails to adjust to the changed realities.

## \* New product superiority is something of a myth

According to the respected UK writer and management commentator, Robert Heller, in his 1984 book, *The Naked Market*, many allegedly marketing-oriented companies still operate on the 'mouse-trap' principle: develop the breakthrough product, they think, and 'technology push' will create the sales. Heller said this was: 'a delusion which has much British industrial blood on its hands. . . . The myth is venerable to the point of decrepitude, disproved again and again.' (1)

In the personal computer market many new entrants have stolen technology marches on IBM. Others have substantially undercut IBM in price, even with superior products. It didn't seem to matter much, IBM still stayed on top – until the influx of a new generation of clones changed the rules, and IBM was forced to adopt a new approach.

Another myth might be termed the 'Mr Muscle' principle: develop a new product – usually a ho-hum line extension – and superior marketing clout will soon move the goods. In today's highly competitive markets, where powerful retail chains now block the way, myths such as these are rapidly being dispelled.

## * A firm's production or operations capability is a key marketing leverage

Prompted by foreign competition and a growing realization that manufacturing productivity was slipping, once again profitable American firms are committing enormous resources – and slashing their payroll numbers – in an effort to drive down costs and improve product quality and production performance.

*Time* claimed in 1984: 'Long US industry's neglected stepchild, subordinated to finance and marketing, the process of making products is suddenly coming into its own, commanding more and more attention from company executives.' When placed in the context of the 'flow of goods' approach to marketing, the manufacturing or operations part of the flow is now seen as crucial for the strategic marketing advantages it can confer. Much has been written about the recent rejuvenation of America's industrial base, as companies pour vast resources into new manufacturing facilities and stock them with a dazzling array of electronic wizardry. General Motors' new Saturn division is but one well-publicized example of the attempt by many American companies to revolutionize manufacturing. This same commitment and experimentation in the operations side of the business is also transforming many service industries as well, from banking to publishing.

## * In many consumer-goods industries the balance of power may be tipping in favour of the retail trade

One of the straws that helped tip this balance was the announcement in early 1984 by Kroger Co., the nation's second largest publicly held grocery chain, with some 1500 stores, that it would ask marketers for a 'slotting' allowance on new products – initially in the Houston market only. A spokesperson for Kroger explained:

> We had recognized for a long time that many suppliers have special moneys (available) to offset (the retailer's) expenses of putting new items in our systems. We know some other retailers were getting this assistance . . . so we identified our costs, which are growing, and formalized the practice. We are merely covering our actual, up-front costs.

A spokesperson for Procter & Gamble said they had no intention of complying: 'The day any customer can tell a manufacturer what his terms must be – that's the end of the industry.'

P & G's concern is understandable. A concentration of chain-store buying power – from computer outlets to supermarkets – has forced the producers of consumer goods to realize they can no longer *market* to the consumer and *sell* to the trade. Rather, they are now finding that achieving distribution through the trade is a strategic issue, deserving the same degree of priority as marketing to the end-user.

Arthur Lawrence ranks 'trade marketing' as one of management's priority tasks in the 1980s:

> Getting trade distribution . . . is an aspect of a company's operations which ranks in importance with the strategies for product marketing, for product development, for manufacturing efficiency and for financial planning. (2)

\*  *With a falling birthrate and an increasingly fragmented marketplace, the past trend of mass-appeal products showing a continuous upward movement in sales as the total population grew, is no longer applicable*

Fundamental demographic and lifestyle shifts, along with a growing income polarization, means that an increasing number of mass markets have reached maturity, with too many competitors. This has led to some fierce and costly market share battles as firms try to hang on to their past sales levels, or to grab sales from somebody else. Many firms are now changing from mass-marketing to segmentation – including regional – strategies in order to escape the crush.

Heller argued that, in overcrowded markets, the 'three-runner rule' applies: 'most markets can only support a leader, a runner-up and one specialist. With more, everybody may suffer – even the Number One'.

Though this may be a rather sweeping generalization, consider the current problems besetting the European mass producers of cars. In a market of some ten million new cars each year, since 1983 only one or two percentage points have separated the six main volume producers: Fiat, Renault, Peugeot, Volkswagen, and the European operations of Ford and General Motors. The industry currently operates at some 20 per cent over-capacity and, as each car maker has struggled to maintain its position, this has led to a welter of new models and constant discounting – and huge cuts in profits as cars are priced below production costs. Only the consumers have benefited, as *Time* pointed out 'they are able to buy some of the world's best-engineered automobiles at bargain-basement prices'.

*Automotive News* reported that in 1985 only Volkswagen and Fiat were firmly in the black – and both firms have had to suffer through Chrysler-like turnarounds in the past decade. No wonder then, that some in the big six have decided that profits are now more important than snatching incremental increases in market share. While GM has recently spent some $3 billion to increase productive capacity in Europe, *Automotive News* in 1986 noted that 'the investment is now being questioned at the highest level of the corporation because all it bought was an extra 3 per cent market share and lower profits'.

On the other hand the six premium-priced car makers – BMW, Mercedes, Jaguar, Porsche, Saab and Volvo – were reaping record sales and profits by exporting to America, where they had been aided considerably by an overvalued US dollar and an increasingly affluent, and growing, target group. *Business Week* reported that, in 1984, the six specialist-producers posted combined profits of $2.7 billion while the rest of the European auto industry lost $1.1 billion.

In the end only the best will succeed. In order to be best in today's intensely competitive mature markets, such as Europe's car industry, an increasing number of firms are showing a willingness to try new approaches to marketing. For example, as Europe divides into two strata – the successful specialists and the mass producers – both groups are moving toward greater flexibility and more collaboration. Though Fiat and Ford could not agree on collaboration terms which would have given them dominance over nearly a quarter of the market, the deal between Japan's Honda and Britain's Austin Rover shows how the smaller companies are trying to pool resources for their mutual benefit. *The Economist* recently argued that, if the other option is government – that is, taxpayer – handouts to prop up uncompetitive car makers, then collaborative deals make business sense:

> A new car model now costs up to $1 billion to bring out (*in fact Ford's Fiesta cost that a decade ago*) and Austin Rover cannot afford to go it alone with a full range of cars on a production volume less than that of a specialist producer like Daimler-Benz. In turn, Honda gets a production base in Europe, from which it can export to other common market countries, notably West Germany.

The world's car industry has become a lattice of collaborative marketing arrangements. And wherever you look, firms – even direct competitors – in industries ranging from banking to computing are doing the same. They are creating this, not in response to set theories or textbook prescriptions, but out of the necessity to survive.

## * The organizational 'climate' is now right for change

*The Economist* reported in 1984 that 'changes are taking place in the management of American business which matter more to companies than the latest swings in economic policy and business policy'. *Business Week* was more to the point: 'The organization man is dead.' A new generation of well-educated (read MBA) management talent is now assuming control of American companies, and their commitment to fostering their organization's culture and spirit of entrepreneurship is encouraging them to reappraise their whole approach to business. For his irreverent style, Donald Burr, founder and chairman of People Express, was virtually canonized by many business schools – prematurely, it turned out. John Scully's rise to the top of Apple Computers shows that, while it takes one entrepreneurial type of executive to get a new venture off the ground, it takes another entrepreneurial type to keep it going – a lesson that sometimes gets forgotten.

As part of the reappraisal process, many executives are questioning the worth and relevance of elaborate and formal corporate planning processes, with their attendant focus on short-term financial results. It is now agreed that what is needed is a planning process that encourages creativity and risk-taking, and does not stifle it in the interests of quarterly profit targets. As a result, a growing number of firms are appointing marketers to the top jobs.

In a 1983 cover story, 'Marketing: the new priority', *Business Week* reported that marketers are:

> now hotter prospects for high-level jobs than executives with financial experience. Companies of every stripe are looking for managers, presidents, or chief executive officers who can not only develop long-term product strategies but also instill an entrepreneurial spirit into corporations that, more often than not, practice risk avoidance.

An executive of a top recruiting firm put it more succinctly: 'Nobody wants bean counters now.'

There is no doubt that the booming American economy has had an impact on America's entrepreneurial spirit. In a 1985 *Fortune* cover story, 'America on top again', Richard Kirkland Jr was exultant:

> Americans certainly have plenty to cheer about. The strongest economic recovery since the Korean war has spawned more than seven million new jobs in two years. US GNP growth since 1982 has left Europe's economies in the dust and even outstripped that perennial worldbeater Japan for two years running – the first time that has happened since scorekeeping began in the 1950s.

Both *Time* and *Business Week* also ran stories in 1985 describing how, at long last, American companies were starting to check 'The Japanese challenge'.

Certainly business confidence has been translated into business investment. Kirkland estimated that R&D expenditure has been growing at more than 6 per cent per year in inflation-adjusted dollars since 1975, compared with 2 per cent from 1970 to 1975. While West Germany and Japan still spend more on civilian R&D as a percentage of GNP (2.5 per cent and 2.3 per cent respectively vs. 1.8 per cent for the US), an economist at the Hoover Institute informed *Fortune* that the US has an enormous advantage in terms of economies of scale – the estimated $109 billion spent on R&D in 1985 would be greater than the combined total spent by West Germany, Japan and France. And by the middle of 1986 American firms had another bonus – the rising yen was beginning to remove some of the cost advantages of many Japanese firms.

Given this confident attitude, and investment volume, it is perhaps not surprising to find that American executives are willing to experiment with new marketing approaches. This means that, should the US dollar stay down, at some stage American firms are also going to be extremely tough competitors in the world's markets.

## * Firms can create their own future

Firms which have 'peered' into the future have come to the conclusion that they need to generate a new gameplan that gives them more control over their own destinies. General Motors, for one, decided that in order to build small cars that would be competitive with the Japanese in terms of cost, quality and technologies employed, it needed to set up a completely new small car subsidiary which would not only sever all connections with the existing corporate culture, but would also change nearly every other aspect of auto-making operations.

When Roger Smith became chairman of GM in 1981 no one imagined he would be a bean counter who turned star gazer. Anne Fisher, writing in *Fortune* in 1984 said that, to outsiders, Roger Smith looked like 'the archetypal man in the grey flannel suit, stamped from the same mold as every chairman since the 1950s: a tradition-bound, somewhat complacent finance man'. Fisher added, however, that 'GM is a whole new company now. Smith is standing history on its head'. In a 1985 interview with *Time*, Smith explained how the company was actually helped by the huge losses it suffered before he assumed control:

> The worse years made it more acceptable to understand that something had to be done. But once we sold that, it was then our turn to say, 'Let's not just go two steps, let's go into the 21st century.' You don't just stumble into the future. You create your own future.

What will the 21st century, GM-style, be like? In a 1985 interview with *Advertising Age* Smith said it would be completely 'market-driven'. If Smith is correct, new car buyers will visit a GM dealership, possibly located in the heart of a shopping mall, and sit in front of a computer terminal to make their selection. Guided by 'user-friendly' instructions, they will compare prices and features of competitive makes, select and tally the cost of different options, have technical details graphically explained, see what different interior and exterior colour schemes look like, and work out monthly payments on their General Motors Acceptance Corp. finance scheme. The computer will be linked to all the local GM dealers, and a quick search will be made to determine whether one is readily available. If it isn't, the customer's order will be placed directly with a GM factory via a Hughes-built satellite communication network, and the buyer told immediately when the car will be built and supplied – probably within two weeks. Likewise, GM's computers will inform all suppliers of parts requirements for just-in-time delivery, probably within hours of the car being built, when payment will be automatically transferred. The same computer system will handle any servicing that customers might need after delivery of the car, such as automatically informing the buyer when warranty servicing is required. All customer complaints will be logged, and used to correct any assembly or servicing faults. There will be virtually no paperwork involved in all these processes. Far-fetched schemes? Not at all. Some are already in practice, and many are planned for Saturn, and other divisions.

While Smith, and others, may be proven wrong, it is this confident attitude toward setting the new rules, plus the willingness to commit massive resources to do so, that sums up why America has entered a new era in marketing.

## New approaches

The remaining chapters will illustrate how apparently isolated changes in the marketing practices of many leading American companies demonstrate that a new era has been entered. Some of the ramifications of this new marketing will be considered – allowing for the problem of trying to predict an outcome when the delineation of an ongoing process is not yet agreed. However, many of the signs are already there. For example:

- Many prominent companies have come to adopt a new approach to marketing now that their previous preoccupation with formal strategic planning is giving way to issues of imaginative implementation. The 'ivory tower' MBA strategists are now learning trench warfare tactics, since this new approach to marketing means, above all, being able to move goods from producer to consumer. As a result many companies have now adopted a more pragmatic and aggressive approach to marketing. 'Satisfying consumer needs and wants at a profit' is a classic objective of packaged-goods marketing. Today's marketers realize this is a pointless sentiment if they can't actually get their goods in front of the consumer in the first place.

- Many companies have recently shed inefficient operations and dumped product lines – and divisions – that were unrelated to their 'core business'. To compensate, they are buying up related product lines – and companies – in order to concentrate their resources on what they do best, and to fend off unwanted raiders. In the process they have achieved a greater 'critical mass' in their operations, and are using every bit of this extra weight to their own advantage. Their smaller and weaker competitors are rapidly disappearing; their bigger but slower competitors are taking a pounding. The resulting industry shakeouts – in soft drinks, wine, family restaurants, home-appliances, telecommunications and airlines, to name but a few – may eventually lead to a situation where 'the battles of the giants' become the norm, and where the 'rules' of competitive practice have yet to be set.

- Many companies have already captured strong positions in highly competitive markets, not by out-marketing their opposition according to the rules and practices prevailing since marketing's go-go years of the 1960s, but by changing the rules. And at the same time, many dominant firms have recently discovered that, ironically, when their position is under threat, a seemingly perilous, tradition-breaking response can be the least risky course of action to take.

## New leverages

But it is not just pragmatism, aggression and risk-taking that characterizes this new approach. Marketers are also finding new ways to gain more control over the key processes involved in the 'flow of goods and services' concept of marketing – which in fact is not a new concept at all. What is new is the way it is now being interpreted and practised. In particular, marketers have come to realize that, to succeed in today's highly competitive markets a company needs to exhibit superior control, or leverage, over *every* stage in the flow – or find a way of compensating when it hasn't got this leverage at some particular stage. As a result, many companies are now rethinking how to manage the processes involved at each of the stages, in order to gain the following:

- *Market-entry leverages*, which equals the superior ways that firms now organize the processes involved in selecting, developing and producing new products or services for entry into the market. For some firms success has come from internal teams of 'intrapreneurs', for others it has come from independent divisions, with freedom to develop their own ways of doing things; for still others it has come from new forms of collaboration – even with one's competitors if need be.

- *Marketplace leverages*, which equals the superior ways that companies execute those marketing tasks now deemed most important out in the market. This involves looking beyond the confines of the traditional four Ps of *product, price, promotion* and *place* in order to provide superior value to their customers, whether they be the final consumers or the intermediary resellers. In particular, companies are placing renewed emphasis on a fifth 'P' – *customer servicing*.

By the end of this book I trust that readers, especially those struggling to achieve even short-term incremental profit and market share gains, will recognize the opportunities inherent in the flow of goods concept of marketing when approached from a completely different perspective. Recent North American experience and examples show that the classical approach to marketing is no longer applicable. We are now in a new era.

# 2    The revolt against strategic planning

The 'new' marketing that is now practised in America emphasizes more the pragmatic and less the philosophical, or even philanthropic, nature of the marketing functions. Compare the definition of marketing offered in the 1983 *Business Week* cover story, 'Marketing: the new priority':

> In essence marketing means moving goods from the producer to the consumer. (1)*

with the definition offered in a leading marketing text:

> Marketing is a social process by which individuals and groups obtain what they need and want through creating and exchanging products and value with others. (2)

Putting this contrast somewhat less equivocally, Robert Heller, in a 1984 *Marketing* article, quoted a top Coca-Cola marketing executive as saying: 'Everything has changed. Before, if you were aggressive – you were out. Now, if you're not aggressive – you're out.' Nowhere is this new aggression more apparent than in the market share battles between Coke and Pepsi.

---

*In fact this definition is based on one first offered some twenty-five years ago: 'Marketing is the performance of business activities that direct the flow of goods and services from producer to consumer or user'. *Marketing Definitions: A glossary of marketing terms*, committee on definitions (Chicago: American Marketing Association, 1960). Interestingly, the AMA recently revised its definition: 'Marketing is the process of planning and executing the conception, pricing, promotion, and distribution of ideas, goods, and services to create exchanges that satisfy individual and organization objectives.' (1985)

The reason for this change in emphasis is not hard to understand. There is no doubt that the consumer is still the final arbiter in the success of a brand – and satisfying wants and needs is still the ultimate test of marketing excellence. But if that brand is copied by a fast-acting competitor even before it comes out of test marketing, or it can't secure and hold shelf or freezer space in the key account outlets that now predominate in so much of United States retailing, or its message gets lost in the clutter of commercials that now clog up network television, then the consumer is unlikely to get much of an opportunity to be that final arbiter anyway. And while building a mutually beneficial exchange process may be an all-important marketing objective, what the textbooks don't tell you is that you may have to crush a few weaker competitors in order to achieve that honourable goal.

While *Business Week* was correct in identifying marketing as a leading force behind the renewed dynamism of American business, it failed to recognize the new approach to marketing that was taking place. For example, adopting the traditional stance, it suggested that marketing:

> starts with finding out what consumers want or need, and then assessing whether the product can be made or sold at a profit.
>
> Such decisions require conducting preliminary research, market identification and product development: testing consumer reaction to both product and price; working out production capabilities and costs; determining distribution; and then deciding on advertising and promotion strategies.

And yet, as *Business Week* insisted: 'Simple as these steps may sound, many of them were all but forgotten in the 1970s, when inflation kept sales pacing upwards and marketing was of secondary importance.'

In today's ultra-competitive, and low inflationary, markets, finding the right approach to successful marketing means much more than treating the traditional four Ps – product, price, place and promotion – as thought they were easily learned and mixed ingredients in a foolproof recipe. Not only have the ingredients changed today, so too have their application.

In 1986 *Business Week* reported that PepsiCo executives recognize only too well that marketing 'is more than a science based on exhaustive numerical analysis. It's a bare-knuckles sport where instincts are important'. This helps explain why PepsiCo tried to buy Seven-Up Co. – and why Coca-Cola was so quick in trying to grab Dr

Pepper Co. in retaliation. As John Enrico, PepsiCo's newly appointed CEO explained, in the beverage market it's 'ready, fire, aim'.

## Planners under fire

One of the earliest group of casualties of this new, rapid-fire 'on-the-ground' aggressiveness that characterizes marketing practices in America today have been the corporate strategic planners who rose in status and power especially during the 1970s. While their stay was brief, their influence was enormous.

The process of strategic planning began to change in the late 1960s when the pressures of controlling large, diversified corporations forced many CEOs to adopt a 'portfolio' approach to strategic planning, with its attendant financial emphasis. As a result, the influence of marketing waned. In its place the SBU – the 'strategic business unit' – became the focal point of analysis, planning and investment decisions, particularly as firms strove to consolidate strong positions and to conserve scarce resources. In a 1983 *Journal of Marketing* article Day and Wensley concluded: 'Increasingly the marketing plan was restricted to a tactical support role at the brand level... and thereby lost its earlier strategic focus.' (3)

Nowhere was the concept of strategic business units more eagerly embraced than at General Electric. In a 1978 *Business Horizons* article William Hall explained:

> It started in the executive offices at General Electric, the world's most diversified company. Corporate management at GE had been plagued during the 1960s with massive sales growth, but little profit growth.... Thus in 1971, GE executives were determined to supplement GEs vaunted system of management decentralization with a new, comprehensive system for corporate planning. (4)

The new concept of strategic planning contained three important components:

- *Strategic business units:* For planning and control purposes it was assumed that large multi-divisional, multi-product firms could be divided into strategic business units – SBUs – with each unit serving a particular product-market grouping.

- *Portfolio management:* It was also assumed that SBUs could be managed as a 'portfolio of business' – analogous to the financial portfolio concept. While each business unit would be expected to develop a strategy to fit its own product-market opportunities, these opportunities – or lack of them – would be evaluated on a commonly applied set of criteria, for example, market growth prospects, company strengths etc.
- *Resource allocations:* By placing each SBU within the context of a portfolio framework, and by applying a common – and comprehensive – set of evaluative criteria, it was also assumed that the firm would be able to balance its cash flows and optimize its investment choices.

Hall argued that:

> The total portfolio of business should be managed by allocating capital and managerial resources to serve the interests of the firm as a whole – to achieve balanced growth in sales, earnings, and asset mix at an acceptable and controlled level of risk. In essence, the portfolio should be designed and managed to achieve an overall corporate strategy.

## New planning

The concept of SBUs gained rapid acceptance in corporate America. As Hall explained: 'Not only did the new system change the direction of planning at GE; it subsequently affected the corporate strategies and the planning processes in hundreds of other diversified firms around the world as well'. In 1981 Walter Kiechel III, writing in *Fortune,* reported that a Harvard Business School study indicated that at least half the *Fortune* 1000 largest US industrial corporations were using the business portfolio matrix in one form or another. Kiechel also reported that: 'These companies may be disturbed to learn that many of the matrix's original champions now view it as outmoded, if not dangerously wrong.'

Yet, only a few years earlier SBUs were being hailed as the answer to every CEO's prayers. The concept was appealingly simple and logical – and it gave the chief executive of a diversified corporation a means of both guiding and controlling his far-flung portfolio of strategic business units.

## Cash generation:
## (relative market share)

|  | High | Low |
|---|---|---|
| **High** | **'Star'**<br><br>Cash generated +++<br>Cash used      –––<br><br>0,– | **'Problem child'***<br><br>Cash generated  +<br>Cash used      –––<br><br>–– |
| **Cash use:**<br>**(market**<br>**growth**<br>**rate)** |  |  |
| **Low** | **'Cash cow'**<br><br>Cash generated +++<br>Cash used      –<br><br>++ | **'Dog'**<br><br>Cash generated +<br>Cash used      –<br><br>–,0 |

*sometimes called
'Question mark'

## Figure 2.1  Cash usage and cash generation

Probably the most famous approach to portfolio planning was that put forward by the Boston Consulting Group. The BCG matrix, as it came to be known, allowed for the classification of a company's products according to their cash usage and their cash generation, along two dimensions: (see Figure 2.1).

According to Bruce Henderson, who was a founder of the Boston Consulting Group:

> To be successful, a company should have a portfolio of products with different growth rates and different market shares. . . . The need for a portfolio of business becomes obvious. Every company need products in which to invest cash. Every company needs products that generate cash. . . . The balanced portfolio has: 'stars', whose high share and high growth assure the future; 'cash cows', that supply funds for that future growth; and 'problem children', to be converted into 'stars' with the added

funds. 'Dogs' are not necessary. They are evidence of failure either to obtain a leadership position during the growth phase, or get out and cut the loss. (5)

Many companies adopted the BCG approach; others drew matrices to suit their own requirements. For example, in 1976, the *Financial Times* presented the matrix used by Shell International, the chemical company part of the giant Royal Dutch/Shell group. Shell at that time was using what they termed the directional policy matrix – DPM – which was built around two axes: one showing the prospects for profitable operation within the particular sector under scrutiny, the other measuring a company's competitive position in a particular sector. Depending on its position on the two axes, any project under consideration could be slotted into one of the nine possible boxes: (see Figure 2.2).

The key, of course, was in having a system for grading each prospective project. As the *Financial Times* noted: 'The technique developed by Shell for deciding how to place projects within the matrix uses a system of stars and grading which owes something to both the *Michelin Guide* and to *Which?* magazine.'

**Prospects for sector profitability:**

|  |  | *Unattractive* | *Average* | *Attractive* |
|---|---|---|---|---|
| **Company's Competitive Capabilities** | *Weak* | Disinvest | Phased withdrawal<br><br>Custodial | Double or quit |
|  | *Average* | Phased withdrawal | Custodial<br><br>Growth | Avis |
|  | *Strong* | Cash generator | Growth<br><br>Leader | Leader |

**Figure 2.2  Company's directional policy matrix**

When asked why they should want to disclose their planning approach, the chairman of Shell Chemicals UK replied that too many companies were embarking on ventures in product sectors in which they had no special advantage. This had led to the construction of excess capacity, thereby depressing prices. He reasoned that if other competitors adopted a planning approach similar to Shell, then companies 'could be guided to choose projects for which they were suited, to the benefit of the industry as a whole'.

If only all competitors could be guided by the logic of SBUs and DPMs! The reality of course was that not all of them were. There was no doubt that the corps of planners, with the backing of top management, certainly tried to impose a top-down discipline on the process of strategic planning. For example, by 1977 GE had 43 strategic business units. As explained by *Business Week* in 1977, GE's corporate plans:

> begin at the top with a team of economic, financial, technological, and marketing experts that assists corporate chiefs in determining areas of growth. Middle or line managers are charged with implementing those plans and providing feedback. And continual monitoring makes certain that projects live up to expectations within a specified time.

According to *Business Week*, the key to GE's success was its process of 'risk containment'. While the most important task of the planners was to determine which growth areas the company should explore, GE also required that something more than a single criterion – such as ROI – be used to justify new projects. As a result any new venture has to undergo GE's much lauded 'appropriation routine'. In fact, the GE grid, developed with the assistance of the McKinsey consulting firm, used similar ideas as the BCG and the DPM approaches, and became the model for many corporations world-wide. The GE matrix used *industry attractiveness* and *business strengths* as the two main axes. These dimensions were then built up from a number of variables. The result was a nine-cell matrix with three main categories of possible strategies: invest/grow; selectivity/earnings; and harvest/divest.

Not surprisingly, one important trick was in finding the right portfolio of operating managers to fit the desired portfolio of strategies – including managers who could operate in a system that had a team of bright (read MBA) young planners calling the strategic shots. In 1980 *Business Week* reported that GE, which categorized its strategic objectives for the company's wide-ranging products in terms of 'grow', 'defend' and 'harvest', also attempted to categorize the required personal styles of general managers in terms of 'growers', 'caretakers' and 'undertakers' respectively. One consultant and GE watcher commented: 'I hear they have a shortage of growers, but they are making great efforts to remove the undertaker types who are heading up growth businesses.'

## New doubts

What is surprising is how quickly the weaknesses became apparent, and the system began to lose its appeal. In 1981 *Business Week* was observing that John Welsh, GE's new chairman and chief executive officer:

> inherits a company that has been systematically honed to financial planning, which has proven itself superior in preventing fiscal disasters and useful in identifying opportunities for new growth.... But GE also houses a corporate culture that has tried to quantify risk so thoroughly, and has been so conservative that it has tended to force less aggressive managers – or less knowledgeable ones – to stick with what they know and to give up easily when traditional methods of competing fail.

According to *Business Week,* GE's failing was typical of many other American firms at the beginning of the 1980s: financially driven firms make poor competitors when the changing markets call for executives to be good judges of technological risk. *Business Week* concluded that GE needed a 'technical renaissance' if it was to play a major role in the high-technology businesses that would be the growth areas in the 1980s.

Yet, as Robert H. Hayes of the Harvard Business School, warned *Business Week,* striking a theme that was to be repeated many times over the next few years:

> A lot of US companies are finding that people without a technological background are unskilled in understanding the nature of technological risk. They substitute a degree of caution and risk aversion because they can't stomach the risk. But you can't quantify and reduce all the risks in technology. You need animal spirits.

The early 1980s saw an unprecedented storm of criticism of corporate planners and the planning process which focused on the concept of portfolio management. In one of the earliest, and strongest, attacks on what they termed 'the new management orthodoxy', Hayes and Abernathy, in a 1980 *Harvard Business Review* article that is now considered a classic, blamed American business's 'marked deterioration of competitive vigor' on an over-reliance on three main factors:

- *Short-term financial measures and control:* which stifled longer-term risk-taking, since managers were afraid of even a 'momentary dip in the bottom line'.
- *'Market-driven' behaviour:* which eschewed longer-term technological superiority in favour of short-term customer satisfaction and incremental product and service improvements.
- *Corporate portfolio management:* 'applied by a remote group of dispassionate experts primarily concerned with finance and control and lacking hands-on experience'. (6)

In a swipe at both management practices and the education system which produces these managers, Hayes and Abernathy argued:

Over the past two decades American managers have increasingly relied on principles which prize analytical detachment and methodological elegance over insight, based on experience, into the subtleties and complexities of strategic decisions. As a result, maximum short-term financial returns have become the overriding criteria for many companies.

## Implementation problems

For some time after that one of the important arguments against strategic planning, and planners, centred on the issue of strategy implementation – or the lack of it.

In a 1982 *Fortune* article, 'Corporate strategists under fire', Walter Kiechel III observed that many of the leading consultants were delivering – via what he termed the 'seagull approach' – a set of concepts that were simple and seemingly powerful enough to be grasped by managers, yet sufficiently difficult to apply that they required the services of a team of bright (read MBA) young consultants.

Unfortunately their concepts may have been inappropriate for the realities of the market place. The main problem, as Kiechel saw it, was one of implementation. Most companies were unable to apply the quick-fix theories such as strategic business units, experience curves and market-share matrices.

Kiechel asked: 'What if you charted your business on a growth-share matrix and found you have only cows and dogs? The grid couldn't tell where your new businesses should come from.' He then added: 'Real live businessmen have learned that the big challenge isn't concocting strategy but making it work.' And to those consultants who countered this criticism with 'the implementation problem' argument – that is, the strategy was perfectly sound, the client just couldn't implement it – Kiechel replied: 'Doesn't the fact that hardly anyone can carry it out say something about the value of strategy?'

## Power struggle

In a 1984 cover story, 'The new breed of strategic planner', *Business Week* also examined this problem of implementation. In the 1970s strategic planning emerged as a separate corporate function and strategic planners became dominant figures in their corporations. However, as their power grew, the influence of operating managers waned. Not surprisingly, hostility between the two groups flared up. *Business Week's* conclusion was that 'few of the supposedly brilliant strategies concocted by planners were successfully implemented'.

An important factor that contributed to this problem was that, as strategic planning groups in company head offices grew in size, sophistication and power, they also grew further and further away from the external world of the market place, where strategic decisions had to be carried out. In 1984 the senior vice-president in charge of GE's Major Appliance Business Group informed *Business Week* that, when he was running the company's dishwasher business many planners made poor decisions, 'usually because they relied on data, not market instincts, to make their judgements'.

He also said that an 'us vs. them' atmosphere had developed – particularly when many of GE's operating people were made to feel 'we were not smart enough to think our way through these things'. And therefore what might have started out as a 'natural resistance' escalated into 'out-and-out hostility,' which meant that 'even when the planners were right, operating managers often would not listen to them.'

*Business Week* reported that more and more operating managers were wresting control of their company's planning function – by the simple but effective strategem of themselves being trained in corporate strategy formulation by business schools and by outside consultants.

The end result of all this guerrilla warfare, claimed Burnett, Yeskey and Richardson in a 1984 article in *The Journal of Business Strategy*, has been that 'planners are being forced off their pedestals and into the organizational trenches'. And the principal reason for this, they felt, was that American chief executives were once again seeing *their* main role as the 'originators or focal points of the corporate strategic planning process', while the planner's role was increasingly becoming that of a 'manager, facilitator and implementator of the planning process'. (7)

Moreover, the man who, in 1984 headed GE's Major Appliance Business Group revealed to *Business Week*, that he no longer has a strategic planning group at all. Instead, he took *his* 'visions' for the future to his senior operating managers who 'hash out a consensus' and then 'drive it through the organization'. As he bluntly put it, 'For any strategy to succeed, you need [operating] people to understand it, embrace it, and make it happen'.

## Mature market problems

Linked to the problem of implementation – or lack of it – another criticism of the matrix approach to planning was that it failed to lead to viable strategies for companies operating in mature markets. As far back as 1978 *Business Week* was cautioning that 'probably the area in which strategic planning has performed the poorist is with the well-established product line that has only average growth potential'. One of the assumptions in approaches such as the BCG matrix is that, while mature products tend to have slow growth rates, they also tend to throw off more cash than young products. *Business Week* said:

> This has led a lot of companies into the trap of not investing enough to maintain market share for so-called mature products. Instead, they have taken the cash flow from the mature products to invest in the young ones.

In 1984 *Business Week* was saying that too often the strategic planning process had become an excuse for corporations buying growth businesses that they did not know how to manage, and 'milking to death mature ones'. As one strategic planner commented: 'If there's a hell for planners, over the portal will be carved the term "cash cow" '.

Robin Wensley, in a 1981 *Journal of Marketing* article, also questioned the assumption that few, if any, worthwhile investment projects will be generated by SBUs operating in mature markets – hence the further assumption that strong units in mature markets can safely be 'milked'. One of Wensley's arguments was that many dominant firms in mature markets could in fact pick up extra sales by investing in new plant and equipment, for example, by making investments which reduced unit costs and led to better price competitiveness. These moves may eventually force the marginal companies out of business. Wensley also said that: 'Such opportunities are reinforced when technical change requires all firms to reinvest in new facilities'. (8)

If, by pouring billions into the Saturn project, General Motors is signalling that it is not only willing to compete in a mature market on cost terms, but that it is going to do so on a new set of technological terms as well, then its competitors will have to spend big just to keep up, or they'll find they're eventually out of the race altogether.

## Japanese planning

Perhaps another factor influencing the mounting criticism of corporate planning was that many American CEOs were learning that their rival Japanese counterparts didn't even have strategic planners as such. What they had instead, according to Kenichi Ohmae, in his 1982 book, *The Mind of the Strategist*, was usually a founder or chief executive who was a 'strategist of great natural talent... with an intuitive grasp of the basic elements of strategy'. In a swipe at the American predilection for formal planning and control procedures, he added: 'Because it is disruptive of the status quo, the resulting plans might not even hold water from the analyst's point of view'. (9)

This theme was echoed by Lee Iacocca when, in his best-selling autobiography, he said, in his own inimitable way:

If I have to sum up in one word the qualities that make a good manager, I'd say that it all comes down to decisiveness. You can use the fanciest computers in the world and you can gather all the charts and numbers, but in the end you have to bring all your information together, set up a timetable, and *act*.... To a certain extent, I've always operated by gut feeling. I like to be in the trenches. I never was one of those guys who could just sit around and strategize endlessly.(10)

## CEOs rule, OK?

No wonder, then, that many American chief executives are now reclaiming what they see as rightfully belonging to them – the job of formulating overall corporate strategy: 'If its good enough for Lee Iacocca and the Japanese ...

Thomas Peters and Robert Waterman Jr, in their widely acclaimed book, *In Search of Excellence* – though it was maligned by many academics on methodological grounds – called their fifth attribute of the excellent companies, 'hands-on, value-driven'. This was because 'we are struck by the explicit attention they pay to values, and by the way in which their leaders have created exciting environments through personal attention, persistence and direct intervention – far down the line'. (11)

The authors also found that the most effective corporate leaders were those who mastered two ends of the spectrum: 'ideas at the highest level of abstraction and actions at the most mundane level of detail'. Perhaps that is why they found that most of the leaders of the 'excellent' companies did not have financial or legal qualifications. Rather, they came from operational backgrounds:

> They've been around design, manufacturing or sale of the product, and therefore are comfortable with the nuts and bolts of the company ... Clarifying the value system and breathing life into it are the greatest contributions a leader can make. Moreover, that's what the top people in the excellent companies seem to worry about most.... It requires persistence and excessive travel and long hours, but without the hands-on part, not much happens.

No wonder, also, that Lee Iacocca, the man who is credited with saving Chrysler, and who may some day try to become the US President, has become such a marvellous contradiction in America today – an industrial folk hero in what is supposedly a post-industrial era. Before moving over to Chrysler, Iacocca was a Ford sales and marketing supremo who eventually became the president – that is, until Henry Ford II told him he was no longer liked.

While the charismatic Iacocca of Chrysler got more headlines, and the technology-struck Smith of GM got more plaudits, Don Petersen, who now heads Ford, was also earning respect for his 'hands-on, value-driven' approach. *Business Week* recently praised him for his product knowledge and his encouragement of staff to take risks, particularly in developing Ford's new 'aero' styling. The editor of *Road & Track* magazine remarked: 'For too long, [top] people in Detroit have been bean counters. But Petersen doesn't sit in the back seat of a Lincoln and get driven around. He drives the cars himself.' There can be no doubt that the new leaders of the 'big three', by their personal styles of management, have played an important part in setting the American auto industry on a more competitive course for the next decade. Perhaps more leaders of Europe's mass producers of cars should drive *their* vehicles?

The lesson to be learned here is that successful companies don't need to adopt the latest in failsafe fads in order to win; they should apply something more fundamental. As Kiechel discovered in 1982, US executives were starting to realize that strategy, by itself, wasn't enough. One planner explained to him: 'What we're moving toward is an integrated theory of management, one that assigns strategy its proper place and identifies the other factors you have to manage to make strategy work.'

The message has not yet sunk in everywhere. For example, in assessing Buck Rodgers' *The IBM Way*, the reviewer in *Business Week* concluded with: 'Despite Rodgers' book, IBM's secret remains secret.' (Books, Jan. 20, 1986) Two follow-up letters to the editor were printed by *Business Week*, and each offers an important insight into what makes an excellent company in the mid-1980s:

> IBM's success is and always has been a result of its uncanny ability to develop managers who think as if they work for a small business. The company's marketing executives work diligently to keep things uncomplicated. But many people don't want to credit IBM's extraordinary success to something so obvious. Consequently they insist on looking for secrets that aren't there.

Like many others, you refuse to believe that the reason for

IBM's great success over the years can be as simple as it sounds: hiring the brightest and most highly motivated people it can find, training them thoroughly, rewarding them generously, and pointing all their efforts toward the singular goal of satisfying the customer. Why is it necessary that the 'secret' be more complex, profound or arcane?

It was no accident that, in 1986, when IBM's sales and profit growth rates began to slow, it immediately set about determining *how* it could increase its commitment to understanding and meeting customers' needs, particularly in the face of strong market-led competitors, such as DEC. One quick way was to move several thousand people from staff and production functions and into marketing jobs (as will be examined in Chapter 3).

## Making strategies work

As Kiechel found in 1982, the biggest challenge for American executives wasn't concocting strategy but making it work. This is where the IBMs excel, and where many others have gone astray.

Thomas Bonoma, in a 1984 *Harvard Business Review* article, stated that many US executives 'find it easier to think up clever marketing strategies than it is to make them work'. He said that when a seemingly effective strategy failed to meet its objectives, it was often because the execution was at fault. He also argued that:

> When unsure of the causes of poor marketing performance, managers should look to marketing *practices* before making strategic adjustments. A careful examination of the *how* questions, the implementation ones, often can identify an execution culprit responsible for problems that are seemingly strategic. (12)

Bonoma also observed that, even though problems with the basic marketing functions, such as sales force management, distribution and pricing – what he calls the 'blocking and tackling' functions – generally outnumber problems at the strategic policy level, most managers still have great difficulties with these basic ones. And yet, 'when functions go awry, it is often because headquarters simply assumes that the function in question will get executed well by someone else, somewhere else, and thus ignores it until a crisis intervenes'.

No wonder then, that Peters and Waterman placed so much

emphasis on the 'hands-on, value-driven' characteristic of excellent companies, and why in the follow-up book, *A Passion for Excellence*, Peters and Austin concluded: 'the number one managerial productivity problem in America is, quite simply, managers who are out of touch with their people and out of touch with their customers'. (13)

Bonoma was not optimistic that managers would ever learn to successfully execute the basic marketing functions.

> The marketing literature is replete with research and analysis to help managers devise marketing strategies tailored to the market place. Yet when it comes to implementing these strategies, the literature is silent and the self-help books ring hollow.

## Unimaginative implementation

Perhaps by the early 1980s the problem had become not one of too much top-down planning by out-of-touch corporate strategists, or too little implementation by untrained and ill-equipped marketing executives, but one of too much unimaginative implementation by risk-averse marketers? One reason for this may have been that there had developed too much of a sameness to marketing education, training and practice.

Academics, students, consultants and managers were all reading the same textbooks and the same articles, had all dissected the same case studies, and had all learnt the same buzzwords and shibboleths. Everyone was looking out their own window of opportunity; they all knew the angle of their experience curve; it was common knowledge that their portfolio should have a cash cow, and no dogs were allowed please. But perhaps knowing the *right* jargon was mistaken for knowing *how* to market? And perhaps a continuous barrage of frenetic me-too marketing activities had become an acceptable substitute for boldness and originality in competitiveness?

The result: in any given market all the main players were making similar, and therefore predictable, moves and counter-moves. A red gel toothpaste brand would be countered by a red and green competitive brand. A celebrity as presenter in a new television commercial would be matched by some other equally famous, and expensive, personality – and both probably had little in common with the product being touted. A toaster given away free to every new customer opening a bank account would be topped by a free microwave oven offered by the bank across the street.

The consequences of this parroting implementation really became apparent when too many firms began to compete for market share in the no-growth markets and a depressed economy at the end of the 1970s. Inevitably there were many losers. Milton Lauenstein, in a 1984 article in *The Journal of Business Strategy*, echoed Robert Heller when he concluded that:

> When several firms are addressing the same business segment, it is not possible for more than one of them to have a reasonable basis for expecting to excel. In such a situation, the 'strategies' being followed by most of them are unsound. Continuing to compete against the company best equipped to serve a specific market segment yields poor results. (14)

This sort of situation certainly developed in the market for personal computers, and Lauenstein's comments were borne out by ITT's late entry, in May 1984, with an IBM-compatible machine, the Xtra, priced at only 5 per cent below the IBM PC list, even though other IBM-compatibles were selling at up to a 20 per cent discount. Critics called it an expensive, late, me-too product. When IBM unexpectedly countered with up to a 23 per cent cut in price, ITT was forced to offer rebates of up to $700 per unit – while still having to give the dealers their normal margin. *Business Week* summed it all up for ITT, and many other hopefuls at the time: 'losses are expected to continue for some time'. The names of the many US companies which have come away reeling after taking on the technically inferior IBM PC now read like a who's who of the computer world.

## New board game

How can companies resolve this dilemma of grand strategies floundering because of unimaginative implementation? By the early 1980s, company after company appeared to be arriving at a similar conclusion: since their present marketing approach was no longer tenable, then rather than tinkering with, and tightening up, the marketing mix components it would be better to dismantle them and start again. As a result, over the past few years many top US marketing firms have begun to rethink both the original premises upon which their success was built, and the crucial processes involved in 'moving goods and services from producer to consumer'.

Linda Daly, writing in *Marketing News* in 1986, told how the UpjohnCo's Agricultural Division of Kalamazo, Michigan, realized they needed to change their twenty-year-old distribution system in order to make it 'more efficient, more responsive to the market place'. However, as Daly observed: 'When systems are used for so many years, it's often hard to create new policies and implement change quickly. In order to make the change, Upjohn set up a twelve-member task force of sales and marketing executives and, with the assistance of an outside 'facilitator', the group set out to:

- Work out why the distribution had to change.
- Define a set of specific distribution objectives – 19 in total were listed – with an importance weight assigned to each.
- Develop a range of alternative distribution channels – seven in total were proposed, including the current channel.
- Assess each alternative – on a 1–10 scoring system – against the list of weighted objectives.

Eventually three alternatives were scrutinized more closely, and one was finally selected. To help the transition to the new system the task force then met with the distribution organization and outlined the processes they had gone through to reach their final decision. Daly said, not surprisingly: 'Their excitement was transmitted to their listeners.' She concluded that:

> The philosophy behind this coaching method is simple: executives have all the information they need to make decisions, but constant exposure can make them lose their perspective.... Upjohn's people had the potential to determine the best solution all along. They didn't need an outside consultant to tell them what to do, or organize an elaborate study. All they needed was an outsider to orchestrate their thinking and keep them on an objective and creative path. Working with a management coach, they resolved – in three days – a critical concern that had been worrying management for months.

There are no textbook solutions to the problems now faced by companies such as Upjohn, and so what is happening is that some very creative and individual approaches are coming from their own executives – often with the help of outside facilitators. In addition, many top US firms have recently decided that, rather than trying to figure out new ways to get around the Monopoly board faster than their rivals, without landing on Park Lane or going directly to jail, they should be playing another board game altogether – *their game*. By reaching this original conclusion they have ushered in a new era in marketing.

The next chapter examines how some companies have recently gained 'leveraging' advantages, not by out-marketing their competitors according to the prevailing 'rules', but by changing those rules.

# 3    Changing the rules

The times of classical textbook marketing and imitative selling techniques are over. Many traditional marketing giants have gained advantages recently, not because they out-marketed their opposition according to the established – and sometimes rigidly imposed – rules of competitive practice, but because they changed the rules to their own advantage.

The rationale for this break from tradition is understandable. Where there are markets – especially mature ones – with many very capable adversaries, short-term gains by one are usually costly to achieve, and are almost invariably countered by the swift, and even more costly, reactions of others. The end result is usually some form of stalemate, with only small changes in market shares until the losers finally start dropping back, or out – not because they were out-marketed by clearly superior competitive strategies or tactics, but because they made too many basic mistakes when placed under sustained pressure.

This situation may not be confined to the US. The European mass market for cars is a good example of such an inevitability waiting to happen. The reasons for this type of situation are many. According to Robert Heller, markets are now 'naked', for three reasons:

- *There's no protection against market forces:* 'The ferocious competition created by differentiated, easy-to-enter and desire-driven markets means that a moment's marketing slumber can easily become the Big Sleep.' (1) Even government bale-out efforts cannot prevent the inevitable, claimed Heller. This may not be entirely true, as witness the turn-around efforts at Chrysler (US), Volkswagen (Germany), and Fiat (Italy). The jury is still out at Austin Rover (UK) – now the Rover Group – and Renault (France).

41

Certainly Bob Lutz, the then chairman and chief executive officer of Ford of Europe, agreed with Heller. In 1985 he asserted in *Time* that, through subsidies, governments are 'supporting companies that in a Darwinian free-enterprise environment would have ceased to exist'.

- *Secrets cannot be kept for long:* Any number of sources – sales reports, published (and unpublished) reports and articles, market research findings, job-hopping executives, industrial espionage – can all provide vital competitive information to the companies willing and able to procure it.

  *The Economist*, in 1986, reported that, although companies have always kept an informal eye on each other, it was the Japanese, with their mania for collecting market and competitive information – not always legally – that first alerted the Americans to this vital function. Sumantra Ghoshal of MIT's Sloan School of Management, submitted three reasons for this:

  > the globalization of business; the shortening life cycles of products and technologies; and the difficulty of finding a competitive advantage when in most industries leading companies are indistinguishable in technology or the scale of their operations.

  An example of one such competitive assessment was provided by Toronto's *Globe and Mail* newspaper, which reported on a 'competitive analysis' of Procter & Gamble carried out by Ogilvy & Mather Inc. of New York for the agency's clients who compete with the Cincinnati colossus. Showing prescience of what was to come over the next couple of years, as will be examined in the next chapter, O&M warned in 1984 that 'Because life has become more difficult for P&G it has become much hungrier. It is more willing to try things it might not have tried in the past. It is more reactive, less predictable and, therefore, even more dangerous.'

- *Most market places are now 'arenas for naked aggression:* Nowhere is this aggression more apparent than in the US beverage market. In a country where, on average, people consume more soft drinks than water, and where 1 per cent of the market is worth $300 million in retail sales, it is not surprising that *Fortune* should conclude that: 'Coca-Cola and PepsiCo don't wage market share battles. They fight holy wars.'

# Cola wars

At the moment Pepsi-Cola USA, the soft drink subsidiary of PepsiCo, is calling most of the shots and, as *Business Week* noted recently: 'The company is on a roll.' No wonder. After more than a decade of the Pepsi challenge, Coca-Cola has seen its lead in the cola market slowly eroded away. Worse, it suffered much embarrassment in mid-1985 when it withdrew, and then brought back, its original Coke flavour, renamed *Classic*. It has also been forced to react to a series of quick-footed moves by its arch rival – such as Pepsi's introduction of Slice, a lemon-lime soda with 10 per cent juice in 1984, and PepsiCo's attempted purchase of Seven-Up Co. in 1986.

Asking 'what makes Pepsi different?' *Business Week* in 1986 concluded:

> A fast-moving, risk-oriented management with an exquisite sense of timing, Pepsi uses the same type of research, advertising agencies, and test-marketing tools as its rivals. But its managers also recognize that marketing is more than a science based on exhaustive numerical analysis. It's a bare-knuckles sport where instincts are important. ... At Pepsi, decentralization creates a highly charged atmosphere that puts great pressure on people to perform.

Added a Pepsi observer: 'These are people who like to win.'

And no one wants to win more than Pepsi-Cola USA's President and CEO, Roger Enrico – the man who replaced John Scully, now of Apple fame. In 1986 Enrico was named by *Fortune* as one of 'America's most wanted managers', and described by the judging panel of headhunters as: 'Tough, wily, inexhaustible. Has fertile imagination, but is deadly serious ... Roger Enrico does not come to the office to make friends.'

Playing its own game against Coke, and winning, has been Pepsi's goal since 1975 when it first launched the 'Pepsi Challenge', based on a series of 'blind' test results which showed that, under test conditions anyway, a majority of Coke drinkers preferred the unlabelled Pepsi flavour over unlabelled Coke.

Comparative advertising is risky, but for the challenger with a convincing argument the payoffs can be enormous, particularly if the brand being challenged is the market leader who makes a mistake when responding. A bad mistake is to acknowledge the challenge; a worse mistake is to give it any legitimacy.

What is most surprising about the Pepsi Challenge ads is that they had any effect at all for, conventional wisdom has it that in 'life-style' markets such as soft-drinks, image and brand 'positioning' take precedence over substance and substantiation. Coke's 'It's the real thing' is a good example of this genre.

In 1981, *Maclean's* said the Pepsi Challenge:

> was one of the most aggressive and effective comparative advertising campaigns ever devised. . . . The Pepsi Challenge has proven to be a classic campaign, breaking new ground in comparative advertising and spawning imitators.

Pepsi challenged Coke on another front as well – distribution. Acknowledging that Coke was dominant in vending machine and 'soda-fountain' businesses – fastfood outlets such as McDonald's – Pepsi put most of its initial effort into securing shelf space in food stores, which accounted for about two-fifths of US soft drink sales. By 1977 Pepsi had captured first place in this sector, and have remained there ever since.

In a 1981 assessment of Coca-Cola, *Fortune*, noted: 'The efforts to halt Pepsi's advance has been a costly undertaking beset by false starts. The Pepsi Challenge . . . proved devastatingly effective. Unaccustomed to serious competition, Coke responded slowly.'

In fact, Coca-Cola responded in a variety of ways, from ignoring the challenge, to ridiculing it, to meeting it head on. One of Coke's first moves was to double national advertising spending between 1977 and 1979. It also brought out a series of amusing ads featuring Mean Joe Green, the legendary Pittsburg Steeler lineman. And then in direct response to the Pepsi Challenge, Coke ran a series of ads featuring the comedian Bill Cosby. In one print ad, which never showed or named Pepsi, Cosby scoffed: 'A lot of colas make claims, but there's only one *real thing.*'

However, in Canada, Coke slipped off its pedestal momentarily when it reacted to a series of particularly aggressive Pepsi ads in 1980 that claimed Gallup poll results were showing a significant brand-switching swing to Pepsi from Coke. In response, one print ad for Coke featured the slogan: *'If there wasn't a champion . . . there would be no challengers.'* As the surprised, but no doubt pleased, marketing director of Pepsi-Cola Canada commented: 'Why Coca-Cola would put the word challenger in their advertising is beyond me.'

South of the border, Coca-Cola USA had gone through a series of presidents without direction until, in 1978, it finally selected Brian Dyson, who had served in the company's Latin American operation, and who described himself as 'a strategy fetishist'. It was Dyson who brought some impact to Coke's advertising by using Mean Joe and Believable Bill, and massively increasing Coke's spending.

And, in a move that even caught Pepsi by surprise, Coke managed to claw back some of Pepsi's lead in food outlets by shifting dollars from national media to point-of-sale displays and price promotions – just at a time when the market was becoming price-sensitive. Perhaps expressing some of the frustrations of many packaged goods marketers over the growing power of the trade, John Scully, who was Pepsi's president at the time, informed *Fortune* in 1981: 'For a national brand to reapportion funds from the support of image to the support of price is a short-term quick fix and not a long-term strategy.'

*(One sometimes gets the impression that in these two companies, as much effort is given to fighting their market share battles in the media as in the supermarkets and fast-food outlets!)*

As it turned out, tossing money at the trade was to continue for a few more years, and it was the lesser companies which, in the end, couldn't maintain the rate.

In 1984 Pepsi switched tactics with its advertising. Deciding to build on its image among the new generation of pop-drinking video viewers – 'the Pepsi Generation' – the company replaced its Pepsi Challenge campaign with an ad costing some $5 million, and featuring Michael Jackson, the Peter Pan of rock. Pepsi also received mega-millions of dollars worth of free publicity when the superstar's hair caught fire during filming. No doubt John Scully would have called this 'event marketing' at its best.

## Classic move?

Coca-Cola meanwhile was preparing the beverage bombshell of the century. In April 1985 the company announced it was changing the flavour for the first time in 99 years – allowing for the fact that Coke's flavour varies slightly in other countries, to cater to local palates. The change did not come suddenly or cheaply. Between 1981 and 1984 Coke secretly carried out a massive taste-testing programme, involving some 190 000 respondents in twenty-five cities in the US and Canada, and costing about $4 million. In announcing the new formula, the company revealed that in various blind-tests the new flavour beat the old by a 55:45 ratio, and when tested against Pepsi the ratio was 56:44. While many companies would not proceed with anything less than 60:40, Coca-Cola decided the new flavour was 'it'.

Showing his *faith* in research, a confident Roberto Goizueta, Coke's chairman, informed *Time* that the new taste was 'the surest move ever made'. Showing his *understanding* of research, a gleeful Roger Enrico told *Fortune* that the new Coke was 'the Edsel of the 1980s'. Other Pepsi executives claimed the change of flavour was a concession that Pepsi *had* tasted better all along.

In the end Goizueta was wrong; it was not the surest move ever made. And no doubt Coke's decision, first to change the flavour, and then to bring back the old one – named *Classic* – will occupy scholars and scribes for years to come. Many will argue the duel decision was smart marketing; others will argue the opposite. By mid-1986 the results for new Coke were no doubt disappointing. Classic Coke was outselling it by a 4:1 ratio, partly because big fast food chains such as McDonald's Corp. and Kentucky Fried Chicken Corp. had abandoned the new flavour in favour of the old.

Whatever the market outcome, Coke did receive one distinction in 1985: *Fortune* put it at the top of its list of 'products of the year' award. *Fortune* proclaimed:

> Testing must be properly conducted and interpreted to have value. Coca-Cola's recent debacle is a classic study in how not to do it. The company decided to retire its flagship Coke formula on the basis of taste-tests that did not discriminate between Coke junkies – the six-pack-a-day types – and occasional sippers. Coca-Cola management not only ignored its best customers, but also failed to anticipate how the public would react to the end of a 99-year symbol of American spirit. For getting people riled up, for sparking general interest in product loyalty, and for providing a rare look at how a major marketer can make a mistake in the quest for a new product and try to correct it, New Coke, and its successor–predecessor Coca-Cola Classic, lead *Fortune*'s list of Products of the Year.

*Fortune* made one slip-up in its assessment. By calling Coca-Cola a 'major marketer' it may not have realized it was critiquing not just that company, but other companies in that elite category. As a 'major marketer' Coca-Cola was only doing what its accumulated wisdom and experience had taught it to do: it was *doing* classical marketing. Had the same situation happened to the number three or four brand in a similar product category, that company would probably have folded – for also *doing* classical marketing. As for Pepsi, it too is a 'major marketer', but it plays by different rules.

Ironically Coca-Cola may have emerged from the debacle in a stronger position to counter the momentum of Pepsi. At the least, with its marginally 'superior' new formula, Coke effectively nullified the Pepsi superior flavour claims. Backed by the momentum of the successful new Cherry Coke, plus its two cola brands – with the new Coke acting as a 'fighting brand' – Coca-Cola can apply even more leveraging pressure on shelf space, thereby pushing off the weaker brand names. Coke's ability to spend in the vicinity of $100 million on advertising (in 1985) is also enough to drown out all but the big-spending Pepsi brands.

And on another level, Cola-Cola stole a page out of Pepsi's book by staging an 'event marketing'. One industry observer pointed out to *Advertising Age* that Coca-Cola was now 'controlling the dialogue'. In other words, for some months afterwards the argument was about new Coke vs. old Coke, not Coke vs. Pepsi. And it showed. *Advertising Age*, which carries out monthly advertising awareness surveys, reported that for several months afterwards, when nation-wide samples of consumers were asked to name the first soft-drink advertising that came to mind from all they had seen, heard or read in the past thirty days, Coke topped their list – thereby stifling a new series of Pepsi ads featuring the rock star Lionel Richie. While John Scully may have started 'event marketing', Coca-Cola executives were quick to learn.

In a follow-up article, *Advertising Age* insisted: 'You can call it brilliant or a blunder, but you can't say it was boring. Coca-Cola's reformulation of Coke may have produced the broadest and fastest awareness for a new product in marketing history.' Eat your heart out, John Scully. So strong was this awareness, that *Advertising Age* reported that Coke's scores were higher than those achieved by Wendy's famous 'Where's the beef?' series of commercials which ran in 1984.

No doubt, much of this increased awareness came from the 'halo' effect generated by the controversial decision of Coca-Cola to try and change the course of American folklore history. So newsworthy was the decision to bring back the old Coke flavour, that ABC-TV interrupted its *General Hospital* soap opera to inform its viewers. *Time*, with its editorial tongue firmly in its cheek, observed in 1985:

> In the noisy confluence of publicity pronouncements, news bulletins, market analyses, gadfly lawsuits and expert pontifications on the momentous Coca-Cola controversy, the Republic seemed to shudder for an instant last week, then right itself and face toward the flag. In the midst of all the foaming and burbling, though, Americans demonstrated some interesting reactions toward the whole process of change.

Equally important, Coca-Cola itself demonstrated some interesting reactions toward the whole process of change. Until Goizueta took over the helm in 1981, critics were saying the old Southern company was drifting, and had become complacent and resistant to serious change. Even in 1984 Pepsi stole a march on Coke by launching Slice, a lemon-lime drink containing 10 per cent fruit juice, thereby creating a new category: sodas made with real juice. In November 1985, PepsiCo entered Canada with Cherry Pepsi – two days before Cherry Coke began test-marketing there. Cherry Coke was also about to commence test-marketing in the UK in January 1986, when instead it was introduced nationally – just as Cherry Pepsi began its launch. And, back in the US, in January 1986, just as Coca-Cola was about to introduce its soda with 10 per cent juice, under the Minute Maid label, Pepsi rolled out three new versions of Slice.

## Ready, fire, aim!

No more of this says Coca-Cola. The company has now served notice to Pepsi that it too is willing to wage marketing warfare the new way: 'Ready, fire, aim!' It is doubtful that Coca-Cola will have a quick reply to PepsiCo's purchase of Kentucky Fried Chicken Co., the second largest restaurant system in the world, with more than 6500 franchised and company owned units. This purchase will allow PepsiCo to convert thousands of outlets from Coke to Pepsi. And since PepsiCo already owns Pizza Hut (acquired in 1977) and Taco Bell (acquired in 1978), thereby giving it some 14000 outlets internationally, the move may eventually help push the company past McDonald's as the leading fast-food franchisor. Only a company like PepsiCo would have the commitment – and audacity – to take on two of the world's top marketing organizations simultaneously.

The holy war now being fought out by Pepsi-Cola and Coca-Cola is an example of the lengths that leading marketing companies are prepared to go to in order to clobber their competitors. If it is also an indication of how marketing is to be practised by *all* companies in the future, then executives in other firms had better start tearing up their old rule books, and looking for new ways to gain leverages. A crucial question many of them may have to answer is, 'Do they want to model their new approach on Pepsi-Cola?' If their answer is 'No', then they had better be prepared to answer the corollary question, 'If their major competitor starts acting *like* Pepsi-Cola, what will they model their new approach on?' For many companies the answer may be: 'Nobody – we'll set our own rules.'

Many other companies in the United States have also discovered that the least risky way out of wars of attrition in mature markets is not to continue with more frenetic 'me-too' activities, but to break some of the established, or most commonly accepted and practised, marketing rules.

## Cookie wars

An only slightly exaggerated hypothetical example will illustrate what could be involved, and perhaps achieved.

Having applied for a patent on its technological breakthrough in soft-centred cookie making – the interior stays soft and chewy while the exterior is crisp and crunchy – company A, a leading packaged goods marketer, quickly rushes its new soft-centred chocolate-chip cookie brand into a mid-western test market area. As it has successfully done so many times in the past, the company saturates the area with television and press advertising, distributes a combined free sample/price-off coupon to selected household clusters, and offers the trade generous introductory rebates. In two months it achieves nearly a 10 per cent share of the total cookie market in the area, and a write-up in *Advertising Age*. Meanwhile another coupon drop is made to introduce a second flavour, peanut butter.

Three months later, company B, another major packaged goods company, and No. 2 in the cookie market, introduces its own soft-centred cookie, with three flavours, into the same test market. It blitzes the area with heavier television and press advertising than had company A; distributes a bigger free sample pack, and a greater price-off coupon into more homes; offers the trade a larger rebate; and also arranges in-store tasting stands.

Two months later the soft-centred cookie share is at 15 per cent, split roughly 60:40 between companies A and B.

Six months after company A's original launch, company C, the No. 1 cookie marketer, introduces its special soft-centred cookie, with four flavours, into two other test market areas.

Company A slaps lawsuits on both competitors, claiming industrial espionage and patent infringement, and begins rolling out a national launch with four flavours. Within a year all three companies have full national coverage, and there are at least four regional brands as well. Company A's lawsuits have yet to be resolved.

A year later soft-centred cookies account for just over 17 per cent of the total cookie market and, although company A is still the market leader, its share and margins are slowly being eroded as a result of costly 'trench-warfare' tactics by all competitors. Its lawsuits are still unresolved.

Company A then decides to change the rules. It starts by creating a new subsidiary, called Sub A. The CEO of Company A is reported in various press reports as saying that he anticipates Sub A will:

> operate independently of the parent company's culture, which has evolved over the past seventy-five years, yet still retain the same commitment to marketing discipline and control that has brought this company to its present success level.... We also expect our new baby will spring a few surprises.

Sub A's first move is to buy out the two bigger regional-brand firms and, although it allows these firms to operate as separate identities, it distributes their products through its own sales force. In this way Sub A now has two separate brands – one national and one regional in the areas concerned – and more leveraging strength to capture shelf space in key grocery outlets.

Sub A's next move is to buy up a recently established chain of nearly two hundred franchised soft-centred cookie and coffee counters, which serve a choice of fifteen flavours of hot, freshly baked cookies. It also hires a top executive from McDonald's to run the chain, with the objective of establishing eight hundred new outlets within two years.

Sub A then announces that it will offer a free microwave oven – having made a special buying arrangement with a major Taiwanese manu- facturer – to every high school, university and hospital cafeteria in each local area where there is one of its cookie counter outlets. The deal is that the cafeterias are to be stocked daily with fresh packs of soft- centred cookie dough, prepared at each cookie counter during the early hours of the morning when customer trading is slowest.

The rationale behind Company A's dramatic change? Having decided that there was a bigger potential demand than that established by its conventional marketing strategies and tactics, the top executives of the company, without the guidance of textbooks, planners or consultants, set about redefining their rules for 'moving goods from the producer to the consumer'.

The results to date? While Sub A's share of cookies sold through grocery outlets is holding roughly constant, its *total* sales volume – and value – from soft-centred cookies continues to grow steadily.

## Computer wars

A far-fetched story? Not at all. Consider GM's current attempts to set up its Saturn division. While there is some speculation over the eventual success of this project, the move does illustrate GM's willingness to use its weight to its advantage, and to introduce some new rules of car marketing. Consider also IBM's introduction of its PC in 1981. One of the most remarkable marketing victories in recent years was IBM's rapid takeover of the market for personal computers. In the process IBM rewrote the book on competing in the PC market.

Yet for five years after the introduction of the Apple II, IBM had sat on the sidelines. When, in 1980, it finally began to make its foray, it set in train a series of rule-breaking decisions which, in retrospect seem so logical, but at the time probably caused much internal anxiety – and certainly caught the rest of the industry unawares.

First it set up an independent unit, in July 1980, and gave it the target of developing a competitive and easy-to-use machine within a year. The group must have also been given the freedom to write some of their own rules, given their tight deadline. Not only did the unit achieve its launch date, it also developed a product that, despite not being technologically innovative – basically it was a compilation of parts from other suppliers – within two years had captured the number one position in the market.

The PC succeeded, not simply because it had 'IBM' prefixed to its name, as some critics have charged, but because the company behind the letters introduced a new level of market intelligence gathering, and marketing discipline and commitment, to what was previously a technology-led market. And no doubt the then President of Apple – and there's a trivial pursuit question – will forever rue the remark he made to *Time* shortly after the PC's launch: 'We don't see anything out of the ordinary. There are no major technological breakthroughs and there isn't any obvious competitive edge.'

In fact, the IBM PC represented many major breakthroughs, both for the company and for the industry:

- It was the first PC with a 16-bit microprocessor rather than the standard 8-bit one, thereby giving it some technological claim. The larger memory meant that the machine had room for more complicated programs which, paradoxically, could make it easier for the neophyte to use it.

- For the first time IBM used outsiders to supply the basic components – for example, the microprocessor from Intel, the floppy disk memories from Tandon Magnetics, the printer from Epson – thereby dramatically reducing product development time, while still obtaining top-quality equipment.

- It was built via highly automated factory systems. The new Boca Raton, Florida, plant was capable of turning out a PC every 45 seconds, thereby achieving significant economies of scale.

- It was the first time IBM ventured outside the confines of its own selling organization, and thereby exposed itself to the world of trade marketing. IBM's research had showed it that one problem with other personal computers was the lack of dealer support – for example, giving adequate advice and instructions to computer-illiterate customers who nevertheless expected to walk out of the store and begin using their new machine immediately. Since the PC's price objective could not justify the cost of personal selling and end-user training by IBM, it decided to sell the PC through selected retail chains, such as Sears Roebuck, Macy's Compushop and ComputerLand, the largest franchise chain, and an Apple mainstay. Even though IBM had to give up some control over customer training, in the end it gained the benefit of a wider distribution network.

- Rather than trying to undercut the market leaders in terms of price, IBM opted to provide customers with a quality and service package that competitors would find hard to match. For example, IBM offered its own service contracts to buyers, in addition to any warranty offered by the chains, such as ComputerLand. As a result, the new machine was priced about 20 per cent higher than the popular Apple II in ComputerLand – though with options added, the PC also provided more than twice the memory of the top-of-the-line Apple.

- It was the first personal computer to be launched as a mass-market product, with TV and print media combining to give an overwhelming advertising blitz. The use of an endearing Charlie Chaplin lookalike to present the IBM PC machinery also introduced an element of creativity previously unknown to computer makers, most of whom were wedded to technology and jargon. In an award-winning series of ads, Charlie Chaplin's triumphant Little Tramp character mollified consumer's fears about personal computers, by demonstrating their ease of operation, and introducing their many applications – mostly in a humorous manner.

  In the process the Chaplin character created a unique position for both the IBM and the PC in a market rapidly becoming overwhelmed by a bewildering array of unknown names and overblown claims. When asked to explain the secret of his success, the actor who plays Chaplin explained to *Advertising Age*: 'The essence of the character is in the vulnerability. IBM is such a big, powerful company. By using Charlie, the element of fear disappears.' IBM – through its advertising – showed the sort of sensitivity towards consumers' feelings and needs that one might have previously expected from makers of cosmetics, but not electronic computers.

- IBM recognized that buyers of personal computers were purchasing a machine not for its inherent technical features, but for what it would *do*. IBM also recognized that an immediate, and large, supply of software would be needed to attract customer attention and make the machine appeal to a very diverse target market. In a move that to some observers was the most important factor in the PC's success, IBM solved these problems by becoming the first computer company to adopt an 'open-architecture' approach. This meant making its machine's technical specifications available to other firms, and encouraging outsiders to write software or build peripheral equipment, leading to the explosive growth in non-IBM hardware and software. The result was that the IBM PC, not the Apple, soon became *the* industry standard. Ironically, five years later, with the onslaught of clones from Southeast Asia, in particular, IBM was probably regretting this crucial decision.

## Think differently

In all respects, IBM rewrote the rules of marketing personal computers, and this allowed the company to 'drive' the market, rather than be driven by it. In turn, IBM obtained important leveraging advantages in each of the four crucial processes: R&D, production, trade and consumer marketing. No other competitor at the time had anywhere near the same degree of control over what it was doing.

An intriguing question, and one that may never be answered, is: did IBM deliberately set out to break so many rules in order to take over the market, or did somebody at the top push the panic button – and breaking the rules become a permissible necessity in order to get into the market before the market slipped away? Whatever the originating circumstances of IBM's success, the end result is certainly not disputed.

Not that the industry leaders at the time of launch showed too much concern. Echoing Apple's President, and also showing his own product preoccupation, a senior executive of Tandy admitted to *Business Week*: 'There definitely is a new kid on the block. But', he added, 'there is nothing that IBM has presented that would blow the industry away.'

In an early assessment of the PC's success, *Business Week* in 1982 predicted that the personal computer market:

> may be the first computer market where marketing savvy, production know-how, and other business skills are more important than engineering talent. Quality engineering talent is merely the price of admission to the personal computer market; playing the game requires a great deal more.

In a later article, in 1983, *Business Week* also predicted that since:

> IBM has so quickly cornered the market its competition could

shrink to ten major players – at most – over the next eighteen
months ... the personal computer market is already taking on
many of the characteristics of a mature market. It is being
dominated by a few large suppliers, and marketing and distribution skills are becoming more important than the latest
technology.

In a 1983 assessment, *Maclean's* gave this synopsis:

During the 1970s the company lost some of its momentum.
While blue-jeaned inventors in Silicon Valley were revolution-
izing the industry, IBM executives seemed by contrast to be
dozing at their desks. Then, over the past three years, the
corporation has awakened determinedly and shaken the entire
industry in the process. Free of the restraints of a 13-year battle
with US antitrust authorities and invigorated by a major internal
reorganization, IBM has become the most aggressive player in
the field.

Perhaps *Fortune*, in 1983, best summed up what the IBM PC
represented:

To its old motto, 'Think', IBM seems to have appended the
word 'differently'. . . . By transforming itself rather than clinging
to old strategies, IBM has increased its command over the
future. When a dominant company's advantage wanes, seemingly perilous, tradition-shattering change can be the course of least
risk.

## Problems with Junior

What is surprising is that IBM then fared so badly with the PC Junior:
launched in November 1983, revamped and price cut in July 1984,
heavily discounted in December 1984, and finally withdrawn in
March 1985. As *Business Week* asked: 'How, in less than a year, could
[IBM] have changed from a personal-computer maker that could do
no wrong to one roundly criticized by dealers and the trade press for
introducing a dog?'

One suggestion is that, by trying to prevent the cannibalizing of PC
sales, IBM 'hobbled' the Junior. It originally had a toy-like keyboard,
which made it unsuitable for word processing, the main application for

personal computers in the office; it could not run many popular business programs without additional hardware; it was inferior to some of its competitors for playing games, the main application for personal computers in the home; and at a price range of $699 to $1269 for various models (without accessories such as a display monitor), it was seen as offering poor value for money compared with many other home computers. In order words, IBM badly positioned the PC Junior – too expensive for casual home users, but not powerful enough for the serious users who could afford a more capable machine.

According to *Business Week*, which described the Junior as neither 'fish nor fowl', IBM made several serious errors in marketing judgement. Unlike the PC, the Junior was 'designed in a vacuum', with little outside technical help. In 'true IBM style', the company seemed more concerned about cannibalization than about 'designing a product that consumers could afford and use'. It was not properly test-marketed to 'determine whether it had features consumers wanted'. Finally, the development programme was 'handicapped by a complex structure of internal product design and marketing teams'. Moreover, the PC was 'pushed' onto the trade, rather than marketed to them.

In other words, many of the lessons learned from the PC launch about breaking the rules seemed to have been forgotten, or ignored, in an effort to compromise on various corporate policies. The PC Junior demonstrates why so many new products fail – not because they are outgunned or out-manoeuvred by their more astute competitors, but because too many internal compromises and mistakes are made. The end result is that not enough leveraging pressure is then exerted where it is most needed.

Needless to state, IBM learned from this mistake. One market researcher, in a later assessment, told *Business Week*: 'PCjr taught IBM humility. IBM now knows it can't win markets simply by showing up. It has made them a tougher competitor.'

## RISC moves

That IBM appears to have learned something is shown by its introduction of the new PC RT – the RT being a corruption of RISC, or 'reduced instruction set computing'. Perhaps borrowing a few tricks from Pepsi, IBM announced in January, 1986, that it would be shipping its new 32-bit RT personal computer in March, thereby preempting Hewlett–Packard's February announcement of a new generation of RISC-based machines.

With its announcement IBM managed to catch both the market, and competitors, by surprise. Most observers expected it to announce a new lap-held computer, its entrant into a growth sector of the generally depressed market for personal computers – the lap-top was finally announced in April. Instead IBM decided to come out with its RT first, and aim it at a highly specialized sector of the industry: the market for workstations, or beefed-up microcomputers used in computer-aided design and manufacturing. This is a market that the company estimated has three million potential buyers, such as engineers, technical draughtspeople and researchers – users who require more computing brawn than brain. General Motors alone is expected to spend some $300 million on workstations. As *The Economist* noted: 'IBM knows how to spot a market. . . . And it will probably be a less fickle and more profitable market than the one for lap-held computers.'

With its announcement IBM became the first mainstream computer manufacturer to take a gamble on reduced instruction set computer architecture. In fact, RISC was first developed by IBM in the early 1970s. Basically it is a computer that has fewer and simpler instructions than most. As such it had previously been adopted only by start-up innovators, and this particular corner of the industry was dominated by specialist companies, such as Apollo, Sun and Digital Equipment.

Perhaps no more. Heller's argument that, in most markets there is room for only one leader, a runner-up and a specialist, may now apply both to the main markets *and* to the niches. IBM, by its announcement of the RT, has served notice that even the specialist niches are no longer safe havens. What the IBMs and the Coca-Colas and Pepsi-Colas are demonstrating, is that they are now out to dominate, not just the middle ground of their markets, but all the edges as well.

And yet, in a remark to *Business Week* that he may long regret, the vice-president for advanced technology at Apollo dismissed the RT as a 'relatively vanilla product, less than we expected'. Perhaps he should study IBM's new approach to marketing more carefully. As *Business Week* noted, in an earlier article: 'When IBM goes after a new market, it intends to win and win big. These days, IBM is foraging for new sources of revenues all over the information-processing jungle. And when it finds them, only the fittest will survive.'

In a 1984 article entitled 'Is IBM playing too tough?', *Fortune* claimed IBM had earlier tended to stay away from some of the industry's more aggressive tactics in order to avoid potential antitrust problems. No more. One competitor complained: 'IBM is actively doing most things it used to prohibit. Its people tell customers about products way in advance so they can chill our sales; they openly disparage us; they even go in after we've made a sale and try to break the contract.'

If IBM competitors were worried about IBM's selling tactics in 1984, by 1987 they were downright terrified. Late in 1986 the company announced that, as part of its efforts to cut down costs, and improve its position in the slumping market, it would shift some 2000 marketing staff into sales positions. This would give it nearly 10000 salespeople, not to mention a few thousand extra serving people, out in the market place – about 4000 more than at the start of 1986. By making this move IBM was also announcing a new era of on-the-ground aggressiveness.

## Clone wars

While IBM may have demolished many of its US competitors who tried to make PC-compatibles, by mid-1986 it was struggling to cope with a new breed of interlopers – the makers of PC clones. These machines often looked and behaved like IBM PCs; they ran on PC software; mostly they came from South-east Asia; they cost about half the price of the PC; and many of them were gaining access to scarce shelf space since they were being sold as house brands by computer dealers. *Time* reported that by mid-1986 IBM's share of the personal computer market was about 33 per cent, compared with the 40 per cent it commanded eighteen months earlier. During the same period, IBM was forced to discount its price of the PC from around $2300 to around $1600. IBM's original 'open-architecture' idea was suddenly no longer such a good idea. Although the PCs accounted for only about 10 per cent of IBM's revenues in 1985, at various stages in 1986 the company talked of leaving what to them was fast becoming a commodity market.

In a 1986 cover story, *Business Week* remarked of the IBM PC:

> The machine, once IBM's exclusively, has become a generic
> product that anybody with a few hundred dollars and some

elementary electronic knowhow can assemble.... Just three years ago the PC symbolized the overwhelming power of the IBM name. Although the machine incorporated few innovations and no distinctive technology, by mid-1983 the IBM logo had made it the dominant personal computer sold to businesses. Now more than two hundred clone suppliers are trying to undo that.

According to *Business Week*, IBM's original strategy was to continually update the PC, and cut prices when required, in order to forestall competitors. But, said *Business Week*, 'IBM didn't execute its strategy well. Instead of a moving target, the IBM PC became a sitting duck.' It didn't change its hardware and software often enough and dramatically enough; it didn't cut its prices fast enough and far enough; and it didn't offer servicing contracts that buyers couldn't afford to ignore, and competitors couldn't afford to match.

Such criticisms were not confined to the business press. By early 1987 IBM was coming under fire from another front – its shareholders – as both its profits and share price fell in 1986.

Carol Loomis, in a 1987 *Fortune* article, 'IBM's big blues: a legend tries to remake itself', said:

Amazingly [chairman] John Akers says the quintessential marketing company lost touch with the buyers.... It persisted in trying to sell them products when what they wanted was solutions – help in getting their thousands of computers to talk to each other, help in wringing both productivity gains and competitive advantage out of their investments in data-processing equipment.

Which is one reason why IBM began moving thousands of executives from factory and staff positions into various marketing jobs. It was a draconian move reminiscent of Mazda Motors of Japan nearly a decade earlier, when that quintessential engineering company found its thirsty wankel-engined cars out of favour. Said Loomis: 'The extra 5000 [marketing staff] will be set to work doing what many of the first 23 000 are being retrained to do: provide the customers with solutions.

## *Ready, aim, fire?*

Despite its commitment to the sluggish high-margin business, and its setbacks in the mini computer market, nobody is underestimating IBM's ability to come roaring back, and even to set some new rules in the process. For example, IBM, which owns some 20 per cent of the shares of Intel, the Silicon Valley chip maker, currently uses Intel's standard chips to make its PCs. Late in 1986, IBM announced it had signed a technology agreement with Intel which would give IBM the rights to incorporate Intel's microprocessor and peripheral chip designs into customized chips. Industry observers said this move would allow the company to build a new generation of personal computers that could not easily be copied by its competitors.

IBM made another move in 1986 that competitors – from any country – will also find hard to match. It introduced its lap-top PC Convertible, and the most outstanding feature of the machine is that it is the first computer to be built entirely by robots – and the factory is located in the heart of the USA. As Bill Saporito observed in a 1986 *Fortune* article:

> But IBM didn't build the breakthrough facility in Austin, Texas, just to get into the lap-top business. The line is designed to make not only the Convertible but any electronic product that is no bigger than 2 feet by 2 feet by 14 inches . . . the technology IBM developed for Austin gives the company a chance to be a competitive player, if not the low-cost producer when the next generation of more powerful PCs arrive in a year or so.

Chapter 6 examines the proposition that manufacturing has become a critical marketing leverage.

In today's high-speed PC market, the three points made by Heller at the start of this chapter now apply. Even if you're IBM, there's no protection against market forces, secrets cannot be kept for long, and the market place is an arena for naked aggression.

What Coca-Cola, PepsiCo, IBM and the hypothetical cookie company have demonstrated is that there's no sure security, particularly for companies relying on past 'formulas', and competing by the traditional 'rules'. New competitors, new technologies, and new regulations – or deregulations – can quickly change the nature of an industry, and overturn the fortunes of its participants. We are in a new era in marketing, and the new rules have yet to be established. Success is likely to go to those companies which can quickly orchestrate, tightly control, and fiercely execute, marketing strategies which break away from the prevailing practices. In the process, they may then realize the leveraging opportunities that are present in the flow of goods approach to marketing. In the next chapter some of these leveraging opportunities will be examined.

# 4 Looking for leverages

While the word 'leverage' is not yet an everyday part of the marketing lexicon, many firms have found it advantageous to concentrate on what can be termed the 'leveraging' opportunities to be found in the flow-of-goods approach to marketing. Certainly the term 'leveraging' is not unknown, though the extent of its marketing possibilities have not been fully explored.

In a 1980 *Business Horizons* article 'Marketing in the 1980s – back to basics', Keith Cox used the term 'organizational leveraging' when writing that firms in different industries have various leveraging strengths in the four functional areas: production, marketing, finance and distribution: 'The results of matching an organization with its environment are referred to as the key leverages of the organization.' He suggested that, for example, consumer-goods firms might stress their marketing and distribution strengths, whereas industrial firms are more likely to stress their production and financial strengths. (1)

However, arguing that the marketing function itself may be an important leveraging strength is an insufficient explanation for *how* a firm is to achieve success in a highly competitive market. In today's high-speed markets it may be *how* a firm manages its marketing tasks – Bonoma's 'blocking and tackling' from Chapter 2 – that will make the difference.

In this vein, Benson Shapiro, in a 1979 *Harvard Business Review* article, 'Making money through marketing', used the term 'points of leverage' when recommending that firms identify and then concentrate on those aspects of the marketing function that are most important:

Marketing is an incredibly complex task.... To do the task well requires concentration on those aspects of the task that are most important, paying relatively little attention to the less important aspects.

This, in turn, means that it is first necessary to identify the important things. By definition, the important things are those aspects of the task in which a little effort generates a lot of return. Activities which reward management in this way are said to have *leverage*. (2)

Shapiro returned to this concept in a 1985 *Harvard Business Review* article, 'Rejuvenating the marketing mix', when he examined the elements of the marketing mix and concluded that they must meet the requirements of consistency, integration and leverage:

To leverage you use the most efficient tools for the market segments being emphasized. (Efficiency, in this sense, relates to the engineering concept of output per unit of input. Thus we might look at unit sales generated per dollar of advertising or personal selling to determine which was more efficient, or what combination of the two was most efficient.) (3)

Theodore Levitt used the word 'differentiation' to refer to something akin to Shapiro's 'points of leverage'. In his 1980 *Harvard Business School* article, 'Marketing success through differentiation – of anything', he argued that the way in which a company manages its marketing function may be the most important way it differentiates itself from its competitors.

What differentiates [companies such as General Foods, P&G, IBM and Xerox] from others is how well they manage marketing, not merely what they market. It is the process, not just the product, that is differentiated. (4)

Levitt explained that companies such as General Foods and Procter & Gamble try, via advertising and promotion, to create consumer 'pull'. They also try to create wholesaler and retailer 'push'. He gave as an example of the latter, General Foods' undertaking a study of retail space profitability and then offering the results to supermarket owners: 'By helping retailers manage their space better, General Foods presumably would gain retailers' favor for its products in their merchandising activities.'

In effect General Foods was trying to achieve trade marketing leverage. John Scully, when he was President of Pepsi-Cola USA, understood the concept well. In 1982, when commenting on Pepsi's introduction of Pepsi Free and Coke's launch of Diet Coke, he informed *Business Week:* 'The more brands we and Coke bring out, the harder it will be for smaller companies to get shelf space. They have no leverage in the stores.' Leverage in this sense is equated with control and power.

Thomas Bonoma, in his 1984 *Harvard Business Review* article, 'Making your marketing strategy work', expressed concern that firms might fall into the trap of 'global mediocrity', whereby they take satisfaction in doing an adequate job on each of the main marketing tasks. 'The best companies have a facility for handling one or two marketing functions and are competent in the rest. (5)

The concept of leverage needs to be considered in terms other than looking for a competitive edge through excelling in one or two of Bonoma's 'blocking and tackling' tasks. In today's 'naked' markets a firm needs to apply continuous pressure on *all* fronts it if is to make a long-term impact on consumers, or if it is to force competitors into tactical errors, which it can then exploit.

## Breaking down the processes

In this sense Walter Kiechel III, in his 1982 *Fortune* article, 'Corporate strategists under fire', came closest to expressing the concept of leverages – without using the term – as explained in this book. Kiechel said that companies need to consider a concept known as 'field theory' whereby, once they decide on which field of activity to compete in, they must then decide on what skills will be required – companywide – to win in that field. Four areas of particular interest are: products made, customers sold to, places sold in, and value added skills:

> Break down the entire process by which your product is brought to market, the new thinking goes, break it down into the individual elements that represent costs or value-added: raw materials, labor in manufacturing, inventory-carrying cost, distribution. Try to do the same analysis for your competitors' products. At any stage, is there something that you can do – and, ideally, that your rivals can't – to make your product more attractive to the customer than the other offerings?

Kiechel mentioned Proctor & Gamble as one company particularly adept at value-added skills. P&G markets its products through grocery and drug outlets. To succeed, 'it needs R&D skills, the ability to link product research with market research, and thoroughgoing knowledge of advertising and promotion'.

Kiechel's view of marketing can be extended, by looking at marketing as a *process*, and in this way the concept of leverage can be included. Leveraging opportunities can be found by re-examining every aspect to do with the process of 'moving goods from producer to consumer'. They may be realized in two ways: first, in the superior ways the firm organizes the processes involved in selecting, developing and producing new products (*market-entry leverages*) and second, in the superior ways the firm executes its key marketing tasks out in the market place (*market-place leverages*).

By concentrating on *all* processes involved in moving goods from producer to consumer, the packaged goods marketer, in particular, is concerned with taking a new product idea:

- From an idea and into a prototype for testing.
- From a tested prototype and into final production.
- From the factory and into distribution and onto retail shelves.
- From the shelves and into consumer hands, repeatedly.

By breaking down the entire process into the individual processes that represent a means of achieving a competitive advantage, leveraging opportunities can be realised at any – if not all – of the following four stages: (see Figure 4.1).

While the diagram is simple, and the logic common sense, the implementation of the ideas suggested by the diagram is not without its difficulties and risks. This has not deterred many US companies from rethinking the processes involved at each of these four stages, now that they realize that it is the implementation, not creation, of strategy that is so important. As a result, many of them are developing significant new ways to gain leveraging advantages over their competitors.

The question they need to ask is: 'Where are our leverages?. . . . Do they come from our innovation and R & D processes? Our production and operations advantages? Our trade marketing expertise? Our consumer marketing skills?' Today's reality is that there is no one best leverage. When marketing is considered from a 'flow of goods and services' perspective, the necessity to win at *all* four stages becomes apparent.

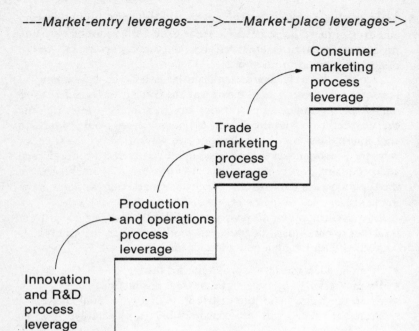

---Market-entry leverages---->---Market-place leverages->

**Figure 4.1 Marketing leverages**

## Rethinking at P&G

Nowhere is the evidence of new thinking more apparent than at Procter & Gamble, the company which practically invented marketing. Although it had managed to double its unit sales volume every ten years prior to 1980, and double its real sales growth every twelve years, by the mid-80s P&G was showing signs of the wash-day blues. After viewing P&G's 1985 results, *Time* reported that:

> For decade after decade Procter & Gamble, the household-products giant, has never failed to show financial results as bright as the clothes in its detergent ads. But when the Cincinnati-based company hung out its latest profit statement last week, there was dirty laundry on the line.

With fiscal 1985 profits down 29 per cent, to $635 million, P&G had suffered its first annual earnings decline since 1952. This was so long ago that *Advertising Age*, in an appraisal of P&G, reminded its readers that 'Harry Truman was president then, the Dodgers were still in Brooklyn, Rocky Marciano was the world heavyweight boxing champion and Gary Cooper won an Oscar for his performance in "High Noon".'

Many P&G observers feel that P&G is beginning to pay the price for a period of complacency. Two companies in particular, Lever Brothers – which Faye Rice in *Fortune* recently described as 'the long-somnolent US branch of the British giant Unilever' – and Colgate-Palmolive Inc. – which *Business Week* once quoted one ex-P&G staffer as saying could always be counted on 'to fall on its own sword' – are now challenging P&G's dominance in several markets.

## Changing environment

In a 1985 *Fortune* review Bill Saporito said that P&G needed to get back in step with a competitive environment that had changed substantially over the past decade:

> A decline in the network television audience has made P&G's primary tool less efficient. Wholesalers and retailers have grown more independent and have begun to balk at P&G's haughty treatment of them. Competitors have narrowed the quality gap that P&G often enjoyed, making premium prices harder to command. These changes have mercilessly pounded some of P&G's most profitable products.

There is much evidence that P&G fell out of step with the changing times. Critics argued it was slow in responding to consumers trading down in the late 1970s; then in the early 1980s it was slow in responding to consumers trading up. Ironically, P&G's internal system of checks and balances – which in times of steady growth was a major strength – may have been a contributing factor to this in-built inertia. And P&G's famous memo system may have been at the heart of the problem. To ensure that decisions were made on facts alone, managers were required to condense proposals to no more than two or three typewritten pages. While this system was originally intended to achieve disciplined decision making, more recently it meant an increasing number of relatively minor decisions took inordinate lengths of time to work their way through the organization. In 1983 *Business Week* reported one P&G staffer as saying that it took two years – as memos worked their way up and down the corporate ladder – for P&G to decide whether it should package Instant Folger's Coffee in 2-, 6- and 10-oz, or 2-, 4- and 8-oz jars.

In 1985 *Business Week* said:

> Procter's problems go beyond temporary business setbacks. They reflect a corporate culture that is stifling at times – and not easily changed. In an age where creative thinkers within big companies often get the freedom to try ideas without interference from above, P&G remains bureaucratic and centrally controlled. Indeed, few companies so large delegate so little.

## Changing nappies

Nowhere was the penalty for caution more apparent than in the nappy business, where Kimberly-Clark Corp's premium-priced Huggies brand (temporarily) ousted P&G's mid-priced Pampers brand as market leader. Although Pampers was not first in disposable nappies, it demonstrated the basic philosophy that guided P&G when developing new products and markets. John Smale, the ex-marketing man who was involved with the successful launch of Crest toothpaste some twenty-five years ago, and who became P&G's chief executive officer in 1981, explained this philosophy to *Fortune* in 1985: 'We first of all determine if we've got a technical right to succeed in a business. Then we look at the total size of the business and its profit margins.' In an earlier assessment of P&G, Faye Rice in *Fortune* had also concluded that 'Pampers seemed to demonstrate what Procter & Gamble does best: develop a product that barely existed yesterday and market it so few people can live without it tomorrow.'

Pampers was one of P&G's greatest success stories. It was introduced in 1961, when real incomes were still rising, and consumers were willing to pay more for demonstrable benefits. Pampers was so successful that, by 1975, it had some 75 per cent of the market by value, and disposable nappies became P&G's second largest business after laundry detergents. However, by the mid-70s, when real incomes began to decline, P&G tried to reduce the impact of sales to lower priced generic and store-owned brands by conventional economy measures – holding down costs and prices on Pampers – not by introducing a budget-priced brand. Instead, in the late 70s P&G introduced Luvs, a premium-priced brand, in order to capture the top end of the market.

According to *Advertising Age* in 1985, by the early 1980s P&G was again misreading the latest market trends:

> In the 1980s, when consumers had more money to spend, P&G was still on an economy kick. It took another company, Kimberly-Clark Corp., Neenah, Wis., to recognize that mothers were willing to pay more for diapers with greater absorbancy and containment, as well as for such conveniences as refastenable tapes. K-C acted on this perception by rolling out Huggies.

So successful was Huggies that, by mid-1985, it had about 32 per cent of the $2.8 billion market; Pampers was down to about 30 per cent, with Luvs at 16 per cent. Yet, in 1981 P&G's total share had been close to 60 per cent.

## Changing manuals

In her 1984 *Fortune* article Faye Rice quoted one ex-P&G staffer as saying: 'Kimberley-Clark stole a page right out of Procter's manual of how to succeed: get an excellent product and execute well.'

Other competitors may also be reading the same manual:

- Lever Brothers recently pushed its Dove beauty soap into the No.1 position in dollar sales, replacing P&G's Ivory soap, which has been available for more than a hundred years.
- Lever's Wisk liquid in 1985 ousted P&G's Cheer as the No.2 brand in the heavy-duty detergents market, though Tide powder still holds the number one slot.
- Colgate-Palmolive beat P&G to the market with both a gel toothpaste and the popular pump dispenser. As a result Colgate's share of the market rose from around 18 per cent in 1979 to about 28 per cent in mid-1985. Crest, which enjoyed about 40 per cent of the market in 1977, saw its share fall to just under 30 per cent by mid-1985.

*Advertising Age* observed that when Lever Brothers and Beecham

Products began succeeding with gels a few years ago, the two market leaders, P&G and Colgate-Palmolive, 'realized the rules had changed'. P&G chose a defensive response, and introduced a new and improved Crest; Colgate chose a more offensive one, and introduced a gel line extension. According to *Advertising Age:*

> What P&G missed was the consumer's willingness to pay more for a toothpaste that tasted better – essentially a cosmetic benefit. The company was late in introducing a gel, and that tardiness left P&G clinging to its No.1 position in the category by the skin of its teeth.

## The myth of product superiority

The toothpaste battles may also illustrate another P&G trait besides slow reflexes – an over-reliance on brand superiority claims based on technological advances. P&G's well publicized failure with Pringles potato chips highlight the problems associated with a pre-occupation with a product's functional superiority. Launched in the mid-70s, Pringles uniformly shaped chips were packed in cans. This was supposed to overcome the traditional problems of freshness and shipping that beset the standard products. Critics claimed that Pringles failed because P&G was again out of step with a changing market: it was seen as too expensive at a time when consumers were concerned with rising prices; it was also perceived as being overprocessed at at time when consumers were moving toward 'natural' foods. In a 1981 *Fortune* article, Carol Loomis observed that: 'The Pringles experience fits a widely held theory that P&G is too intent on the function of its products to succeed in areas like taste and fashion.'

## The myth of marketing transfer

Procter & Gamble has also come up against another harsh reality: marketing superiority in one product-market area doesn't mean the same techniques can automatically be transferred to other areas. Over the past decade P&G has attempted to enter new markets via acquisition rather than internal product development. The result has been a series of head-to-head confrontations with a new set of competitors, many of whom have proven equal to the challenge.

Procter & Gamble's entry into the chilled and frozen juice markets via its acquisition of the Ben Hill Griffin citrus processing operation, and subsequent launch of the Citrus Hill orange juice brand in both frozen concentrate and refrigerated, ready-to-pour forms, has brought the company into direct conflict with market leader Coca Cola – with Minute Maid – and number two Beatrice Co – with Tropicana.

Using technology developed in the coffee industry to preserve the natural taste and aroma of coffee beans, P&G claimed it had a superior product – pulpier, better flavour, better texture, and more aroma. Less than two years after launch, and after spending some $125 million in advertising in fiscal 1985 , *Time* announced the brand had 'gone flat'. *Advertising Age* quoted analysts claiming that, although P&G anticipated a 15 per cent market share, by the end of 1986 they'll probably not achieve much above 10 per cent in a market that is dominated by generic and private-label brands – plus Minute Maid and Tropicana. In 1985 *Business Week* reported that critics believed P&G was mistaken in trying to establish a premium brand in what was essentially a commodity market. As one former P&G manager told *Business Week:* 'We're not dealing with a product where you can lay it down and say, "This shirt is white." ' P&G's problems with Citrus Hill may also stem from its relative inexperience in selling into freezer space, as opposed to the more familiar shelf space territory of a supermarket.

Procter & Gamble's entry into the over-the-counter drugs market has brought it up against the likes of Sterling Drug, Bristol-Myers, American Home Products and Johnson & Johnson. In June 1984, P&G launched Encaprin, a new encapsulated aspirin that the company claimed was 'a better way to treat arthritis than plain aspirin'. President John Smale called over-the-counter drugs 'a P&G kind of business', meaning that it is big, and it combines high technology with heavy consumer advertising and promotion. Despite spending $35–50 million on advertising and promotion to launch the brand, *Fortune,* in late 1985, stated that the results to date were 'unimpressive.' This was not surprising, since Encaprin's entry into the $1.2 billion analgesics market was quickly countered by the introduction of new ibuprofen-based pain killers from Bristol-Myers Co. (Nuprin) and American Home Products Corp. (Advil), with each company spending more than $50 million in advertising and media support.

Procter & Gamble entered the cookie business nationally in 1984 with the launch of its Duncan Hines soft-centre cookie, but by mid-

1985 had only about 5 per cent share of the market. *Advertising Age* predicted: 'P&G may have bitten off more than it can comfortably chew by entering the $3.1 billion ready-to-eat cookie market in 1984 with a product that's now considered a parity product at best.

Procter & Gamble believed its baking technology would give it a significant form of product differentiation – the product's emulsifying agents are claimed to prevent crystallization of the sugar solution, thereby keeping the cookies crisp on the outside and soft on the inside. What P&G failed to anticipate was that its competitors in the market would respond so quickly with similar brands. In fact, two forces, the No.1 company, Nabisco Brands Inc. – with Almost Home – and the No.2 company, Keebler Co., a subsidiary of United Biscuits PLC of Britain – with Soft Batch – came up with the same kind of product based on the same kind of technology, even before P&G had completed its test marketing programme in Kansas City, in 1983. Nabisco was the first to react and, as one market analyst revealed to *Marketing:* 'They saw soft cookies were where the growth was. They had to participate and had the time – P&G, for example, stayed in Kansas City forever.'

Procter & Gamble's patent-infringement suits against Nabisco and Keebler, and also against Frito-Lay, the snack food subsidiary of PepsiCo – with GrandMa's Rich'n Chewy line – are still outstanding. P&G's big problem as put to *Advertising Age* in 1985 by one industry watcher, was that:

> The food and beverages markets are very different from detergents and toothpaste. Almost anybody can copy what anybody else makes. And in this case, neither Frito-Lay, Keebler nor Nabisco is going to go away just because P&G is in the market with what is essentially the same kind of cookie.

## The 'New! Improved!' P&G?

But neither is P&G going to go away, if some recent moves are evidence of its ability to bounce back. There can be little doubt that P&G – unable to hold, let alone build, market share and profits in many of the categories it has dominated for so many years – has been forced to introduce new approaches to marketing. The evidence from the past few years suggests that these new approaches reflect a massive, highly structured and tightly controlled organization now being prepared to break its own rules in order to come to grips with the realities of a different set of market rules. As noted in Chapter 3, Ogilvy and Mather Inc., in a 1984 'competitive analysis' study of P&G, observed:

> Because life has become more difficult for P&G it has become hungrier. It is more willing to try things it might not have tried in the past. It is more reactive, less predictable and, therefore, even more dangerous.

This is a far cry from an earlier assessment of P&G. In a 1981 report Ogilvy & Mather maintained that the company was 'disciplined and consistent', and that its executives 'plan, minimize risk, and adhere to proven principles'.

Bill Saporito, in his 1985 *Fortune* article, agreed with Ogilvy & Mather's more recent observations:

> P&G is scrambling in many ways as it tries to break out of more than half a decade of stumbling meager growth. Competitors think they are seeing a new Procter & Gamble – and they are...the Cincinnati colossus is attacking simultaneously on more fronts than ever before, and in so doing has adopted several tactics that are distinctly un-P&G.

In her 1986 *Fortune* article on P&G, Faye Rice reported that three changes to its strategy are contributing to the revival:

- it is beating competitors with superior new products, rather than matching them with parity ones;
- in an unprecendented burst of line extensions, it is exploiting the strengths of its established brands by introducing new products with old, familiar names; and
- it is recognizing the importance of trade marketing leverage.

## Thinking big

In 1985 Bill Saporito in *Fortune* had concluded: 'P&G's scrappy new ways – and its diminished status – are most evident in the battle for babies' backsides.'

In January, 1985, P&G announced a $500 million upgrading of its nappy production facilities in order to market a 'new generation of Pampers' that it claimed would be more leak-resistant. Industry observers were predicting that, in order to inform consumers of the benefits of its new range of nappies the company would spend some $225 million on advertising and promotion over the next two years. One analyst told *Advertising Age* in 1985: 'In my fifteen years covering P&G I don't remember any other undertaking of this magnitude. The size of the restaging of Pampers world-wide is mind-boggling.'

Procter & Gamble first introduced new Blue Ribbon Pampers with a leakproof waistband and elasticized legs in early 1985, and followed this with Luvs Baby Pants. Its biggest move was in February, 1986, when it announced new Ultra Pampers. *Business Week* said that, for P&G, the launch was:

> vintage hoopla. There was the new product: a superabsorbent disposable diaper.... Scientific studies on diaper rash.... An endorsement from a national pediatric association....The product introduction showed that P&G – a marketing king that has suffered some humiliations of late – is on the march again.

The fact that the company is marching to a drum beat reminiscent of the one that originally launched Crest – which was endorsed by the American Dental Association – is probably no coincidence, given Smale's association with both products.

Rice said that Ultra Pampers 'are transforming the industry'. The older nappies were made of paper pulp, while the new ones are made of a highly absorbent, granulated polymer which turns to a gel when wet, thereby soaking up the wetness. They are also much thinner than the older products. Ironically, the unpatented technology was first developed in Japan, though P&G was the first American company to adopt it. In fact, it has locked up a supplier of the scarce polymer material by assisting a Japanese vendor to finance a new plant, thereby achieving a production leverage that its competitors cannot yet match. In six months P&G's total share of the nappy market was nearing the 60 per cent mark and, said Rice, 'Kimberly-Clark is scrambling to match Ultras'.

## Thinking small

Procter & Gamble is also beginning to think small. Until recently it had concentrated on developing truly new products for potential major markets, rather than dissipating its massive resources behind extensions of existing brands, competitive-parity products or minor brands. All that has now changed. P&G has started to introduce a range of new products under established brand names, a defensive move that, to some industry observers, signals a major shift in strategy.

For example, P&G has capitalized on the strength of its Ivory soap image – despite its ousting from the number one slot by Dove – by introducing, in 1984, a new Ivory shampoo and conditioner. Within a year it had captured an estimated 5 per cent share of the market in unit sales. P&G's Head & Shoulders shampoo, with 10 per cent, is considered the market leader.

In late 1984 P&G introduced Liquid Tide which, one senior executive insisted to *Fortune,* 'is the first liquid we've developed that's had the quality of cleaning performance that we felt comfortable putting the Tide name on'. Eighteen months later Liquid Tide had become a star performer in its own right. Rice reported that it was 'locked in a fierce battle for the No.2 position' with Lever Bros.' Wisk, with powdered Tide holding onto the No.1 slot in the total detergents market.

Early in 1986 P&G began test marketing Tide Multi-Action Sheets, a combination of detergent, whitener and fabric softener packaged in a single quilt-like sheet, and used in both the washer and the dryer. In total, in 1986 P&G had five separate detergents, either in test markets or nationwide, and all bearing the Tide name.

In a 1984 interview with *Advertising Age,* a spokesperson for P&G explained the new thinking: 'With line extensions, we don't have many of the concerns and problems associated with introducing a brand-new product.' And, while recognizing the risk of damaging the existing brand if the line extension fails, she added, 'with the market more competitive we feel it's worth the risk'.

In a 1986 interview with *Advertising Age,* another spokesperson commented on the Tide detergent pouches by arguing:

> The name Tide is respected as the standard of cleaning excellence among detergents, and this product is a major advance of laundry care worthy of the product name.... It's a premium price compared with detergent, but not when compared to detergent used with other laundry additives.

In a later *Advertising Age* article Laurie Freeman added that P&G were capitalizing on an environment in which consumers were once again willing to pay more for familiar brand names. Said one analyst: 'This is an environment P&G thrives in. All of its sophisticated marketing caused grief when consumers didn't want to pay for that technology. Now, consumers are trading up.'

To the casual observer, transferring a brand name from one product category to another may not appear to be a particularly risky move. For some packaged goods marketers it is akin to moving heaven and earth without divine guidance. This author recalls, as a brand manager with Unilever New Zealand some dozen years ago, sitting in on a presentation to a group of senior marketing co-ordinating gentlemen from head office, London. Local managers were seeking permission to use the Sunlight name on a budget-priced shampoo, in order to counter the growing threat from store-owned brands. Despite reams of research evidence that showed the Sunlight name to be most acceptable as a shampoo brand, the proposal was turned down, and the locals were told in no uncertain terms that Sunlight was a name associated with detergents, not toiletry products. Not that it mattered. The name Pears Shampoo was chosen, and the brand became an immediate success.

Other 'new-old' products recently introduced by P&G have been Spic & Span pine-scented liquid cleaner, Ivory liquid soap, Folger's new decaffinated coffee and Crest Tartar Control Formula toothpaste.

Besides introducing a number of products that exploit existing brand names, largely to capture or hold retail shelf space and preserve market share, P&G has also made other un-P&G moves recently. It has introduced bargain-brands to compete at the low-priced end of the market – for example, Banner, a defence against no-name toilet tissue. It has also introduced products that lag far behind consumer and/or competitive trends – for example, Crest toothpaste in pump dispensers in 1985. Needless to state, the pump dispenser was introduced with one traditional P&G trait – a massive advertising and promotional blitz of some $20-25 million.

## Thinking fast

The once super-cautious company is also taking un-P&G risks. It is now bringing products forward into national launch much more quickly, thus eschewing the long test-marketing programmes that previously characterized their methodical approach. In today's environment P&G has found traditional test marketing to be too slow, too expensive and too open to sabotage – as evidenced by their Duncan Hines cookie crumble in Kansas City.

Whereas P&G used to spend years test marketing a new product, in mid-1985 it introduced nationally Crest Tartar Control formula toothpaste – a dental formula that helps prevent the build up of hard surface deposits on teeth – after only three months in test market. It also tested Encaprin for only three months before going national, and put Folger's instant decaffeinated coffee into national distribution without any formal test marketing programme.

Procter & Gamble's moves reflect a trend away from conventional test marketing techniques. In 1984, *Fortune* observed that a 'revolution is coming to test marketing' in the form of simulated techniques, such as Burke Marketing Services' 'BASES', or the more sophisticated scanner-based test marketing programmes, such as A.C. Nielsen's 'Testsight'. These changes will be examined in Chapter 9.

## Thinking creative advertising

Procter & Gamble is now encouraging its advertising agencies to think creatively and strategically in directions it would never have countenanced a few years ago. One agency executive suggested to *Advertising Age* in 1983:

> If there is a single trend developing, it appears to be that P&G is beginning to recognize that confidence and a positive feeling are more motivating today than fear (of spotty glasses or stained clothes). There is the acknowledgement that there are not as many fanatical cleaners around – there appears to be the recognition that a whole different set of emotions trigger a response today. And those are feelings of confidence, pleasure, happiness and reward, not fear of insignificant mishaps.

As a result of this new awareness P&G is now prepared to move away from traditional approaches – such as efficacy claims, product demonstrations and testimonials – and rely more on imagery and emotion in certain commercials.

Procter & Gamble is also thinking more creatively in its media usage and expenditure allocations. In 1984 it spent $872 million on advertising, making it the nation's largest spender. It normally commits roughly half its budget to network TV, especially its own-produced daytime soap operas. That may all change. In 1984 P&G set up a media task force, with each member responsible for a specific medium, to find alternative ways for the company to remain, not just the biggest spender, but the most cost-effective as well. This massive review results from the company's concern, both about the continued erosion of ratings strength of its soap operas on network daytime TV, and about the ever-rising network costs. Although specific trends in the reallocation of monies are not yet apparent, *Advertising Age* in 1984 said that the group's presence 'has resulted in a whole new way of looking at the media world from P&G headquarters . . . they're telling their agencies that the world is bigger than network TV', and predicted that any shifts in the way P&G spends its vast pool of money will also 'shift the fortunes of the media world itself'.

Procter & Gamble is thus using Shapiro's definition of leverage – achieving maximum output per unit of input – in order to remain the most cost-effective buyer of media. While there is nothing new in this objective, what *is* new is the way P&G has set out to achieve it.

## Thinking trade marketing

One of the most significant turn-arounds in P&G thinking is their new approach to dealing with the retail trade. There is little doubt that P&G once exploited the enormous 'pulling' power of superior brands backed by massive advertising, a power that, according to Saporito in *Fortune*, allowed them to view 'the middlemen who sell their products as interlopers standing between them and the consumer. Not long ago wholesalers and retailers had to put up with the shabby treatment they got from P&G because the company's products were in such high demand'. Saporito cited several examples of this attitude, such as P&G salesmen restricting the quantity of discounted products that super-markets could buy, and of salesmen insisting that supermarkets always stock all sizes of a brand – if not, they wouldn't get it when it was discounted.

No more. As Saporito predicted: 'The day of the imperious P&G may be ending as the company adapts to some radical changes in consumer retailing.' The most radical change is the concentration of retail shelf space into fewer and fewer hands, which in turn gives the retailers greater leverage when negotiating with manufacturers. One result is that more and more consumer-oriented companies, including P&G, are discovering that it pays to be trade-oriented as well.

Procter & Gamble recently reformulated Tide powder detergent. While still giving the consumer the same number of washes per pack, the change allowed P&G to shrink its pack size. In turn, the outer container now carries 14 boxes instead of 12, thereby reducing handling costs both to P&G and to retailers.

Procter & Gamble's nappies, Ultra Pampers, are much thinner than conventional diapers, despite their greater absorbency abilities. While some consumers may be hesitant to buy, thinking that thickness equates with absorbency, *Business Week* predicted they would be a hit with retailers: twice as many Ultra Pampers will fit in the same shelf space as other diapers.

Saporito reported that, after running profitability studies with various retailers, P&G redesigned its Ivory shampoo bottle, from the teardrop shape used in test markets, to a squarer, barrel-like look. The new shape, which takes up less case and shelf space, saves the distributors 29 cents a case. This new-found attention to the trade's needs by P&G prompted one retailer to exclaim to *Fortune:* 'It's been a quantum change'. In Chapter 8 the importance of trade marketing will be examined in detail.

## The 'old!, improved!' P&G?

If P&G is prepared to change the shape of a new bottle of shampoo in order that the trade sector saves 29 cents a case, then surely marketing *has* entered a new era? P&G's willingness to shorten test marketing programmes, to pour enormous resources into new production facilities, to introduce me-too brands, to show new concerns about trade needs, and to rewrite media and advertising formulae all suggest that the company is undertaking a thorough reappraisal of its approach to marketing. Yet, when asked by *Fortune*, in a 1986 story, 'America's most admired corporations', to comment on P&G's future, Smale began by maintaining: 'What we're doing now is what we've done in the past'. *Business Week* echoed this comment in 1986 when, after reviewing the launch of Ultra Pampers it commented: 'Procter has gone back to basics: marketing product performance'.

Has P&G really gone back to so-called basics in order to find new leveraging opportunities in all stages of moving goods from producer to consumer? If so, will it succeed by repeating the past? In 1986 Rice announced 'the wounded lion has come roaring back. In the past 12 months P&G has racked up stunning market share gains in diapers, toothpaste, and detergents, products that account for over half its earnings'. Rice also admitted that success had not come cheaply, adding: 'Competitors grouse that P&G has simply bought market share to recapture prominence in major products and refurbish its reputation.' She quoted analysts' estimates of up to $1 billion being spent on advertising to launch the two new versions of Pampers, not counting the $500 million spent on the new plant. However, P&G's competitors have similar products already, thereby possibly denying it the advantage of a long-term technological edge.

In mature markets short-term gains are always possible. One of P&G's strengths has been its willingness to think – and act – in terms of decades, especially when traditional marketing practices prevailed. Perhaps it will require one of its main competitors to start behaving like a PepsiCo, for P&G to realize that it really is in a new era of marketing, and that it will not succeed simply by going back to the basics of marketing product performance.

While one market analyst claimed in 1985 that P&G 'took their eye off the ball', the diagnosis is more fundamental, and complex, than that. By the early 1980s Procter & Gamble had begun to lose its prior leveraging power and control: it could no longer count on long-term product superiority based on technological advantages; its competitors were making it look slow and cumbersome; it could no longer count on protracted R&D and test marketing programmes to hone its marketing mix skills before going national; it was running out of significant new product ideas, anyway; it was having to come to grips with the new reality of dealing with the trade on something closer to equal terms; and its tried-and-tested advertising approaches were falling behind the times. In effect, P&G's 'proven principles' of marketing had become inappropriate to the tumultuous market places of the 1980s.

Only a fool would deny Procter & Gamble's ability to develop new leveraging strengths. In its own deliberative fashion it is changing its approach, as are so many other US marketing giants. And, many of them *are* making quantum changes, not incremental ones. Nowhere is this more apparent than in their approaches to innovation and product development, the first of the four processes in the 'flow of goods' approach to marketing. The importance of R&D leverage will be considered in the next chapter.

# 5    Leverage in R&D

Though there does not appear to be a collaborative effort, in company after company the traditional approaches to innovation and product development are being re-examined and revised, if not replaced altogether. Not so long ago it seemed unlikely that such a turn-around would occur. What is perhaps most surprising is how quickly it *has* occurred, and how completely it has affected many companies.

## Gloomy future

The 1980s opened with an air of gloom and despondency following the second oil crisis. The once mighty US industrial base seemed unable to stem a flood of less expensive and better made imports, particularly from Japan. Critics claimed that US industry had lost its competitive edge. For example, *Time*, in a 1980 cover story, 'Detroit's uphill battle', announced: 'A generation of neglect has sapped Detroit's competitive strength'. This comment could have been aimed at a host of American industries. Steel, automobiles, footwear, machine tools, textiles and television manufacturing were thought by many to be moribund. A frequently mentioned alternative to mass production was that the US should develop into a combined high-technology/service-based economy.

One vocal dissenter from this alternative vision was Lee Iacocca. If the country wanted to save millions of jobs, and maintain national security, he argued, then basic industries had to be preserved. Besides, these were the ones that created markets for both the service sector and for high-technology:

Close down autos and you close down steel and rubber – and

then you've lost about one of every seven jobs in this country. . . .
Where would that leave us? We'd have a country of people who
serve hamburgers to each other and silicon chips to the rest of the
world. (1)

In order to restore America's industrial vigour, one debate centred
on whether or not US firms should be 'market-driven' or technology-
driven'. In market-driven firms the main direction for R&D is from
marketing in the form of conventional new product research techniques, such as concept testing, prototype testing and test marketing.
In technology-driven firms R&D provides the stimulus and the
marketing task is to find applications and create demand out of the lab
breakthrough – an approach which, in many respects, characterized
the 1950s. In many respects it is also an approach which characterizes
Japan in the 1980s.

Proponents of each of these two approaches found themselves at
loggerheads during the late 1970s and early 1980s.

## Market-driven approach

Many 'market-driven' supporters argued that the real problem with
innovation was that not enough US companies had adopted a
marketing 'philosophy'. And the reason for this, as suggested by one
entrepreneur in a 1983 *Business Week* article, 'Listening to the voice of
the marketplace', was that American firms were run by 'custodians',
not visionaries. Top US executives were unwilling to take the risks
needed to stimulate innovation because their jobs were 'too pre-
cariously balanced on this quarter's results'.

In its 1983 cover story, 'Marketing: the new priority', *Business Week*
summed up the problem. Despite advances in new product testing
techniques, and the vast sums of money required to launch a national
brand in a major category – $50 million in 1983 – two-thirds of new
products still fail, a casualty rate that was 'astonishingly high'. 'At
those odds and prices', claimed *Business Week*, 'companies are
understandably wary about committing themselves to high-risk
endeavors. They are demanding more research, more strategic
planning, and more "review" committees to weed out problems. More
often than not, however, the result of all these checks is total confusion
and inactivity.' The president of one ad agency was more truculent:

'There are more and more people [at a company] who can say no and very few who can say yes'.

In the earlier *Business Week* article, John Rockwell, a senior vice-president at consultants Booz, Allen & Hamilton, had suggested that this attitude was changing: 'More and more companies are understanding that the match of corporate capability with marketplace needs is what the game is all about'. He predicted that since growth in the future would be market-driven, the successful companies would be those that 'figure out how to drive that change instead of just reacting to it'.

## Drive that change

'How to drive that change' means knowing how to identify unarticulated market needs, and turning the findings into successful new products. This has encouraged the development of some highly advanced market research approaches, as practised by the top

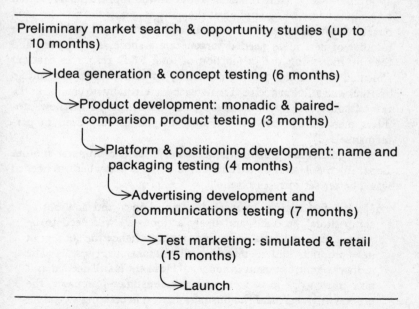

Preliminary market search & opportunity studies (up to 10 months)

└→Idea generation & concept testing (6 months)

  └→Product development: monadic & paired-comparison product testing (3 months)

    └→Platform & positioning development: name and packaging testing (4 months)

      └→Advertising development and communications testing (7 months)

        └→Test marketing: simulated & retail (15 months)

          └→Launch

**Figure 5.1 Step-by-step development of new brand**

marketing companies. Edward Warren, Senior Market Research Manager with Clairol Inc., in a 1983 article in *The Jounal of Consumer Marketing*, reported that his company followed a multi-stage, sequential process to develop a new brand. Clairol's textbook approach (see Figure 5.1) could equally apply to any number of packaged-goods marketing firms. Despite this careful, step-by-step approach, Warren admitted that 'the odds of developing a successful brand are (only) 50:50'. (2)

This pessimism echoed the comments of Rockwell and Particelli, in a 1982 *Industrial Marketing* article, 'New product strategy: how the pros do it'. They reported that the success rate of commercialized new products had not improved, on average, during the past two decades. Studies carried out by Booz, Allen & Hamilton concluded that, in the period 1963–68, 67 per cent of all new products introduced were successful – success being measured by both financial and strategic criteria – while in the period 1976–81, a 65 per cent success rate was obtained.

What had improved, according to the authors, was management's appoach to R&D. More financial resources and sophisticated research techniques were being applied at the early stages of the new product development process. As a result, companies were reducing the number of new ideas needed to generate a successful product, and thereby increasing the proportion of total R&D resources that get allocated to products that are ultimately successful. Yet, as admitted by Rockwell and Particelli: 'There has been virtually no change in the rate of successful introductions.... Improvements in the new products management process has only helped us stay even in performance'. (3)

'Market-driven' proponents such as William Sommers, another Booz, Allen & Hamilton executive, maintained that what was needed was a better set of research tools.

> Market forecasting, interviewing techniques and analyses of competitors' products and likely actions – all will need to be refined and orchestrated to improve the chance for success of new products and to minimize unpleasant surprises.... The individual entrepreneur is not dead. He or she is still needed, but now must work in concert with the consumer-purchaser, the process engineer, and the business analyst in creating a product that is tailored to the buyer's needs and desires. (4)

## Technology-driven approach

Not so, argued proponents of the 'technology-driven' approach. It was this over-emphasis on 'buyer's need and desires', and a preoccupation with scientific measuring devices, that had led to the stifling of America's innovative skills in the first place.

Peter Riesz, in a 1980 *Business Horizons* article, 'Revenge of the marketing concept', warned:

> By moving from 'science push' to 'market pull' research and development, we've sacrificed much creativity, technological parity, thoughtful product strategy, and a commanding market position.... Marketing and marketing research are not substitutes for the creativity, insights, and imagination of a group of well-trained scientists. (5)

Edward Tauber, in a 1979 *Business Horizons* article, 'How market research discourages major innovation', and later at the 1981 American Marketing Association Annual Conference, questioned the market researcher's assumption that attitudes of consumers – at the earliest stages of their exposure to either a product or its concept – are indicative of their future purchasing behaviour. He argued that when consumers perceive, and articulate, a new need, it is usually for a simple product improvement:

> Major innovations and the need for them are beyond the forsight of masses of people.... Is it surprising that line extensions and flankers dominate the packaged goods areas? Could anything else get through our maze of screens and safety checks? (6)

In a 1981 *Business Horizons* article, 'The misuse of marketing: an American tragedy', R. Bennett and R. Cooper observed that between 1960 and 1977 America had spent a relatively constant percentage of its GNP on advertising, while the proportion allocated to R&D had fallen:

> We have decided that it is easier to talk about our new products than actually to develop them.... In the world of new products we have become a society of tinkerers and cosmeticians rather than true product innovators. (7)

## Car tinkerers

Bennett and Cooper singled out the American automobile industry as representing all that was wrong with a market-driven R&D strategy:

> Pundits claim that the auto industry is in trouble because of cheaper imports that get better fuel economy. This is too simple an answer. A more incisive diagnosis reveals the hard truths. The European and Japanese car makers have simply been better competitors.... While domestic auto makers regarded small cars as low-technology, cheaply designed products aimed mainly at buyers unable or not willing to purchase a larger vehicle, the foreign manufacturers produced high-quality small cars that were recognized as better by the American consumer.

The authors claimed that between 1955 and the late 1970s, Detroit's car makers pursued a 'non-product' strategy on the premise that cosmetic changes and style updates, backed by intensive advertising and promotion, and aggressive selling, would keep their products moving: 'After all, how can one go wrong simply doing what the customers say they want?'

In fact, this diagnosis was too simplistic. The American auto industry lost its competitive edge not because it was too market-driven but, like so many other sectors, it had become too 'finance-driven' – and consequently was unable, or unwilling, to adjust as the market whip-sawed after the two oil crises of the 1970s. This was one of Iacocca's complaints about Ford.

> That's what happened at Ford during the 1970s. The financial managers came to see themselves as the only prudent people in the company.... What they forgot was how quickly things can change in the car business. While their company was dying in the market place, they didn't want to make a move until next year's budget meeting.

Top GM executives have also admitted to being 'production-driven', not 'market-driven'. Anne Fisher, in a 1985 *Fortune* article, 'Courting the well-heeled car shopper', said that in the late 1960s and early 1970s, 'Detroit's automakers managed to mislay an entire generation of moneyed customers'. These are the buyers of top-end imports – mostly European – such as Audi, BMW, Jaguar, Mercedes-Benz and Volvo. It is a highly profitable and growing sector, and one that has begun to attract upmarket Japanese entrants as well. Fisher noted that the scramble for 'market niches' – a marketing rallying-cry for the 1980s – has finally aroused US car makers to try to discover the requirements of this upscale group. This is understandable. Detroit's research will have shown that once buyers move to the specialist imported cars, they are unlikely to buy American again. Which is why one GM executive told Fisher: 'We're all trying to be a lot more market-sensitive. We're saying, "Let's not just turn out the iron and hope they buy it. Let's ask what they want first"'. To which Fisher replied: 'Better late than never'.

As for Chrysler, given its model line-up, its market share, and its financial state by the end of the 1970s, anyone who labelled the company as either market – or financial-driven would have been considered highly irresponsible. Judging by what Iacocca found when he arrived there in late 1978, Chrysler had some good engineering talent and a solid dealer network, and not much else. At the most charitable level, it might have been classified as a company driven by a 'move-the-metal' mentality.

## Car innovations

Quite suddenly, these attitudes have changed. Detroit's car makers are now scrambling in a variety of ways not just to catch up with the pack, but to move ahead of it, and they are committing mind-boggling sums of money in order to do so. The attempts by General Motors, in particular, to achieve R&D and production leverages are illustrative of the lengths to which some large, bureaucratic American corporations are now prepared to go in order to regain their innovative edge.

Technological innovation in the auto industry does not happen by chance. Nor is it realized overnight. And it is fraught with risks. One risk is that, while the new technology may be superior to existing proven alternatives, it fails because of unforeseen side-effects. Even some Japanese companies have faced this problem. Mazda's commitment to the wankel engine nearly bankrupted the company when, in the mid-1970s, its performance was overshadowed by its unacceptable fuel consumption. Another risk is that the total vehicle package incorporating any new innovations is not seen as compatible with the existing product line-up, especially the one it might be replacing. This could result in it appealing to a very narrow market sector. Ford, for one, took the calculated gamble that the 'jelly-bean' shape of its new fleet of cars, starting with the Thunderbird, would become widely accepted, given that the public's 'taste' in aerodynamic styling was beginning to move from the 'folded-paper' to the 'contoured' look.

According to the authors of *The Future of the Automobile*, (8) technical advances are the result of three conditions:

- *a dramatic change in the operating environment.* In the late 1970s the important changes in the operating environment of American car makers were government-legislated mandates for safety, lower emissions, and improved fuel economy. All of these factors demanded that new design approaches be adopted, yet at the same time, done in a manner that wouldn't leave the final buyers and users feeling too compromised.

- *intense competition in the market place.* Innovation is likely when there are many firms with a technical orientation trying to hold, or grab, market share in a mature market. By the late 1970s American, European and Japanese carmakers found they were all arriving at this same, over-crowded place.

- *exogenous development of new technologies with applications in the auto industry.* The most far-reaching innovation of late has been the microprocessor, developed originally for defence applications. For car makers, its possibilities began to be realized in terms of improvements in driver comfort, control, safety and entertainment. And these are early days still.

These a priori conditions could equally apply to any number of industries: for example, airlines, banking and financial services, cameras, home audio equipment and personal computers. In other words, in all these industries the most significant forces driving them may not be market related.

However, a fourth condition, which *is* market related, can be added:

- *significant demographic and socio-economic shifts.* Several crucial shifts occurred in the 1970s. In particular, the enormous baby-boom cohort hit the labour market and, linked to that, women also began to enter in record numbers. By the mid 1980s these two groups would become important segments of the new car buying market. Yet, as a top Ford executive admitted to *Business Week* in 1980: 'We are dealing, or about to deal, with a generation that is inherently anti-big. We still don't know what compromise in vehicle size this younger generation will accept.' Ironically, six years later GM's Cadillac division was having big trouble coming to grips with what compromise in vehicle size the older generation of luxury car buyers would accept, as will be examined shortly.

## Introducing new technologies

Car makers prefer to introduce new technologies to one area at a time, in order to build on the experience gained. For example, microprocessors have been introduced in the following order: engines → transmissions → suspensions. Likewise, designers prefer to introduce new advances into the fringes of the market, and gradually work on developing a wider acceptance. Four-wheeled drive vehicles, as bought mainly by urban dwellers, have become popular in the following sequence: recreation 'jeep-type' vehicles → utility or pickup trucks → performance cars. Such 'steps' are preferred and, the authors of *The Future of the Automobile* claim: 'It is not surprising that the vehicle designer's nightmare is the prospect of putting an entirely new technology into the whole product line on short notice.' This is exactly what happened to U.S. auto makers during the 1974 and 1975 model years, when emission controls were federally imposed.

What is perhaps unique in American auto history is that, in the late 1970s and early 1980s, all four conditions were present.

Now add two more dimensions to the car maker's woes: fickle consumer tastes, and the time it takes to develop a new car, depending on what is meant by 'new'. An executive vice-president at Ford informed *Automotive News* in 1985 that: 'An all-new car from the ground up, including engine and transmission, is now a five-year program, assuming you've done a year and a half of advance work'.

Russell Mitchell, in a 1986 *Business Week* article: 'How Ford hit the bull's-eye with Taurus', described the traditional, sequential process of developing a new car:

First, product planners come up with a general concept. Next, a design team gives it form. Their work is then handed over to engineering which develops the specifications that are passed on to manufacturing and suppliers. Each unit works in isolation, there is little communication, and no one has overall project responsibility.

What this means is that by the time a truly 'new' car gets launched, any or all of the original conditions for developing it may well have changed. It is not surprising that a senior sales executive at Chrysler should have admitted to *Business Week* in 1980: 'Ten years ago you could tell market changes three years ahead, but in today's world, you're really tossing a coin.' While critics would probably argue that Detroit's car makers have been calling the wrong side of the coin over the past decade, this is too simplistic a criticism.

Many critics of the US auto industry may not know that in Japan and Europe a combination of consumer buying power constraints, road and traffic conditions, government fuel tax and other official policies all combine to influence car buying requirements, and therefore design and performance specifications – to an extent unheard of in America. Japanese buyers, for example, pay twice the normal car taxes, whether registration, road tax or local tax, if their car is over 1.7 metres wide, 4.7 metres long, and the engine exceeds 2 litres. This explains why most Japanese cars sold in Japan are below 2 litres, and their dimensions are so similar. Consider the model line-ups for Mazda and Honda as shown in the table:

| Make | Model | Length (cm) | Width (cm) |
|------|-------|-------------|------------|
| *Mazda* | 323 range | 399–420 | 165 |
|  | 626 range | 443 | 169 |
|  | RX-7 | 430 | 169 |
|  | 929 range | 469 | 170 |
| *Honda* | Today | 320 | 140 |
|  | City | 356 | 162 |
|  | Civic range | 385–414 | 163–164 |
|  | Shuttle | 399 | 165 |
|  | Accord range | 434–454 | 170 |
|  | Prelude range | 429–437 | 169 |
|  | *Legend** | 481 | 174 |

*Only with the new Legend, its new luxury car aimed at North America and Europe, has Honda recently broken the 'mould'.

Tight design parameters such as these probably help explain why Japanese manufacturers have become so adroit at the 'packaging' of their small cars, and why they have gone for diversity of configurations (3-door/5-door hatch, 4-door saloon, 2-door coupe etc.) around a common sized platform, in order to segment their markets. This in turn may help explain why flexible manufacturing is so important to Japanese car makers.

They may also help explain why Japanese – and to a similar extent European – manufacturers were better placed to take advantage of American buyers moving to smaller cars after the first oil crisis in 1973. That scare, plus government efforts to legislate car makers' average fuel consumption figures, was expected to curb the American buyer's appetite for large cars. It did, except that importers were the first to benefit. Ford reacted to the federal fuel-economy standards by having its new car designs use as many existing components as possible, thereby saving costs, and preserving some of their big car look.

General Motors and Chrysler eventually brought out their first generation of 'downsized' cars – basically they were uninspiring copies of overseas designs – just in time for the oil glut of 1978. And with gas prices artificially held below world prices by the Carter administration, not only did American-produced small cars prove hard to sell in the late 1970s, demand for competitive imports sagged as well. Detroit's large car plants were working overtime and, as *The Economist* commented in a 1981 article, 'The downsizing of Detroit': 'Ford's policy of overhauling its big saloon designs rather than its smaller models seemed vindicated'.

Not for long. By 1979 Americans were once again rejecting big cars when gas prices soared after the second oil crisis, and drivers were forced to wait in long queues for scarce supplies. No wonder that *The Economist* predicted: 'The American gas-guzzler motor cars, already an endangered species, should have disappeared altogether by 1985.' In fact, by the mid-1980s gas prices were once more on their way down and GM, for one, may have tossed its coin the wrong way to suit its traditional customers who hankered after the big, softly-sprung cars Detroit affectionately termed 'luxoboats'.

In the 1986 model year GM's new range of downsized luxury models – the Cadillac Eldorado and Seville, Buick Riviera and Oldsmobile Tornado – suffered a 51 per cent decline in sales over its older 1985 lineup. 'What went wrong?' asked *Business Week* in a 1987 article, 'GM's new luxury cars: why they're not selling', and said that GM blamed the unexpected drop in energy prices. 'When these cars were being developed, gasoline was projected to rise to $2 a gallon' bemoaned one top Buick executive.

*Business Week* observed:

> What a difference a few years and some big marketing mistakes can make. Today, GM's latest luxury lines . . . languish on dealer lots. In trying to broaden the cars' appeal, GM wound up alienating its core customers without attracting new buyers.

The new models are some 20 inches shorter and over 600 pounds lighter than the older ones and, as *Business Week* noted: 'GM's traditional customers think the new models are small and plain, younger import-oriented buyers find them unsporty, and everyone complains that they cost too much.'

*Business Week* also suggested that the cars were too similarly styled – a common criticism of GM for some years now. Moreover: 'The E/K models also bear a remarkable resemblance to a line of much cheaper GM compacts – the Buick Somerset-Regal, Oldsmobile Calais, and Pontiac Grand Am – that were introduced a year earlier.' GM's vice-president in charge of the recently created Buick, Oldsmobile, Cadillac Group admitted: 'We've got some short-term problems here.' Given that it currently takes anywhere from four to five years – depending on the company – to design and build a new car, that 'short-term' problem is probably going to stay around for what seems like a very long time to GM.

## Innovations at General Motors

Yet, GM in its own labyrinthine way had attempted to put together a coherent new car development programme over the 1970s and 1980s, mainly in order to 'downsize', but with mixed success. In the early 1970s, as part of a design centralization policy, GM set up 'project centres' – teams of engineers from different divisions and staffs brought together to co-ordinate each new car design and engineering. Their task was mammoth: completely redesigning GM's product line within a decade, by bringing out a series of smaller cars based on what became known as the X-, J-, and A-bodies. While the project centres could cut across divisional and staff boundaries, the weaknesses of this system soon became apparent. Charles Burck, in a 1983 *Fortune* article, 'Will success spoil General Motors?', explained:

Besides separating design and manufacturing still further, the project centres badly blurred responsibilities. A centre might, say, choose Chevrolet to design an engine; if the design came up short, neither the centre nor the division could be held accountable, particularly since a centre disbanded the moment it handed a car over for production.

The start-up problems encountered by GM were gigantic, and would probably have overwhelmed any lesser car maker. According to *Business Week*, in a 1984 cover story, 'GM moves into a new era', producing small cars from scratch demanded development and manufacturing processes quite different from the traditional large cars that GM had been pumping out. Smaller cars meant switching to unitary body construction, front-wheel drive, more fuel-efficient engines and new transmissions and, most important, stylish designs that looked smaller from the outside, but inside gave a feeling of roominess, comfort – and value. Because of such conflicting demands, *Business Week* claimed:

GM's old structure began to break down. Approval for even minor changes in a part ended up requiring huddles between hosts of manufacturing, parts, marketing, and body engineering executives. New-car introduction dates began to slip, quality suffered, costs rose. And when the cars finally came to market, GM discovered that customers had a tough time telling one division's model from another.

Critics were most vocal about the styling of the J-cars, which cost some $5 billion to develop. In order to save costs all five GM divisions were required to share nearly identical bodies. The points of difference were to come from 'badge engineering' – own names, cosmetic exterior differences, individual ride and drive characteristics, separate interior specifications, and different prices. In a 1984 article, 'Mr Smith shakes up Detroit', *Time* revealed how a Cadillac engineer, when asked to explain the difference between the Cadillac Cimarron and the Chevrolet Cavalier, two J-cars, replied: 'Oh, about $5000.'

## Marketing nonsense at GM?

In *The Naked Market* Robert Heller maintained that the fact that the divisional marketers had no real responsibility for the models they were required to market was 'marketing nonsense literally of the first order'.(9)

*Time* observed: 'By blurring the distinction between competing car lines, GM was violating a cardinal rule of Alfred P. Sloan Jr.' His 1920's restructuring, which had centralized planning and decentralized operations, was designed to produce 'a car for every purse and purpose: Chevrolet for the hoi polloi; Pontiac for the poor but proud; Oldsmobile for the comfortable but discreet; Buick for the striving; Cadillac for the rich.'

Not surprisingly, by the early 1980s GM had lost the marketing advantages of product differentiation – which was why the five divisions were created in the first place, and why Sloan had originally centralized planning and decentralized operations. GM also began to slip in market share. And one other reason for this slippage was that GM's new downsized cars didn't have that extra *something* that American buyers were beginning to demand: in-built quality and reliability, as borne out by their higher warranty claims when compared with Japanese makes.

GM's X-cars, developed at a cost of some $2.5 billion, and marketed as the Chevrolet Citation, Pontiac Phoenix, Oldsmobile Omega, and Buick Skylark, came under severe criticism for their many defects. Charles Burck, in a 1980 *Fortune* article, 'A comeback decade for the American car', noted:

> The X-cars were the beneficiaries of the most massive attempt ever in the U.S. to build a high-quality small car. Those efforts included endless testing and close attention not only to basic design but to the layouts of assembly lines. Nonetheless, plenty of X-car buyers are disappointed with what they got.

In his 1983 *Fortune* article Burck added:

> In large measure, GM's quality problems can be traced to the company's extraordinary efforts during the 1970s to clean up emissions, meet new safety regulations and downsize the entire product line – all at once. The company overestimated its ability to manage these tasks.

Many of GM's problems with trying to manage a maze of conflicting tasks were still in evidence by the mid-1980s. One analyst informed *Business Week* in 1984 that: 'They lost the marketing advantage of differentiation, and they still had poor costs.' In 1985 *The Economist* stated: 'Put rudely, GM's cars are seen by too many as boring and second-rate. In every segment of the market some other company produces a better car.' Even Buick's general manager confessed to *Automotive News* in 1985 that: 'Our products look alike, they feel alike and they drive alike.' The launch of GM's new luxury cars in late 1986 confirmed the company's worse fears – too many customers were staying away from GM showrooms until they could be lured there by financial incentives, such as low interest loans. Industry observers were beginning to question whether this was the best way for the world's largest auto maker to run a business.

## The General picks technology

That may all change, if one man has his way – and the time. In 1980 GM lost $760 million, its first red ink in sixty years. In 1981 Roger Smith took over. Anne Fisher, in a 1984 *Fortune* article, 'GM's unlikely revolutionist', reported: 'To outsiders he appeared to be stamped down from the same mold as every chairman since the 1950s: a tradition-bound, somewhat complacent finance man.' However, right from the start Smith had his own, non-traditional, vision of GM's future. This was revealed to *Fortune* as far back as 1981: 'Technological leadership is what will keep us ahead in world competition, and it's also one of the things that is going to make the difference between high and low profit margins.'

*The Economist*, in 'General Motors: survival of the fattest', said that:

Though Mr Smith's immediate reaction was to reach for an axe it quickly became apparent that the knee-jerk response of cost cutting would never alone make up the gap. . . . GM had by then become the classic hierarchical bureaucracy. Conformism and mediocracy dominated. Entrepreneurship was all but extinct.

Smith brought in McKinsey, the management consultants. They stayed two years. Their recommendations, and Smith's determination to carry them through, will affect GM's fortunes for the rest of this century. As described by *The Economist*: 'From industrial dinosaur to technological leader. It is an epic change for General Motors.' And there is no guarantee of success.

## GM's first moves

In 1982 GM took steps to bring design, engineering and the manufacturing processes closer together. It abandoned the project centre approach and in its place new car development was assigned to new teams responsible for everything from defining a car's market to overseeing its production. In this way GM intended that its new models would be developed by teams that included not only product and production engineers, but also market researchers, stylists, finance staffers and material management specialists.

This change was taken a large step further in early 1984 when a new reorganization plan was announced. The move lumped Chevrolet, Pontiac, and GM of Canada into one super division (CPC), with an emphasis on small cars, and Buick, Oldsmobile and Cadillac in the other division (BOC), with responsibility for larger cars. The Fisher Body and GM assembly divisions would be integrated into both groups. Each group would operate as self-contained business units and be responsible for engineering, manufacturing and marketing their own cars. Each would also be accountable for quality, performance and profitability. Fisher called it 'the first sweeping change in GM's structure since Alfred P. Sloan split the company into five competing car divisions in the 1920s'.

## R&D leverage

The objective of this restructuring was R&D leverage. James McDonald, GM's President, explained to *Business Week* in January, 1984: 'How can you execute a car in the US and get it to the market faster? That's what this is, pure and simple.' In July, 1984, in another interview with *Business Week*, he admitted that no one wanted to abolish the five divisions, but they recognized they had to co-ordinate their product development process better in order to reduce the obvious shortcomings of the present approach. 'We wanted to find a way to execute a car from concept to market place sooner, at the same time meeting objectives of cost and quality.'

*The Economist* in 1985 said the main purpose behind the move was 'frontloading', in order to reduce the time taken to develop a car from five to three years:

> Frontloading means spending more money at the start of a new model programme. The idea is that designer and engineer work together from scratch. Previously a designer 'designed' a car. The engineer then had to adapt the design to comply with the practical constraints of mass production.

The head of the CPC Group explained the process to *Fortune* in 1985 by describing how a new car, code-named GM80, would be developed:

> We have full-time marketing people over at the GM80 project center; we've got the product design and manufacturing people too, and they're all working for the same boss . . . on that team of close to 600 people we now have a totally integrated car company. So the decision on what the car ought to look like – the components, the chassis layout – all that didn't go up and down the organization as it would have in the past.

In 1985 *The Economist* predicted the new structure would end duplication and make management more accountable: 'Cars will be sold under different names, be it Chevrolet or Cadillac. The difference is that if a car turns out a dud top management will, in theory, know whom to blame.' *The Economist* also praised GM for its willingness to change:

> That the company's management is prepared to make this act of faith and tolerate the current [1985] profit decline speaks volumes. In the past, GM was notorious for being run by its finance officers, mesmerized by the need to issue upbeat quarterly reports to shareholders.

Michael Brody, in his 1985 *Fortune* cover story, 'Can GM manage it all?', said there were no precedents that GM could follow. 'No company of even remotely similar size has attempted such an overhaul.' GM's goal, as stated by Smith, was clear: 'to move our decision-making closer to the market place'. One result of GM's do-it-yourself approach (with a little help from consultants) is that each group has been structured differently. According to David Whiteside, in a 1986 *Business Week* article, 'Roger Smith's campaign to change the

GM culture', BOC has a decentralized structure based on four product groups, each of which is an integrated business, while CPC is more centralized and based on functional lines, though coupled with a 'matrix management' to facilitate communication channels between functions. According to Whiteside, Smith has placed his bets two ways in terms of what structure will best fit GM's new risk-taking culture, and move decision making 'closer to the market place'.

How dramatic is the change? Shortly after the restructuring was announced *Business Week* quipped: 'Once the new organization charts are done, GM will be ready to do what it has not done in nearly twenty years: develop cars roughly as other companies do.'

Unfortunately for GM, Ford has already demonstrated the success of its new development process, called the 'program management' approach. As Russell Mitchell said of the Taurus and Sable in 1986: 'A team approach borrowed from Japan has produced the hottest US car in years.' According to Mitchell:

> Representatives from all the various units – planning, design, engineering, and manufacturing – worked together as a group. The team took final responsibility for the vehicle. Because all of the usually disjointed groups were intimately involved from the start, problems were resolved early on, before they caused a crisis. For instance, manufacturing suggested changes in design that resulted in higher productivity or better quality.

In terms of this new approach, one market researcher informed *Business Week*, Ford 'hasn't just been talking about it; they've been able to execute it.... They've really forced GM to play catch-up'.

Smith doesn't want General Motors to catch up; he wants it to get ahead. His most ambitious change – and one that originally had the business writers searching for new superlatives – was the setting up of the new Saturn subsidiary to market a new generation of sub-compact cars. Saturn began in 1982 as an in-house engineering project to find a new way to make a small car that would be competitive with the Japanese in cost and quality terms. In January, 1984, it became a separate company with its own headquarters and management and, after much wooing from many states, GM decided to locate its $3.5 billion plant facilities in Tennessee. The first cars were expected to roll off the state-of-the-art assembly line in 1989, a year before Smith was due to retire.

By 1986 GM's plans were coming unstuck, as sales and profits failed to meet expectations. While Saturn was still talked of as a manufacturing break-through, as will be discussed in the next chapter, it had also become a questionable marketing proposition.

## Can GM succeed? (Part 1)

General Motors has staked its future on a belief that a strategy that homes in on technological leadership is superior to one that over-emphasizes financial performance. Can it succeed?

There are many who *hope* it succeeds. *Time*, in a 1985 article, 'GM picks the winner', claimed: 'If GM succeeds, American industry will have proved that it has not lost its vision and verve.'

GM still has a long way to go. Michael Brody, in his 1985 *Fortune* article, 'Can GM manage it all?', pointed out that while GM had the grand plans, Ford and Chrysler were gaining the sales: 'Is GM so preoccupied with its spectacular plans for the year 2000 that it's neglecting to build and sell the right cars in the here and now?'

David Whiteside, in his 1986 *Business Week* article, claimed:

Despite a four-year drive to reinvigorate the auto maker, many managers are still groping for a clear understanding of their new roles. Costs remain so high that the company's return on sales is the lowest in the industry. GM's market share remains below its 1978 level. Earnings are expected to fall 15 per cent this year.

Whiteside then quoted one industry observer: 'GM will be around in the year 2000. The question is, will it be competitive?'

William Hampton, in a follow-up *Business Week* article, 'Down-sizing Detroit: the Big Three's strategy for survival', disclosed that GM was having doubts about Saturn's 'dazzling display of advanced production technology' as the key to fighting lower-cost imports. Apparently GM discovered from its joint venture facility with Toyota in California – where the Chevrolet Nova, a derivative of the Corolla, is made and where productivity is twice that of the GM norm – that it is possible to achieve 'Japanese-like efficiency with careful management rather than exotic automation'.

In a late-1986 article, *Business Week* described the creeping malaise at GM. Even as it was set to be the first company ever to top $100 billion in sales, its overhead costs continued to rise, its plants were as much as 20 per cent less productive than Ford's and Chrysler's, and it was still reliant on super-low (under 3 per cent) financing deals to move excess stock. As a result:

> Profits are down, market share has eroded, and GM Chairman Roger B. Smith's much-ballyhooed corporate reorganization seems mired in GM's bureaucratic morass.... This is nowhere more evident than at GM's Saturn Corp., where a revolutionary blend of robots and new management techniques was created to meet the Japanese head-on. The project has slipped a year – production is set for 1990 – and climbed upscale a notch. No longer the basic import-fighter, Saturn will be a $10 000 compact car. Five years to design a car? 'We won World War II in four and a half', snorts (H. Ross) Perot.

Perot was the owner of Electronic Data Systems, the big computer services company which GM bought. Even though he sat on GM's board the feisty Perot became one of its most vocal critics. 'Revitalizing GM is like teaching an elephant to tap dance', he explained to *Business Week*. 'You find the sensitive spots and start poking.'

In the end Perot's poking proved too irksome for GM and, in a much-publicized and roundly-criticized deal, he was bought off for some $700 million. *Business Week* observed in a 1986 article: 'GM hasn't bought much peace.... Getting rid of Perot only highlights the carmaker's basic problems.' *Business Week* then added in an editorial:

> Chrysler and Ford, which were in far worse shape than GM several years ago, have used the trade respite (with Japan) to far greater advantage.... Smith and GM may be better off without Perot, but it will be a major loss if they remain reluctant to admit the company's problem and fail to move quickly to increase efficiency and competitiveness.

*Time* commented:

> No longer will Perot sit on GM's board and offer suggestions on how to manufacture cars more efficiently in the high-tech age. With or without Perot, the biggest challenge facing Roger Smith remains the same: to prove that he can turn around GM's sagging fortunes.

# Can GM succeed? (Part 2)

Despite GM's 'sagging fortunes', the important point is that Smith has hit the market-driven vs technology-driven argument right on the head. In today's naked markets, where the consumer is only one force influencing strategic change, he has shown that it is no longer a question of choice – firms must be both market-driven *and* technology-driven if they are to achieve competitive leverages. When *Advertising Age* selected Roger Smith as their 1985 'Adman of the Year', his attempt at this dual approach was summed up as follows:

> Since taking over as chairman on Jan. 1, 1981, Mr. Smith has steadily moved GM toward the global, technology-based, marketing-oriented shape he envisions. Along the way, he is changing the rules on how cars will be produced and sold by the entire industry.

It is not surprising that the management of technology and innovation became a preoccupation with Smith, and a source of frustration with Perot. James Quinn, in a 1985 *Harvard Business Review* article, 'Managing innovation: controlled chaos', summed up the potential dilemma facing any company, large or small, trying to manage the process:

> Innovative companies tie their visions to the practical realities of the market place. Although each company uses techniques adopted to its own style and strategy, two elements are always present: a strong market orientation at the very top of the company and mechanisms to ensue interactions between technical and marketing people at lower levels.(10)

This may be one of GM's weak points. Smith is a finance expert, and *The Economist*, in 'General Motors: survival of the fattest', noted that despite GM's efforts to 'meet the competitive challenge through technological leadership', its marketing people lack status. The most senior of them is responsible for forward planning, but is not on the board. 'Chrysler in contrast is run by a salesman', it added.

Quinn also argued that management practices in innovative companies need to reflect the 'realities of the innovation process'. This process is often opportunistic in its start-up, and individually motivated – which is why some companies have adopted a 'product champion' approach. Other companies use internal 'skunkworks' –

small teams of engineers, technicians, designers, and model makers, placed together with no intervening organizational barriers – to develop a new product. Arrangements such as these show mangement recognizing that the process of innovation may be tumultuous and non-linear – which is a far cry from the clearly delineated, sequential decision-making approach to new product development as shown in most texts, and illustrated at the beginning of this chapter.

While GM may still not tap dance like an elephant, Chrysler certainly seems to have found some new agility. Iacocca revealed how, in 1982, with Chrysler healthy again, he decided to have an experimental convertible built by hand from a Le Baron model. He then drove the car around in public. The immediate response was so favourable that: 'Back at the office, we decided to skip the research. Our attitude was: "Let's just build it. We won't make any money, but it'll be great publicity. If we're lucky we'll break even."' In its first year 23 000 cars were sold – not the three thousand that were first planned.

The introduction of Chrysler's family minivan was equally opportunistic. The original concept was developed at Ford in the mid-1970s, and early consumer 'clinic' tests showed it had much potential. However it was rejected by Henry with: 'Forget it, I don't want to experiment.' This prompted Iacocca to write:

> In my book, if you're not number one, then you've got to innovate. If you're Ford, you've to find market niches that (GM) hasn't even though of. You can't go head to head with them – they're just too big. You've got to outflank them.

Iacocca took the minivan concept with him to Chrysler and launched, in 1984, the Dodge Caravan and Plymouth's Voyager; each sold over 80 000 units in 1985. The concept proved so popular that GM, once it was in the market, postponed the production start-up of some new station wagons in order to reconsider their prospects. Ford, meanwhile, entered the market in 1985.

Iacocca's team now have a reputation for intuition and quick reflexes. Steven Flax, in a 1985 *Fortune* article, 'Can Chrysler keep rolling along?', said that the company has successfully launched a series of sporty variants of basic cars to tap into 'hot new markets':

> From management approval of design to the first car off the assembly line, the company brought out its Shelby Charger in

six months, its Omni GLH (the initials stand for 'goes like hell') in eight months, and its street-racer Charger Turbo in 12.

This may not be true 'innovation', but at least it works for Chrysler.

## R&D flexibility

Quinn argued that while top management can plan overall directions and goals, they need to allow for surprises and changes.

> Innovative companies keep their programs flexible for as long as possible and freeze plans only when necessary for strategic purposes such as timing. Even then they keep options open by specifying broad performance goals and allowing different technical approaches to compete for as long as possible.

He cited Sony as one company which encourages several competing prototype programmes to run in parallel – for example, ten options in videotape recorder technology were pursued by different teams. According to Quinn:

> Such redundancy helps the company cope with uncertainties in development, motivates people through competition, and improves the amount and quality of information available for making final choices on scale-ups or introductions.

Quinn also said that some companies structure a 'shoot-out' among competing approaches *after* they reach prototype:

> They find this practice provides more objective information for making decisions, decreases risk by making choices that best reflect market place needs, and helps ensure that the winning option will move ahead with a committed team behind it.

This approach is at variance with one that focuses on weeding out potential losers at the idea/concept generation, screening and evaluation, and business analysis stages. The rationale is obvious – to keep one's options open for as long as possible.

GM is attempting something similar to the above 'shoot-out' approach by developing what it terms 'generic vehicles'. It plans to build a series of 'platforms' containing various chassis, engine, transmission, and suspension options, upon which a variety of new models might then be grafted and 'clinic' tested on an on-going basis. If successful, GM will be quicker, not only in spotting changing demand requirements, but also in turning out finished products, by cutting the engineering lead time needed once a final design is approved. GM's target is to produce a newly styled car in three years instead of five. This will give them enormous R&D leveraging advantages if competitors are still working to the standard four- or five-year development cycles.

## Can GM succeed? (Part 3)

For GM to tap dance successfully to the tune of its innovatory abilities it may have to learn the new skills of 'high-speed management' and 'experimental' marketing. The implications are that other firms following the same technological score will need to do likewise – all the while knowing there is no guarantee of long-term success.

Susan Fraker, in a 1984 *Fortune* article, 'High-speed management for the high-tech age', said that what with rapidly changing technologies, unexpected competition, quick market saturation, and shorter product life-cycles, 'managing well, in the classical sense, isn't enough. You have to manage differently. The skills that make up the new technique – call it high-speed management – aren't easy to master. Business schools don't teach them'.

### Rule 1: think new products, and again, and again

Fraker believed that firms adopting a high-speed management approach have recently learned several lessons. One is to constantly think about new products, 'and then to back this thinking with investment – fast'. The idea that a company can spend several years developing and perfecting a break-through product in order to generate several further years of continuous – and predictable – income, is no longer valid. New products now go through their life-cycle stages too fast, and the practices that once characterized mature markets – such as a proliferation of competitors, cut-throat price competition and comparative advertising – occur so quickly that they can wreck a company if it is dependent on the single new product with no fast follow-up. One marketing director in the computer industry informed Fraker: 'If you become complacent in this business, you're dead. It's the next product and the next and the next that keep you alive.' Some analysts have suggested that IBM was not fast enough in adopting this approach, and that hastened the cloning of its PC.

In the car industry, the Japanese success in America did not suddenly occur. The current vehicles are the result of several generations of product learning. The early entrants from Datsun (Nissan) and Toyota were not suited to the American demands for prolonged driving at high speed. Even the next generation, which arrived in the mid- to late-1960s, were still being treated as basic and cheap forms of transportation. However, by the mid-1970s, the Japanese had begun to 'package' cars that successfully blended design, reliability, comfort and, most important, economy. Then, by the mid-1980s they were ready to begin moving upmarket, where the Europeans had the sector to themselves. The fact that the Koreans and East Europeans were threatening them from below, was an added incentive to do so.

Mazda Motor Corp., which began as a precision engineering firm, is one Japanese car company which thinks in terms of the next car, and the next. Pulled back from the brink of bankruptcy in the mid-1970s because of its over-commitment to the thirsty wankel engine – Mazda's production staff even went selling door-to-door – the company steadily refined and improved a new series of cars: 323, 626, 929, and RX-7, to embody what it terms a 'joy of driving' promise.

Within a decade Mazda has evolved its philosophy, its strategy and its tactics into a coherent new car development programme – largely based on four-year replacement cycles – that could continue into several more life-cycles. It is this 'total family' approach that – perhaps not surprising given its ties to Mazda – Ford not GM is now coming closest to achieving in the US. And while America is Mazda's target for measuring sales success, West Germany seems to be its target for achieving industry awards for automotive excellence. In 1984 the Mazda 626 was the first Japanese car to be chosen the best imported car in the sub-compact car category by readers of the big German motoring magazine, *Auto Motor Und Sport*. It won the award in 1985 and 1986 as well and, more important, was the top selling Japanese car in West Germany in 1984 and 1985.

Honda Motor Corp., which less than twenty-five years ago, didn't produce automobiles, and is now Japan's third largest auto maker, also thinks in terms of generations of cars. Honda's attention to quality has meant it consistently achieves among the highest ratings in various customer satisfaction studies carried out in America and elsewhere. To maintain its engineering edge, the company spends proportionately more on research and development than its US competitors.

Some of this research is as 'hands-on' as it is possible to get. J. David Power of J.D. Power & Associates, the large auto research firm, told *Time* in 1986 that Honda do less 'clinic' research before a model is launched, but more hands-on research in the market place after the car is introduced. He cited one Honda design team that spent several days at a California shopping mall observing and talking to shoppers as they loaded grocery bags into their cars. One result of this study was a redesigned Civic hatchback, introduced in 1983, that had a lower rear 'lip' than its predecessor. Honda's pragmatic approach seems to be to continually develop new models as logical extensions of the previous, while at the same time retaining a distinctly – yet constantly evolving – 'Honda' look, from the Today to the Legend.

## Rule 2: think 'experimental' marketing

A second lesson, said Fraker, is that a firm must stay close not just to consumers, but to competitors as well, in order to keep up with their investment strategies and costs. It must then be prepared to push through new products, even if the engineers are asking for further improvements. As one consultant suggested: 'The new ideas can be included in the next generation.'

Roland Schmitt, in a 1985 *Harvard Business Review* article, 'Successful corporate R&D', claimed that many Japanese firms, particularly in audio and video electronic products, have adopted this 'experimental' approach in their marketing: 'They have taken chances by introducing still questionable product innovations, listening to customer's responses, and tailoring the product accordingly.' Schmitt was especially critical of the American predilection for conducting:

> one market research study after another, with none giving sufficiently clear answers to support an unequivocal management commitment to go to market.... The professional literature bulges with methodologies for R&D project evaluation.... For slow-moving and protected industries, these methods have been successful. For fast-moving and worldwide industries, they

have been a disaster. The Japanese and Western entrepreneurs have outflanked and overwhelmed companies relying on such hands-off analytical models. (11)

Shanklin and Ryans Jr, in a 1984 *Harvard Business Review* article, 'Organizing for high-tech marketing', agreed. Their research indicated that innovation-driven, high-technology firms mostly rely on qualitative marketing research techniques, such as focus groups, to assess new product potentials. (12)

Some of Sony's competitors use 'experimental' practices in order to nullify its painstaking approach to R&D. Fraker commented that:

> Sony is still a brilliant innovator. But it has little time to reap the
> rewards of innovation because rivals follow hard on its tail with
> better-selling products – in the videocassette recorder business,
> for example.

In 1975 Sony introduced its first Betamax videotape recorders. Two years later Matsushita launched a cheaper recorder that worked on a rival technology, known as VHS and which used different-sized tapes that could make longer recordings. According to *Time* in a 1984 article, 'Max troubles for Betamax': 'Matsushita then outmanoeuvred Sony by adding extra features to its recorder, providing licences to other companies that wanted to enter the business and concluded aggressive marketing pacts with such companies as RCA and General Electric.' Although Sony improved Betamax, it had lost the tactical initiative – and eventually market leadership to VHS.

## Filmless cameras

Some of these issues appear to be having a replay in the market for filmless cameras. In 1981 Sony introduced the Mavika, which looked liked a conventional 35-mm camera, but which stored pictures on a miniaturized computer floppy disk similar to those used in computers. While the resolution was poor, Sony and other Japanese electronics firms continued with the development. In 1984 one firm, Hitachi Ltd, offered the marketing rights to Polaroid Corp. The offer was rejected, and one of Polaroid's top scientists revealed to *Business Week* in 1985: 'The prints aren't very good. A true photographic company can't come out with a product that's mediocre.' The editorial director of *Modern*

*Photography* added: 'It'll be the year 2000 before people get a decent electronic image from a printer.'

Despite Polaroid's refusal, Hitachi said it would proceed alone. At the time it was estimated that Hitachi's camera would cost about $2000 – well above the prevailing price for 35-mm cameras. From the Japanese point of view, an unproven technology and a prohibitive initial price is not a deterrent. As the president of Sony Corp. of America informed *Business Week*:

> We never worry about price points for new products and new technologies. If the idea has merit, there's always some segment of the population that will buy it, regardless of cost. Then we can refine it and bring down the price.

In mid-1986, Otis Port, in a *Business Week* article, 'Filmless cameras: pictures on a floppy disk', reported that Canon Inc. had beaten both Sony and Hitachi in introducing the first fully electronic 35-mm camera. 'The all-electronic age of still photography has arrived', claimed Port. Canon's new camera would transmit light into electronic signals that are stored magnetically on a 2-inch disk which and then be placed in a recorder in order that the pictures can be viewed on a tv screen, printed out on a special ink-jet colour printer or transmitted down a telephone line via a special transceiver.

While the end picture would still exhibit some granularity, and the whole system would cost some $32000, Port said that Canon hoped to target the 6000 press companies in the US, where speed of capturing late-breaking news was expected to be more important than cost. Port added that Canon's priority was to improve picture reproduction and, to do so, it 'hopes to sell some cameras now to help fund development of better imaging chips'. No doubt, like many of its high-speed competitors, Canon will probably do much of its 'hands-on' experimental research out in the market place, not back in its labs. Inevitably, the end result will be a range of better-quality and lower-priced camera systems, plus a flock of new competitors.

## Rule 3: manage creativity

A third lesson, said Fraker, is that companies need to manage creativity, even if it means wrenching changes to the existing corporate culture:

Companies that have mastered high-speed management try to keep the mental light bulbs on by establishing small teams to design, manufacture, and market new products. Whatever they're called – entrepreneurial groups, independent business units, skunkworks – these teams remove the bureaucratic straightjacket from product development. . . . To be successful, independent business units must be small, hard working, and preferably located away from the normal corporate premises.

In other words, the high-speed management of creativity requires a high-pressure organizational culture.

This was the approach adopted by IBM in order to get the PC on the market quickly and, as noted by Whiteside in *Business Week*:

Smith is counting on Saturn and his high-tech subsidiaries (Hughes Aircraft and Electronic Data Systems, in particular) not only for their knowhow but also for the cultural changes they can bring to the core business. Saturn is combining the latest in factory- and office-automation technology *(that is, production and operations leverage)* with participatory management, which Smith says he wants 'Saturn to sell by example' to the rest of GM.

Only six months later, doubts were being raised about Smith's chances of getting the GM elephant to tap dance.

## Rule 4: manufacturing is marketing's secret weapon

Fraker insisted a fourth lesson was that marketers, designers, and product engineers need to be closely involved with the manufacturing process: 'Companies in which the design team continues to toss a product over the wall to manufacturing risk adding years to development.' Harry Gray, Chairman and CEO of United Technologies, in a 1985 article in *Research Management*, 'Research and manufacturing should be partners', shared this view: 'For new technology to produce results in the factory, both the research and the production people have to be committed to making it work. . . . Not only do we need innovative products, we need products that can be made innovatively.' (13) Chapter 6 will explore the proposition that innovative approaches to manufacturing and operations are, more than ever, crucial to marketing success.

Fraker's 1984 theme that the management of innovation requires a complete rethink was continued by *Fortune* in a 1987 special report, 'The economy of the 1980s'. For example, the founder and chief executive of Analytical Devices, a Massachusetts-based maker of specialist systems of components that link sophisticated measuring instruments to computers, stated in *Fortune* that high-tech by itself is no guarantee of success of high growth:

> While the technologies we develop and market are quite new, our management practices are quite archaic. We've been managing through vertical department structures that seem to work quite well. But we've done a miserable job of linking the disciplines across the organization – engineering, manufacturing, and marketing – in a way that yields the best product for the customer.

He then added:

> Once you awaken to that challenge and decide to do something about it, you may face a five- to ten-year correction exercise. And you may wind up replacing a whole generation of people in one discipline before you're through.

Despite his efforts, six years after taking over the chairman's role, Roger Smith may be finding his 'five- to ten-year correction exercise' more complex and difficult than he originally imagined. In a 1987 *Fortune* article, 'Detroit's cars really are getting better', Jeremy Main concluded:

> Being the biggest and richest of the Big Three, GM tried to meet the Japanese by doing too much. GM spent $53 billion to upgrade its plants and build new ones. At the same time, it tried to remake the corporation's culture and structure, introduce fleets of entirely new models, equip its cars with elaborate electronic doodads, and meet emission and fuel consumption rules.

As one top executive, responsible for quality at the Chevrolet-Pontiac-Canada Group admitted: 'We had an unbelievable amount of stuff on our plate, and we thought we could handle it, but we ran into problems.'

By early 1987 GM was still remaking its structure, in yet another attempt to get the right product for the customer. It announced that the Buick-Oldsmobile-Cadillac Group would be reorganized, with Cadillac being given its own engineering, design and manufacturing capacities.

## Can GM succeed? (Part 4)

'High-speed' management, 'experimental' marketing, a 'high-pressure' organizational culture, and 'innovative' manufacturing may be part of what gave so many Japanese companies the edge over their American competitors – all honed by the fiercely competitive nature of their own market. Penny Sparke, in the UK magazine *Design*, wrote that like America in the 1950s, Japan in the 1980s is in the midst of a product development boom that pays great attention to fashion and lifestyle. Under these conditions, good marketing strategies are important, but superb tactics are crucial:

> There is a naive enthusiasm about Japan's current frenetic rate of product innovation and the energetic consumption which fuels it. Products have short life-cycles. Sharp calculators, for example, are usually around for about six months before they are plagiarized and have to be replaced by a new model. The demand for novelty, whether of technology or design or both, is perpetual.

This comment could apply equally to Japanese cars, given that there are nine local car makers competing in a market less than half the size of America's. Can GM succeed against these competitors, when only their best products reach the US, the market that now keeps them financially viable? It is pinning much hope on its technology to stem the Japanese onslaught. The great weakness of this approach is that its Japanese competitors are now its equal technologically.

For many years the conventional wisdom was that the Japanese car makers were supreme copiers but not innovators. The Europeans led the way in designing quality cars with superb high-performance engines and road holding characteristics, and the Americans were best at building large, comfortable gas-guzzlers, laden with gadgets. According to Alan Kennedy, in a 1986 article, 'Car-makers out to catch the Europeans', in the Australian weekly magazine, *The Bulletin*, the role assigned to the Japanese 'was that of makers to the mass market. Cheap and reliable but hardly the leading edge of car design and technology'. To some extent this was true, but at the 1985 Tokyo Motor Show there were enough high-tech 'concept' cars on display for Kennedy to say they 'must have left the rest of the world's car industry worried'. As a Mazda executive and engineer pointed out to Kennedy: 'The show is proof that our engineers want to create instead of imitate others.' Certainly Detroit car makers were impressed. The director of product development at Chrysler told *Time* in 'A look into the crystal ball': 'The advanced cars here give us a clear picture of what's coming in the very near future.'

## Wrong car from GM?

What's coming from Japan is a new generation of larger, high-performance luxury cars that even the Europeans will eventually need to worry about. The irony is that GM, when it decided to build Saturn, may have picked the wrong end of the market upon which to stake its technological future. With Saturn, the risk for GM is that just as its grand plans to 'reinvent the wheel' come to fruition, the high-speed Japanese will be preparing to compete with it on their *own* techno-logical terms – at the other end of the market. Not to mention Ford, Chrysler, the Europeans and perhaps even some others. After two oil shocks, and massive efforts to 'downsize' its models, by 1987 GM had realized that it was at the top end of the market that its new model mix weaknesses were most exposed.

To be market-driven or technology-driven? The question is now redundant. GM's experience demonstrates that the larger players need a high-speed R&D policy that is both market-driven *and* technology-driven, in order to cover every possible sector of a constantly shifting market. This now seems to be the strategies of Procter & Gamble and IBM, as discussed in earlier chapters. The smaller players may have no choice either, if they don't want to get squeezed out of their own niche markets. A flexible approach to innovation and R&D also requires a flexible approach to production and operations. Now more than ever, US companies in both the services and manufacturing industries are looking for marketing leverages in the areas of production and operations, as will be seen in the next chapter.

# 6 Leverage in production and operations

The gloom and despondency that characterized the beginning of the decade for US industry has vanished. A sense of confidence and optimism now prevails, spurred on by the strongest economic recovery since the Korean war, a GNP growth rate better than its main trading rivals, and a falling dollar that eventually should help boost export earnings. Investment in plant and equipment is at record levels, fuelled by the strength of the economic recovery and by the 1981 business tax cut. American business once again feels it is capable of competing on the world stage. Even the Japanese are now considered beatable at their own game – the production of technologically superior goods. And this time the rules are seen to be not so stacked against the Americans, particularly since the Japanese yen has risen to what are considered to be more realistic levels.

## Diagnosing a marathon runner

What has surprised some observers is that the decade of the 1970s was not so bad either, given the magnitude of the transformations that had taken place. Schwarz and Volgy, writing in a 1985 *Harvard Business Review* article, 'The myth of America's economic decline', claimed that 'The impression that the US economy from 1970 to 1980 performed poorly compared with a more glorious era such as the 1950s is wrong'. (1)

According to the authors, the US economy had to confront two major challenges – the enormous surge of young workers entering the labour force, including married women, and the price of oil, which more than tripled between 1974 and 1981. At first glance the American economy appeared unable to cope. Even though the number of new jobs grew at unprecedented rates, the unemployment rate climbed throughout the 1970s. Although real GNP and real personal income rose, inflation soared to more than double the rates of the 1960s. While real investment grew at a normal pace, the rate of productivity stopped improving. And as industry after industry faltered, the U.S. trade balance deteriorated. Yet, maintained Schwarz and Volgy, these signs were not the signals of decline. Rather, and although most observers misinterpreted them, 'the four symptoms masked the impressive economic performance that was actually taking place'.

This performance was impressive even in America's supposedly weak area – manufacturing. Although there were some declining industries, such as steel and rubber, the 6 per cent growth in manufacturing employment during the 1970s was greater than all other major competing nations, including Japan (2 per cent growth) and Germany (which had a decline). What caused the sluggish productivity performance was that the impact of all the new workers – a 40 per cent growth rate between 1965 and 1980 – meant that the amount of investment per worker declined. In fact, US manufacturing productivity increased at an average rate of 2.8 per cent per year during the 1970s, compared with a 2.3 per cent annual rate during the supposedly golden years of the 1950s. As a result, asserted the authors:

> the period of presumed economic decline was a time of unrecognized success.... We mistook the symptoms of a perfectly normal economy undergoing the rigors of a long-distance, uphill run for an economic heart attack.

## Running again

There is no doubt that by the mid-1980s, the uphill slog was beginning to pay off. Richard Kirkland Jr, in a 1985 *Fortune* article, 'America on top again', exclaimed: 'Confidence and optimism have come roaring back, fuelled by a growth rate better than Japan's. And this boom is built on some solid foundations.' In a 1986 article, 'Now, R&D is corporate America's answer to Japan Inc.', *Business Week* reported the director of one top research centre as saying: 'Industrial research has become the principal driving force behind the process of technological change.'

US capital spending has been booming, spurred by the continued strength of the economic recovery, the 1981 business tax cuts, and the spurt in the venture capital market in the early 1980s. Investment in research and development by business had grown by more than 6 per cent per year in real terms since 1975, vs 2 per cent from 1970 to 1975, claimed Kirkland. And while West Germany and Japan still spent more on civilian R&D as a percentage of GNP (2.5 per cent and 2.3 per cent respectively, vs 1.8 per cent for the US), 'playing the percentage game obscures the magnitude of the US advantage', he added. *Business Week* reported that in 1985 the 844 companies included in the magazine's annual R&D 'scorecard', spent $48.8 billion, an increase of 10 per cent over 1984. In an earlier 1986 article, *Business Week* had reported the Battelle Memorial Institute as estimating that industrial R&D spending should increase by over 9 per cent, to approximately $58 billion in 1986.

In another 1986 article, 'America can beat anyone in high tech. Just ask Bruce Merrifield', *Business Week* reported the Assistant Commerce Secretary as affirming that 'The climate for entrepreneurship and productivity is bringing about a total restructuring of the economy'. Merrifield added that new companies had been starting up at a rate of almost 700 000 a year, creating, directly or indirectly some ten million new jobs over the previous three years. Yet most of this was going unnoticed because 80 per cent of these new outfits employ fewer than twenty people, and Census Bureau statistics, which cut off at twenty-five employees, fail to pick them up – which prompted a strong denial from the government agency. He also assured *Business Week* that there were impressive productivity gains being made by big manufacturing companies, as they replaced outmoded plant and equipment with up-to-date production facilities.

*The Economist*, in a 1986 article, 'America manufactures still', agreed with this assessment, and added that the US was far from losing its industrial base, as was being predicted by many at the beginning of the 1980s. While manufacturing's share of value added, at current prices, fell from 26 per cent of GNP in 1970 to less than 20 per cent in 1985: 'The same thing happened in all industrial countries as higher productivity cut the price of manufactured goods compared with services, while consumers spent more of their growing incomes on services instead of goods.'

*The Economist* reported that manufacturing productivity rose at an annual average rate of 4.7 per cent in the three years 1983–5, vs 1.7 per cent in the rest of the non-farm economy over the same period: 'The biggest increases were in old industries, which got rid of their worse plants, and in mass-production, e.g., of consumer durables, where firms automated fast to cut costs.' Certainly the car industry was one to slim down, and speed up. In an earlier article, 'A puzzlingly poorly productive America', *The Economist* said that the US auto industry had an annual productivity increase of 4 per cent in the five years to 1984, vs 3 per cent in the past thirty years. This is not surprising, given the billions of dollars that had been poured into new plant and equipment.

Robert Lawrence, in a 1984 book, *Can America Compete?*, insisted that the manufacturing slump after 1973 was a worldwide pheno- menon, and even though the growth in labour productivity in the US was not as rapid as in other industrial countries, 'US productivity levels in manufacturing and the US share of R&D spending in value added for manufacturing remain the highest in the world'.

Lawrence argued that the superior performance of American manufacturing may also be due to a more mobile and flexible labour force – and one more willing to trade wage cuts for employment. One result has been that the proportion of manufacturing employment in high-tech industries has increased more rapidly in the US than in Germany or Japan. Lawrence also noted another couple of important recent trends:

> Although American investment flows have shifted toward manufacturing, in the manufacturing sectors of Europe and Japan the share of total investment allocated to manufacturing has declined significantly. Profit rates in manufacturing have fallen considerably less in the United states than they have in Europe. (2)

No wonder that Robert Hayes, co-author of the important 1980 *Harvard Business Review* article 'Managing our way to economic decline', should inform *Fortune* in 1985: 'The US has won the battle with Europe. I can't think of a single high-technology industry where we are concerned about Europe's leadership.'

It is not just the Europeans that American manufacturers want to beat. Judging by some recent reports they are once again ready to take on the world. In late-1986, in 'Are America's manufacturers finally back on the map?', *Business Week* proclaimed:

> The battered US manufacturing sector is fighting back. A

leaner, more efficient industrial base is emerging from years of brutal cost reduction and massive consolidation forced by imports.... Since 1981, when manufacturers first realized that their goods were less and less able to compete with imports, they have stepped up capital spending, acquired new technology, and slashed costs.

By 1987 the results of this effort were beginning to pay off. Even the much maligned US automobile industry was able to report an improvement in product competitiveness. Jeremy Main, in a 1987 *Fortune* article, 'Detroit's cars really are getting better', claimed that, led by Ford, the Big Three have all raised their quality levels since 1980. Concluded Main:

> The tumultuous, expensive revolution in technology, management, labor relations, and corporate culture forced on Detroit by the success of Japan is beginning to pay off. Some of the best-built American cars, such as the big Lincoln Town Car and Mercury Grand Marquis, are within reach of world-class quality, as defined by Honda, Mercedes, and Toyota.

## No resting

Both observers and participants agree the US cannot now afford to become complacent. Even though the American economy is expected to grow faster than Europe's total for the rest of the decade, the Japanese remain their main threat. For while output per hour in manufacturing in the US is still higher than in Japan, the gap is narrowing. *The Economist* stated that American firms will not give up their lead without a fight: 'Efficient, more automated production is now a top priority at companies from IBM and General Motors to smaller, specialist manufacturers like Intel.'

*Business Week*, in a 1985 cover story, 'Fighting back: it can work', gave the results of a survey carried out by Louis Harris & Associates Inc., in which senior executives at 301 large US manufacturing companies facing Japanese competition were asked to name the step their company was *most* likely to take to become really competitive with the Japanese. According to the executives polled, their best response to the Japanese challenge is increased capital investment and improved marketing, especially the quality of customer servicing.

Knee-jerk reactions, such as reducing wage costs and/or cutting margins in order to maintain market share, were low on their list of priorities:

*Percentage saying:*

| | |
|---|---:|
| Invest in more efficient plant and equipment | 27% |
| Invest more in research and development | 23% |
| Improve the quality of service to customers | 23% |
| Adopt more aggressive marketing tactics and strategies | 14% |
| Reduce wage costs | 6% |
| Cut profit margins in order to keep market share | 2% |
| All of the above | 1% |
| Not sure | 3% |

What is also important is that US firms are not replacing outdated plant and equipment with 'more of the same, only faster'. They are replacing it with plant and equipment that is 'completely different, and faster'. At the same time they are adopting Japanese practices, such as better management of inventories. In the process they are rewriting the rules of marketing, by introducing innovative manufacturing and operations.

In a 1986 survey, 'The titans of high technology: Japan and America', *The Economist* observed that:

> conventional manufacturing is limping out and new computerized forms of design and fabrication are muscling in ... high technology is making the whole notion of the special-purpose factory – with its automated equipment purring smoothly along as it churns out millions of identical parts all made to the same high standard of precision – a relic of the smokestack past. The market place is much more competitive today, no longer accepting the 10–12 year product life-cycles needed to justify the investment of such dedicated plants. The pace of technological change is demanding that manufactured goods be replaced every four or five years; in consumer electronics, every two or three years.

*The Economist* predicted that high-tech American manufacturers would eventually overcome the Japanese challenge, for a variety of reasons – a greater supply of brain power, more diverse and flexible sources of finance, a bigger and more acquisitive home market and, most important, the pace of innovation itself:

High-tech products tend to have two things in common: they fall in price rapidly as production builds up (they possess steep learning curves) and they get replaced fairly frequently (they have short life-cycles). The trend in high-tech is toward things becoming steeper and shorter. So the competitive advantage of being first to market is going increasingly to outweigh almost everything else.... This spells an end to the traditional low-risk, low-cost approach that Japanese companies have used so successfully to date – coming in second with massive volume and forward prices after others have primed the market. Henceforth, Japanese firms are going to have to take the same technological risks – and pay the same financial penalties – as everyone else. And that puts the advantage decidedly on the side of Yankee ingenuity.

No company in America is spending more, and risking more, to overhaul the way it produces things than General Motors. Perhaps ironically, the way it *used* to produce cars was a key factor in explaining its long-running domination of the US auto market. Charles Burck, in a 1981 *Fortune* article, 'How GM stays ahead', said:

> The genius of the old GM lay in manufacturing: it stretched the lifetime of its machinery and tooling over great unit volumes, and drove down costs through constant improvements in production processes. It did a superb job of making cars better by honing conventional technologies, and it made a lot of money for a long time.... But it was neither a big spender nor much of an innovator. Whether for fear of antitrust action (shades of IBM?) or because there was no market for innovation, the company took few risks.

This is now changing and, *The Economist* noted, between 1981 and 1985, GM alone spent no less than $40 billion on 'factories of the future'. And that may be only the start.

# New production philosophy

In a 1983 cover story, 'Detroit's merry-go-round', *Business Week* pointed out that despite recent sales and profits lifts, Detroit's car makers had yet to 'pick up ground on the world standard of success: Japan'. The way to do that was to 'create a philosophy that questions almost every traditional operating and management assumption and concentrates on establishing solid profits on existing market share'.

General Motors, for one, is trying to create such a philosophy. *Business Week*, in a 1985 story, 'How GM's Saturn could run rings around old-style car makers' said that the technology that made the assembly line synonomous with Detroit 'may be reaching the end of the road'. And the reason for this was GM's decision to set up its new Saturn subsidiary:

> Just as Ford Motor Co.'s assembly line became the mainstay of US industry, General Motors Corp.'s new Saturn Corp. subsidiary may pave the way for the elusive 'factory of the future'.... GM's Saturn subsidiary is a $5 billion bid to do nothing short of revolutionizing automobile manufacturing.... By replacing the assembly line with a fully computerized production system that extends from the dealer to the factory floor, GM is betting that it can close the estimated $2000-per-unit gap between its production costs and those of its Japanese competitors.

Saturn is the first new US passenger car manufacturing division within GM since 1918. *Business Week*, in a 1985 article, 'GM's bold bid to reinvent the wheel', claimed:

> GM no longer sees Saturn as a means to find engineering and manufacturing tricks but as a way to induce radical rethinking in every aspect of the car business – from corporate administration to dealer franchises.

It is perhaps not surprising that GM came to realize it needed to set up Saturn as an autonomous division. *The Economist*, in a 1985 article 'Saturnalia', perceptively noted:

> It would be a mistake to interpret the (Saturn) announcement just as a sign that GM thinks it can now produce small cars more cheaply than the Japanese.... The real reasons for Saturn are, first, marketing – a car being hyped as revolutionary can hardly be sold under the boring old Chevrolet nameplate. And, second, management – Saturn is a hotbed on which GM can try out new ways of running itself.

In other words, unfettered by GM's bureaucracy, Saturn's managers were to rethink the whole process of moving goods from producer to consumer. Saturn would not only change GM's approach to product development and manufacturing, it would also set up its own dealer network – and *Business Week* speculated that some outlets may be located in non-traditional locations, such as shopping malls. Whether Saturn's sales people will go as far as the Japanese, and sell door-to-door, is another matter.

## Flexible manufacturing

While Saturn may be the factory of the future – though, as noted in the previous chapter, there is now some doubt that Saturn's start-up date will be met, and that cost targets will be met – some of GM's Japanese competitors have been running factories of today. These factories are also based on principles contrary to the previous notion of economies of scale. This is a system known as flexible manufacturing, or FMS. As explained by Gene Bylinsky, in a 1983 *Fortune* article, 'The race to the automatic factory':

> Flexible manufacturing systems . . . complete a process of factory automation that began back in the 1950s. First came numerically controlled machine tools that performed their operations automatically according to coded instruments on paper or Mylar tape. Then came computer-aided design and computer-aided manufacturing, or CAD/CAM, which replaced the drafting board with the CRT screen and the numerical control tape with the computer. . . . The new systems integrate all these elements.

In a 1981 *Fortune* article, 'A new industrial revolution is on the way', Bylinsky explained how CAD/CAM worked: 'The CAD of CAD/ CAM is basically designing, drafting, and analysing with computer graphics displayed on a screen.' Of course this involves more than merely 'drawing' a three-dimensional picture, and rotating it on the screen, separating it into bits, or enlarging and shrinking it. It also means subjecting the designs to various tests and simulations, such as stress tests, thereby saving enormous time and expense in building and testing mock-ups. Bylinsky continued: 'CAM, the other side of CAD/CAM, refers to something that has come to be commonplace in manufacturing plants – computer control of production machines.' These machines can range from a single lathe cutting away in a closet machine shop, to a row of welding robots darting and sparking in harmony all along a darkened assembly line.

Bylinsky said that CAM provides 'speed, accuracy, tirelessness, and dependability that human operators cannot match', and added:

> But the potentialities are greatly magnified when CAD and CAM are joined together. . . . When the linkage works smoothly, the on-screen designing and testing of a product generate a bank of computer instructions for manufacturing it – or making the tools, dies, and moulds used in manufacturing it.

The payoff comes from reducing the time between design and production; moreover 'it is less costly to move to new models, make mid-stream design changes, customize products, set up short production runs'.

Flexible manufacturing takes this linkage one step further by integrating all the elements. *The Economist*, in a 1985 article, 'What comes after quality circles?', noted that the aim of flexible manufacturing is a reduction in the production run necessary to make an assembly line profitable and:

> The tool for doing this is the computer: in automated assembly lines, inventory control, design (CAD) and manufacturing (CAM), and through integration of a company's office engineering and factory computer.

The marketing advantages are enormous, as explained by Bylinsky in 1983:

> Flexible manufacturing is the ultimate entrepreneurial system: it will allow fast-thinking manufacturers to move swiftly into brand new fields and leave them just as swiftly if need be – at the expense of less agile older producers.

Writing in *The McKinsey Quarterly* Bolwijn and Kumpe claimed in 1986 that while the benefits of flexible manufacturing systems and factory automation have been well publicized:

> so far, though, the slip-ups probably outnumber the successes, mainly because companies have tried to introduce automation without thinking through the far-reaching effects of the new technology on every aspect of the operation.

According to the authors, among other things, most companies view flexible manufacturing mostly as:

a matter of automating the individual segments of their business systems – the chain of functional operations, beginning with product design and materials procurement and ending with physical delivery and after-sales-service.... In other words, they have typically used automation to optimize individual links in the chain rather than refashioning the chain as a whole.

In order to realize the real benefits of flexible manufacturing, top management need to replace functional thinking with a view that spans the entire business system, said the authors. The implication is that to successfully introduce the FMS concept, firms virtually need to rebuild themselves from the ground up – a mammoth time-consuming task that many US companies have now embarked upon.

If so, they are building for good reasons. Bolwijn and Kumpe said that since market forces are forcing companies to shift towards shorter product life-cycles, shorter production runs, and higher product quality, manufacturing flexibility is now a necessity. One important benefit is that it helps speed up the introduction of products incorporating the latest technologies, thereby increasing market competitiveness. Another is that it helps reduce work-in-progress and finished goods inventories, thereby improving profitability.

## Fast starters

One example of the potential of flexible manufacturing was provided by *Business Week* in a 1986 article, 'The fully automated factory rewards an early dreamer':

> Take Allan-Bradley Co. A year ago it threw the switch on a highly automated assembly line: 50 machines – all untouched by human hands – that turn out a wide variety of starters for electrical motors. Bar codes in the bases of the starters tell the assembly machines what other components are needed for each unit, so the computer-integrated lines can randomly skip from one type of starter to another – a total of 143 variations can be assembled on two sizes of bases. Now the Milwaukee company is getting set to add three more base sizes to span the bulk of the foreign market.

*Business Week* claimed the system is so flexible that it is worthwhile making only one copy of a particular starter, and added that President

O'Rourke expects to leverage A-B's $15 million investment into a 30 per cent share of the worldwide market by becoming the world's low-cost producer'.

While flexible manufacturing systems were developed in the US as far back as the early 1970s, Bylinsky wrote in 1983 that it was the Japanese who 'have become the implementers par excellence of this new type of factory automation not because they are great technical innovators... but because they have moved fast in putting the new systems into their factories'.

A principal reason for this acceptance, claimed Bylinsky, was that 'a technology like flexible automation is a logical extension of a manufacturing philosophy that views the production of goods as a seamless activity that starts with product design and ends with support in the field – a philosophy, as the Japanese put it, of "making the goods flow like water"'. A top executive of a large US farm equipment supplier added: 'Japanese management takes a holistic view of manufacturing.... They apply logic and common sense to their problems rather than laboratory investigations and discounted cash flow calculations.'

*The Economist*, in 'What comes after quality circles?' agreed, and referred to an unpublished study by four American business school professors to show where the main Japanese advantage exists. According to the authors of the study of the manufacturing strategies of some one thousand companies in America, Europe and Japan, the Americans and Europeans are concentrating on yesterday's manufacturing problem – quality and delivery times – whereas the Japanese have moved on to tomorrow's – computerized production control in order to realize the advantages of flexible manufacturing. The key to the success of flexible manufacturing is the computer, and here the Japanese and Americans part company as well. The impetus in America, say the professors, is coming from computer specialists; in Japan the drive for factory computerization is coming from the process engineers. This should not be surprising if the flow of goods concept is implicit to the Japanese thinking.

## Flow of cars

Virtually all car manufacturing firms have had for some time sections of automated production, where tasks such as stamping, welding or painting have been performed by robots. Flexible manufacturing system is the attempt to link these sections, especially the final, assembly stage, into a continuous flow. A crucial advantage, especially when the system is linked to a just-in-time delivery system, is that it allows the same equipment to manufacture several different car body styles on one assembly line, thereby allowing the company to cover a greater part of the market with a range of vehicles from the one plant. It also forces a redefinition of the notion of economies of scale based on long production runs of a single body type, since FMS potentially allows for shorter production runs which are more profitable.

Mazda is one Japanese car maker which has adopted this approach. Its Hofu plant in Japan, which began operating in 1981, can simultaneously produce up to nine different types of car bodies. With the help of computer-controlled production and just-in-time delivery of components from suppliers located nearby, Mazda is able to quickly adjust its product mix in response to changes in consumer needs. Another advantage, claimed by the company in its 1982 annual report is that the system also minimizes the downtime for switching to the production of a new model, an advantage few plants at the moment could claim. Its flexible manufacturing system thus gives Mazda a major production and operations process leverage, a key determinant of success when a market is characterized by sudden fluctuations in demand, or when a company wishes to serve the diverse requirements of a global market. In this latter case, flexible manufacturing demolishes another recent marketing myth – that of the trend towards the standardized 'global car' concept.

Another advantage claimed of flexible manufacturing is the shorter time it takes to change over to new models. Honda's Marysville, Ohio, plant is capable of turning out some 320 000 cars annually, at the rate of 100 cars a year per worker, or about a third more than the most modern US plants. In a typical US-owned plant a model changeover would normally take up to several days – or even weeks – of costly downtime. When the Marysville plant switched from building the 1985 Accord to the 1986 model, *Time* reported that the changeover was done without any loss of production: 'Not bad for a company that less than three decades ago had yet to build its first car', reported *Time*.

## Linking R&D and production leverages

The big payoff occurs when the planning, designing and production of a car are linked together into a continuous process, rather than being performed as sequential, but discrete, functions. How Mazda handles this process gives some pointers to the way the flow of goods approach to R&D and production now works in one Japanese car company anyway.

Traditionally it has taken about five years to *plan, design* and *produce* a new car, which is then expected to stay on the market for anything from four to ten years without major modifications. Some manufacturers, such as Mazda, currently work on four-yearly launch-relaunch cycles, with possibly a minor cosmetic face-lift in the second year. This means that when one model is being released its replacement is already being planned as a concept. This new car development process, in a simplified form, can be shown as follows: (see Figure 6.1).

With the computer-assisted design (CAD) process being integrated with computer-assisted manufacturing (CAM), it now takes about two years to convert a design into a showroom product, illustrated above. In other words it takes as long to develop and test the designs as it does to produce the car. Arguably, this makes the design concept the most critical decision in the new product development process. The manager of Mazda's design division recently remarked, in an in-house publication, that it hasn't been too many years since the word *design* replaced *styling* in automobile technology. The impact of this semantic change reflects a complete change in the concept of car design – and the result is that new cars are now being developed and marketed in a different way. No matter where we look in the flow of goods approach to marketing, there has been a recent upheaval in the way a particular task is carried out, or even defined – and the supplanting of *styling* by *design* is an example of this.

## Styling vs design

According to Mazda's design executive, the term styling, especially in the US, 'tended to mean designs aimed merely at attracting customer attention and spurring sales' – what Walter McQuade, in a 1982 *Fortune* article, 'The shape of cars to come', termed the attraction of 'chrome-grimace styling'. That has now changed because of techno-

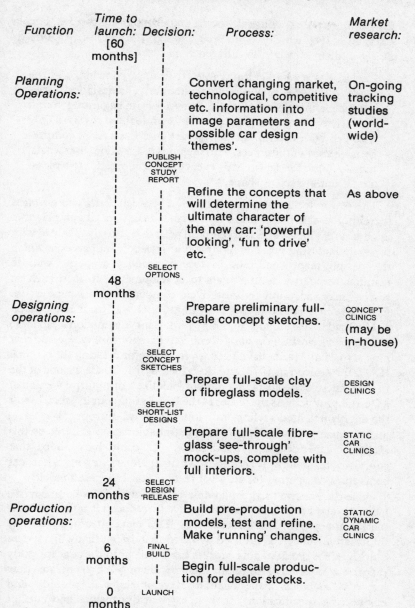

| Function | Time to launch: [60 months] | Decision: | Process: | Market research: |
|---|---|---|---|---|
| Planning Operations: | | | Convert changing market, technological, competitive etc. information into image parameters and possible car design 'themes'. | On-going tracking studies (world-wide) |
| | | PUBLISH CONCEPT STUDY REPORT | | |
| | | | Refine the concepts that will determine the ultimate character of the new car: 'powerful looking', 'fun to drive' etc. | As above |
| | 48 months | SELECT OPTIONS | | |
| Designing operations: | | | Prepare preliminary full-scale concept sketches. | CONCEPT CLINICS (may be in-house) |
| | | SELECT CONCEPT SKETCHES | | |
| | | | Prepare full-scale clay or fibreglass models. | DESIGN CLINICS |
| | | SELECT SHORT-LIST DESIGNS | | |
| | | | Prepare full-scale fibre-glass 'see-through' mock-ups, complete with full interiors. | STATIC CAR CLINICS |
| | 24 months | SELECT DESIGN 'RELEASE' | | |
| Production operations: | | | Build pre-production models, test and refine. Make 'running' changes. | STATIC/ DYNAMIC CAR CLINICS |
| | 6 months | FINAL BUILD | | |
| | | | Begin full-scale produc-tion for dealer stocks. | |
| | 0 months | LAUNCH | | |

**Figure 6.1 Mazda's model development process**

logical innovations, political, social, and economic pressures. Nicola
Crea, in a 1985 article, 'Styling and design', in the journal *Auto &*
*Design* explained what the difference means:

> Design has a socio-cultural role. It implies knowledge in the
> fields of art, science and socio-economics. The designer carries
> out the planning of an object and its uses from beginning to end;
> the stylist works with just a part. And while the stylist is mainly
> involved with exterior shape, the designer has a more compre-
> hensive view of the object. This includes its function, uses, costs,
> mass-production feasibility – everything combined into a pleas-
> ant, if not attractive shape.

The reason for making this distinction between *design* and *styling* is
to reinforce the point made by Susan Fraker, in Chapter 5, that
designers, engineers and marketers all need to be closely involved with
the manufacturing process. As Fraker affirmed: 'Companies in which
the design team continues to toss a product over the wall to
manufacturing risk adding years to development.' In fact, such an
analogy may apply only to Western car companies. In a Japanese auto
firm there may not be any such organizational 'wall' in the first place.

McQuade also noted another important distinction – Japanese
design teams work on the basis of collective responsibility. He said that
nine stylists at Mazda have been given credit for creating the original
RX-7, introduced in 1978, and described by McQuade as 'one of the
first Japanese-styled cars that did not look like a diminutive version of
a Detroit product'. As the leader of the RX-7 group put it, Japan hasn't
the highly talented styling individualists as in Europe: 'We have,
instead, many individuals who have reasonable capacity. Based on this
reality, teamwork makes good sense.' He could have added that
complete teamwork is *essential* when there are eight other car
companies competing for survival in the local Japanese market.

Once the planning stage is completed, design and development of a
new car take up to four years and, once introduced it must retain its
market appeal for several more years. This makes it crucial that the
information collected and used will lead to a design that will not date
quickly, since the designing process can't start until the concept study
report is completed. This report includes not only market-related data
but also technical data, such as developments in plastics, and
engineering specifications, such as exterior dimensions and interior
space requirements. Marketers, designers, planners and engineers

must cooperate in preparing this report and, as noted in Chapter 5, General Motors in the early 1980s began a massive structural overhaul to ensure that new car development teams became responsible for everything from defining a car's market to overseeing its final production. They needed to. McQuade pointed out that, in the past, it was not uncommon for GM stylists working on the front of a new car to be kept ignorant of what was being done with the sides or back, for security reasons. 'Which may or may not have helped the overall result', suggested McQuade.

## Key words

Out of the concept study report must then come the agreed image of the vehicle. This image will be determined first by the important design 'themes' that are predicted to influence – or dictate – car design, such as the need for aerodynamic lines for less wind resistance, in order to conserve fuel. Second is the selection of key words, such as 'powerful', 'rugged' or 'fun to drive', which will determine the final image or 'personality' of the car, as well as its potential target market. These key words are then translated into design terms as the image takes shape. At the same time the selected key words must meet the requirements of the company's overall development policy – assuming the company has one – in order to tie together the entire model line-up. According to a 1985 Mazda publication, its policy is: 'The pursuit of the ultimate pleasure of driving.' Some design teams will try to apply the key words to products other than cars, such as buildings or clothes, to put the concepts being considered into a wider context. Agreeing on the 'right' key words is thus a crucial step in the development process because succeeding operations, including manufacturing, grow out of it. This exercise cannot be done in isolation, and it is not surprising that it may take up to a year to complete. It is interesting to speculate what key words IBM's designers selected when the PC Jr was being developed, and what key words GM has now adopted for its Saturn Project.

Most auto manufacturers eschew radical design changes. As a GM design chief explained to McQuade: 'When you totally redesign a car, you can't leave your last year's customer stranded. He must still feel a member of the family.'

Mazda is one Japanese manufacturer which has adopted the

European practice of evolutionary design changes. Manufacturers such as Audi, BMW, Mercedes Benz, Jaguar, Peugeot, Porsche, Renault, Volvo and VW, deliberately refine and evolve their designs, particularly the exterior styling, so their products maintain a consistent, but ever-developing, image or brand 'personality'.

## Designed in the USA

To keep up to date with the US market, Mazda – along with Honda, Nissan and Toyota – has a design centre in California, considered to be the bell-wether state for the rest of America, and certainly the state most receptive to imported cars. According to Peter Nulty in a 1984 *Business Week* article 'Ford's fragile recovery', this is why Ford also selected California to carry out much of its design development research on its new Thunderbird, launched in 1984. Ford's design objective was a car that would lead the rest of the US market, with California the necessary starting point.

Mazda is attempting to achieve product research and development leverage in the American market. And since hologram technology is now available it is not difficult to envisage Mazda's combined Japanese–American design team in the United States – there is also a design centre in Belgium – testing design concepts on US car buyers in what are called 'car clinics', and relaying their findings via satellite directly into their flexible manufacturing operations back in Japan – or in Michigan, where Mazda has located its new US plant.

One implication is that, by linking one technological breakthrough (consumer testing using holograms of new car designs) with another (CAD/CAM and flexible manufacturing), the more innovative and 'high-speed' Japanese car makers will gain both R&D *and* production leverages over their American rivals. Not only would they be able to turn out a wider range of top-quality cars to suit changing consumer requirements and tastes, they would also be able to design and produce these cars in much less time than previously.

## GM's factory of the future: made in the USA

GM is not giving up without an expensive fight. Its Saturn division will change nearly every aspect of auto-making operations, claimed

*Business Week*, in the 1985 article: 'How GM's Saturn could run rings around old-style carmakers.' One of Saturn's goals is a three-year product development cycle and, if GM's cut back in investment doesn't jeopardize this goal, that will make the division very competitive even by Japanese standards.

One of Saturn's main departures – and one that has important implications for other manufacturers – is that component production and assembly operations will be performed on one site. This means a fully integrated line that will, for example, cast engine blocks, machine, and assemble them, and then automatically feed them directly into the final body assembly operation when required. Likewise, many parts suppliers will set up plants within the Saturn complex in order to be linked directly to the central computer controlling the production process, thereby giving GM the benefits of just-in-delivery. This will force a complete rethinking of GM's relationship with suppliers who, in the past would have been played off one against the other, usually for cost concession reasons.

Rather than putting together a car bit by bit as it moves along an assembly line, Saturn cars will be built from 'modules' – such as the complete dashboard, probably built by outside contractors rather than as a sub-assembly on the main track – which, once in the main plant, get delivered by computer-controlled vehicles to a final assembly line where they are combined into the finished cars – probably using robots to a greater degree than ever before. The end result, originally claimed by GM, will be a higher-quality car built with no more than forty hours of labour – with much of this costed at the cheaper outside contractors' rates – compared with the estimated Japanese input of about a hundred hours, including suppliers' labour.

A marketing strength of this system will be GM's ability to turn out a virtually unlimited range of customer orders. Further, at this final stage of the flow of cars process, Saturn is expected to break more new ground. Anne Fisher, in a 1985 *Fortune* article, 'Behind the hype at GM's Saturn', reported that distribution accounts for 25 per cent or more of the cost of a small car. To reduce this, GM is likely to set up a new distribution network – something the Japanese do frequently when completely new lines are introduced – one reason being to ensure greater control over dealer after-sales servicing, currently a weak link in the GM chain, as borne out by consumer surveys. Fisher said this will allow GM to capitalize on a major advantage over its Japanese rivals – its plant is closer geographically to its end customers. This potential advantage, however, is rapidly disappearing. By 1990 Japanese car companies could be assembling close to two million units in the USA, in no less than six plants scattered about the country.

GM also announced it was developing a computer system to cut down the lead time between order and delivery of a new car. Customers can go to a Saturn dealer and choose a new car, complete with any number of options, by entering their selections on a computer terminal at a Saturn dealer. This information will be relayed directly to the plant and, theoretically, the car could be built within days, rather than weeks, as currently. GM has already experimented with this approach, in fact it has taken it one step further, by sending diskettes to a sample of Apple home computer users in California. The diskette listed information about features and options on GM's cars. Fisher said that: 'By popping a diskette into his Apple II computer, the user can assemble the car he wants, and get an idea of its price, before he goes out to see a dealer.' Those customers without a home computer can pop into their local Saturn dealer which, according to Fisher, could be a small storefront in a shopping mall, a form of distribution that is now being used in parts of Europe.

## Overhauling GM

By the end of 1986, GM's profit, product, and market share deficiencies were such that some industry observers were questioning the company's ability to compete. William Hampton, in a *Business Week* article, 'Reality has hit General Motors – hard', quoted Maryann Keller, one of America's most respected auto industry analysts, as warning that 'GM will continue to lose market share unless it improves the appeal of its products with more distinctive design, higher quality, and better marketing'. She added that these tasks could take years to accomplish.

GM's problems are not unique. In 1986 *The Economist*, in a major feature on Fiat's turnaround, said that over the past dozen years a number of major car companies – Volkswagen, British Leyland, Jaguar, Peugeot, Fiat and America's Chrysler – have all managed to carry out massive recovery programmes. Renault still has a question mark. In all the cases strong leaders were necessary prerequisites for success. Given the problems in selling its newest models, even with low-interest incentives, its steady decline in market share in the US, and the wide swings in its profit results, General Motors may be the next company to undergo the radical restructuring that necessarily accompanies the recovery process.

If so, will GM under Roger Smith succeed? *The Economist* believed that the car industries of America and Europe, rather than facing inevitable conquest by their Japanese and South Korean rivals, can in fact survive by learning a few key lessons. These lessons apply equally to GM and its Saturn mission.

One lesson, stated *The Economist*, was that: 'Europe and America will never revive their manufacturing employment until they realize that the technological revolution means mainly that they can make yesterday's things more ingeniously and more cost-effectively – but only if they change yesterday's attitudes among the workforce.' Perhaps *The Economist* should have spelled out that the 'workforce' includes the cadres of middle and upper management as well. Equally: 'The turnaround men in car making have all had to relearn the first lesson from Henry Ford – that the product beats everything else in determining success or failure. . . . And all the recovering companies . . . have had to relearn the importance of quality control.'

If *The Economist* is correct, the Saturn mission will succeed, not just by its CAD/CAM and its FMS breakthroughs, or its new MAP – (manufacturing automation protocol). Gene Bylinsky, in a 1986 *Fortune* article, 'GM's road map to automated plants', said GM's MAP was a recently developed standardized communications system that lets all the computers, robots and machine tools converse in a common language, and will perhaps ultimately lead to the 'paperless factory'. While these systems are becoming essential, the real measure of GM's factory of the future will not be the technology but the results. *The Economist* indicated that, ultimately Saturn will succeed by its finished product – and the way the product is presented to a market that will already be saturated with quality-built small cars when it finally gets launched. As one industry researcher said to Fisher in 1985: 'The product is all important. If Saturn turns out to be another Honda, GM has hit a home run. But if Saturn is a shrunken Chevy Cavalier, they're dead.'

Perhaps not surprisingly, by 1986 GM had decided to produce a slightly larger car than originally intended – and had already incurred the penalty cost of adding at least another year to its development process time. In late 1986 GM announced further revisions. Saturn's budget was being cut from $5 billion to about $2 billion, and its output slashed from 400000 cars annually, to about 250000.

Added to GM's woes was the discovery that its best-built car in the US was the Chevrolet Nova, built in the Fremont, California, plant under a joint production agreement with Toyota. In 'General Motors: the Toyota touch', *The Economist* said in 1986 that: 'Fremont is teaching GM that it does not need robots and layers of agreements with unions to produce quality cars.' Noting that sales of GM's luxury cars had stalled, *The Economist* added: 'Now that Toyota has taught GM to build better cars, it needs to start teaching the Detroit car company how to sell its better cars better.'

## GM's mission

GM's mission statement reads:

> The fundamental purpose of General Motors is to provide products and services of such quality that our customers will receive superior value, our employees and business partners will share in our success, and our stockholders will receive a sustained, superior return on their investment.

It is interesting to speculate whether, from this mission statement, the GM design team working on Saturn have now got their '*key words*' right.

Despite its early setbacks, Saturn may indeed become the 'factory of the future' and, as a result, achieve leveraging advantages for GM at all four stages in the 'flow of goods' approach. Certainly if its attempts to revolutionize – and integrate – the flow of cars *and* the flow of information are successful, GM will dramatically change the process of car marketing into the next century. If so, then the innovative thinking that led to this change is likely to be applicable to firms in other industries.

As *The Economist* concluded, while the car industry is a mature industry, decline is not inevitable. Rather, it is:

> an industry with more technical variety, more scope for imagination, more unfinished business, more ways to survive, and more ways to put together a winning product than ever before. Car making in the West has now run through a dozen years of its post-Japan revolution. The lessons from this period are therefore reasonably clear, even when they have not been

accepted. Other old manufacturing industries that need a tonic for the tough years ahead can heed the carmakers' example, and take aim and take heart.

One such industry is among the oldest of them all.

## Production and operations leverage in the clothing industry

The Italian firm, Benetton, is Europe's largest producer of woollen knitwear. Sales in 1985 were $500 million, up 30 per cent 1984. In 1985 its ten factories turned out 40 million garments which were then sold through 3500 outlets in 54 countries. There are 450 outlets in the US, five of them on Fifth Avenue. Since 1983 the family-owned company has been opening new stores at the rate of one a day. All advertising is centrally co-ordinated under the slogan 'United colours of Benetton', which is always in English. The company's success can be put down to three factors: innovative design, production and distribution. Together these factors make the company's brightly coloured garments 'flow like water'.

*Time*, in a 1986 article, 'The sweet colors of success', described how the factors work:

Benetton has more computer programmers than seamstresses on the payroll. Stylists design shirts and pants on video terminals. Computers lay out patterns for cutting, reducing waste material to only 5 per cent. In the knitting plants, computers coded with up to 300 colours work out print, weave and colour combinations for sweaters, permitting designers to add decorations with the touch of a sensor pen. When the design is done, the computer punches out a program for the knitting machine, which automatically weaves the pattern.

Automation also aids distribution. In most of Benetton's European stores, computerized cash registers permit the company to receive instant inventory feedback, right down to style and colour. To keep up with the mercurial taste of younger buyers, the firm also produces a portion of its sweaters in uncoloured natural fibres. As daily sales reports flow into Treviso headquarters, these garments are dyed in the season's most popular hues and rushed to stores within ten days.

Last year Benetton opened a $25 million distribution centre in nearby Castrette di Villorba that the company claims is the most modern in the world. Except for a handful of maintenance and security men, the operation is run entirely by computers. Robots store garments as they arrive from the factories. Then, when orders come in, the machines retrieve the correct number of each style, in the right sizes and colours, with price tags in the appropriate currency, and deliver the shipments to the warehouse dock.

*Time* concluded: 'In the changeable world of Fashion, Benetton seems to have found a sure formula for success.'

At the other end of the spectrum is Custom Vetement Associates, the New York subsidiary of French clothing maker Vestra. In a 1986 article, 'How high-tech tailors are saving a stitch in time', *Business Week* revealed how the firm is achieving total operations leverage in what is a very custom-tailored business:

CVA is giving retailers terminals made for the French national videotex system and marketed in the US by Honeywell Inc. These link retailers with the main manufacturing operation in Strasbourg. . . . Tailors take key measurements from customers and plug them into a terminal. Every night the data are sent to a central computer in New York and beamed via satellite to France. In the morning, after nine inspectors look at different pieces of the data, a computer-controlled laser cutter selects the appropriate material and cuts the garment. A staff of tailors does the finishing touches, and the suit is shipped within four days.

*Business Week* said that ten retailers, including Saks Fifth Avenue, had signed so far and CVA expects to be serving 150 more stores by the end of 1986.

To requote from Chapter 1, *Time*, in a 1984 article, 'Manufacturing is in flower', correctly concluded: 'Long US industry's neglected stepchild, subordinated to finance and marketing, the process of making products is suddenly coming into its own, commanding more and more attention from company executives.' Whether we look at how companies make cars or clothes, we see that never before has manufacturing been so flexible, so innovative – and so vital a link to their market success. Further, rather than surrendering their manufacturing superiority to foreign competition, we also see that a growing number of American companies have come to realize that *MADE IN THE USA* is their marketing secret weapon.

The production and operational process parts of a company's business are now recognized as crucial leverages to gain a strategic marketing advantage. Yet, as many companies discover they haven't the means, or the time, to achieve these leverages on their own, they have turned to others – including their main competitors – to obtain them. No matter where you look, somebody is making a joint-arrangement with somebody else. Some may argue that collaborative efforts do not make for sound marketing long term. While that may turn out to be true, there are currently a great many companies willing to take the risk, as will be shown in the next chapter.

# 7 Collaborative marketing

Theodore Levitt, the Harvard Business School professor who has been referred to as the Copernicus of American business, in *The Marketing Imagination* reminded marketers to continuously ask: 'What's new in the market?' According to Levitt, the way to now deal with 'what's new' is to be widely informed, and to 'think straight':

> Picking easy formulas or exotic models out of textbooks or other people's heads may be convenient or even occasionally helpful, but it does nothing for your mind or for your ability to deal effectively with the constantly emerging new realities. To 'think straight' successfully in a world full of smart, straight-thinking people requires thinking with a special quality, transcending the ordinary and thus reaching imaginatively beyond the obvious or merely deductive. The future belongs to those who see possibilities before they become obvious and who effectively marshall resources and energies for their attainment or avoidance. (1)

In Chapters 5 and 6 we saw how firms, such as those in the automobile industry, were attempting to achieve new leverages in their R&D and/or production processes by completely rethinking, and then managing, these processes in ways that are superior to anyone else.

Their reasons for a complete rethinking are not difficult to understand. *Business Week*, in its 1983 cover story, 'Detroit's merry-go-round', concluded: 'US auto makers realize that concentrating on plants, equipment, and product will not be enough to solve all their problems. A more important and more difficult metamorphosis, industry leaders say, must take place within their own managements.' As was noted in the previous chapter, *Business Week* added that they needed to question 'almost every traditional operating and management assumption' about developing and building cars.

One such assumption is that, by rethinking their internal R&D and production processes, they can still develop new cars from scratch on their own within cost and time constraints – and with enough in-built flexibility to cope with fast-breaking changes in the market place. An alternative approach is to strike a deal with someone else who already has done the rethinking. Critics might argue that today's marketers have not reached 'imaginatively beyond the obvious or merely deductive' in their willingness – and sometimes haste – to enter into collaborative marketing arrangements, especially with direct competitors, in order to achieve quickly and relatively cheaply a combination of R&D, production, and distribution leverages. What might surprise many people is just how widespread this practice has become, and not just in the automobile industry. It may be popular, but is it sound marketing?

## Australia's own – from Japan

In the November 1985 issues of the *Australian Women's Weekly* – which is actually a monthly magazine – GM-H, or General Motors-Holden, the No. 3 Aussie car company, and one that for many years was No. 1 and prided itself as 'Australia's Own', ran an advertisement with the following headline:

> *'HOLDEN HAS THE BEST RANGE OF FUEL EFFICIENT*
> *4 CYLINDER CARS IN AUSTRALIA.'*

Part of the body copy read:

> *'That's right.*
> *Your good old Aussie Holden now has the best range of 4-cylinder cars in Australia. The range to beat those petrol prices that keep going up, and up.'*

GM-H listed five models as making up their new range. What the reader wasn't told was that all five were mostly designed, developed and/or built outside Australia:

| | |
|---|---|
| *Barina:* | is a badge-engineered Suzuki Swift |
| *Astra:* | is a badge-engineered Nissan Pulsar |
| *Gemini:* | is a joint Isuzu/GM-derived car |
| *Drover:* | is a badge-engineered Suzuki Sierra 4X4 |

*Camira:*     is the Australian version of the world J-car, which GM
            originated in its West German subsidiary, Opel

Not shown in the advertisement was the Holden Commodore, the flagship in GM-H's fleet, and which was being remodelled and prepared for relaunch in early 1986. That car is Opel-derived and is powered by a Nissan-built 6-cylinder engine. 'Aussie's Own' has now become a smorgasbord car company. Not that it really matters that much. Ford, now No. 1 in Australia, markets a range of models, many of which were developed in collaboration with Mazda.

## Joint deals

One of the most significant marketing changes in the past few years has been the upsurge in collaborative arrangements. In a 1986 article, 'Corporate odd couples: beware the wrong partner', *Business Week* announced:

> Welcome to Corporate America's version of the singles bar. It's where the cash-rich meet the funding-starved. Where the blue-jeaned meet the pin-striped. Where smokestacks meet high-tech. Where Yankees meet foreigners. Where once in a while perfect matches are made.... In simpler times these liaisons were called joint ventures. They've got a fancy new name now – 'strategic alliances'.

They may be popular, but do they make for good marketing? *Business Week* also warned: 'The rage for joint ventures has its pitfalls – a lot of them don't work out.'

In a 1984 cover story, 'Drastic new strategies to keep US multinationals competitive', *Business Week* explained the dilemma facing American firms, from car makers to construction equipment manufacturers, trying to compete internationally at the time:

> For several years, US business has been losing share to foreign rivals at home and abroad, as declining productivity and high labor costs have priced it out of market after market. But the dollar's 33 per cent surge in the last four years adds a new dimension to the fight for global competitiveness. Growing numbers of executives believe that the dollar's increase represents a structural change requiring big strategic adjustments in their business.

As discussed in Chapter 6, many US companies facing lower-cost foreign competition were responding to the challenge by accelerating their planned capital expenditure programmes in order to improve productivity. *Business Week* gave the example of GE, which had obtained work-rule concessions from its union in one plant; in return GE agreed to build in the USA 'a new, fully automated aircraft engine-parts plant that was expected to boost productivity by 100 per cent. The chairman of Booz, Allan & Hamilton informed *Business Week* that the strong dollar 'is forcing everyone to wake up to the potential of the factory of the future'.

For many companies in the early 1980s, working on the assumption of a permanently overvalued US dollar and undervalued Japanese yen, the factory of the future was to be located outside the US. As the executive Vice-president of Ingersoll-Rand explained to *Business Week* in 1984: 'Strategically, I'm betting on a strong dollar – and shifting more and more manufacturing abroad.' As the director of international operations at Beckman's bioanalytical-systems group replied when questioned about setting up operations in Ireland and Scotland: 'It is a permanent shift.'

*Business Week* also noted another trend:

Several other major US manufacturers – once symbols of the country's worldwide economic dominance – are not merely moving manufacturing to their own foreign plants to be competitive but are also ceding production of key products to foreign companies altogether and essentially acting as marketing agents.

By 1986, in a special report, 'The hollow corporation', *Business Week* was raising the alarm over what was seen as a dangerous trend:

A new kind of company is evolving in the US – manufacturing companies that do little manufacturing. Instead they import components or products from low-wage countries, slap their own names on them, and sell them in America. Unchecked, this trend will ultimately hurt the economy – retarding productivity, innovation, and the standard of living.

## Wheel deals

In the 1984 article, *Business Week* said that most 'dramatic example' of the out-sourcing of production was the automobile industry, and singled out GM for special mention. In a follow-up 1986 article, 'Downsizing Detroit: the Big Three's strategy for survival', *Business Week* repeated that, in order to give customers what they want, Detroit had increasingly turned to sources outside the US.

A decade ago the idea of joint arrangements was anathema in Detroit. In his autobiography Iacocca disclosed how, in the late 1970s, he realized that he had no small car in the development pipeline to counter the growing threat from the Japanese, and the anticipated small car entries from General Motors and Chrysler. His original solution was to build a car based on Ford of Europe's immensely successful small car, the Fiesta, developed at a cost of a billion dollars in slightly over three years. Henry Ford vetoed the plan on the basis of the enormous cost of developing both a completely new car and engine in the US, with no guarantee of market success. Iacocca then went to Japan to meet with Honda, and returned with a deal whereby Ford would purchase engines and transmissions from their Japanese competitor at a cost far less than could be produced locally. According to Iacocca his boss promptly rejected it with: 'No car with my name on the hood is going to have a Jap engine inside.' (2)

In 1982 Iacocca was still convinced that the concept made sense, especially for Chrysler, which had shipped some 111 000 Mitsubishi sourced cars to the US the previous year. As he told *Business Week* in 'US automakers reshape for world competition': 'You've got to have a Japanese partner. If Mitsubishi can build the low end of the US auto business and nobody in the US can make a bundle on it, then some combination of joint venture or modest imports is a good program.'

By then the new Ford hierarchy were also in agreement with him. *Business Week*, in a 1981 article, 'Autos: distress that won't go away', reported that Ford was trying to come to a joint production deal with Toyota, the No. 1 Japanese car company. *Business Week* reported that of the four US car companies only GM seemed to be rejecting the need for any small car partnership deals. As GM's newly appointed chairman, Roger Smith, stated: 'From what I see from now until 1985, GM has everything covered.' Apparently Smith also had a rethink for, within two years, he was announcing an agreement to produce as many as 250 000 Toyota-designed subcompact cars – eventually marketed as the Chevrolet Nova, but basically a Toyota Corolla – at its mothballed factory in Fremont California. In fact GM began making so many joint arrangements that, in 1984, Chrysler's executive vice-president remarked to *Business Week*, in 'GM moves into a new era', that Smith 'has more partners than Zsa Zsa Gabor'.

## Small car margins

According to *The Economist*, in a 1984 article, 'America's carmakers: labour's love regained', the US car industry had probably changed faster than any other mature industry in the previous four years. The reasons given were: cuts in capacity, overheads and stocks, the introduction of many new models, plus protection from imports. As a result, said *The Economist*, American car companies 'are bringing their engineering, design, assembly methods and parts-management up to Japanese standards'. *The Economist* also noted that the Japanese still produced cars more efficiently than their American competitors and, as a result, 'GM, Ford and Chrysler make little or no money on their small cars'.

In a 1984 *Fortune* article, 'Ford's fragile recovery', Peter Nulty agreed, saying that while Ford's Escort was the best selling small car in the US, domestic or imported, in competing with Japanese imports on price, the company was losing about $400 on every unit sold. 'A company can't afford many successes like that', concluded Nulty.

It was not surprising that *Business Week*, in a 1984 cover story, 'The vanishing all-American small car', should report that while Detroit's auto manufacturers would continue developing and building their own mid-size and large cars, they were turning over the making of their smallest cars 'to an array of joint ventures with foreign competitors, mostly Japanese. . . . The US automakers are taking to the idea like guests at a buffet dinner. No one wants to be first in line, but no one wants to be last either'.

## Lining up cars

By the end of 1984 every US car manufacturer had some form of collaborative arrangement with a foreign supplier:

*General Motors* had the most comprehensive network of deals, ranging from the bottom of the market to the top. In addition to its arrangement from Toyota, GM had announced plans to import a subcompact car, the Spectrum, from Isuzu Motors Ltd. (34 per cent owned by GM), and a minicar, the Sprint, from Suzuki Motor Co. Ltd (5 per cent owned by GM). It has also made a deal with Daewoo, the No. 2 South Korean car maker, to build 165 000 small cars a year, starting in 1986. GM said that half the volume of cars, to be designed by Opel, would be shipped abroad, mostly for sale by GM in America. In 1984 GM also announced a $600 million deal with Pininfarina Spa, an Italian vehicle stylist, who would build some 8000 two-seater convertable bodies that would then be air freighted to the US and outfitted under the Cadillac marque name.

*Ford*, which owned 25 per cent of Mazda Motor Corp., announced it would replace its Mercury Lynx compact in 1988 with a car built in Mexico and based on Mazda's 323. Ford had a particular reason for choosing Mexico, besides its low-cost labour. According to *Business Week*, in a 1984 article, 'Ford's better idea south of the border', in 1983 the Mexican government decreed that foreign auto companies balance their trade accounts. As a result, 'Ford needs those exports to work off its foreign exchange imbalance with Mexico. Failure to do so would mean Ford could not produce and sell cars in that nation'. In an attempt to win back sales in the imported specialty class, Ford also said it would import cars, such as the Merkur XR4ti, based on the Sierra XR4i, from its West Germany subsidiary.

*Chrysler*, which owned 15 per cent of Mitsubishi—since increased to 20 per cent—was already bring in about 140 000 subcompact Colts and Ram 50 mini-pickups from its partner for resale through its domestic dealers. Observers were also predicting that Chrysler's replacement for the ageing Omni and Horizon subcompacts would also be based on a Mitsubishi model. Following GM's deal with Pininfarina Chrysler announced it would be entering into a similar styling arrangement with Maserati.

*American Motors Corporation*, which was controlled by Renault, had its popular – at the time – Alliance and Encore sub-compacts developed by the state-owned French automobile manufacturer.

The rush of collaborative deals has continued since 1984. So much so that *Business Week*, in its 1986 article, 'Downsizing Detroit: the Big Three's strategy for survival', concluded: 'Traditional distinctions between 'domestic' and 'imported' cars are blurring as Detroit abandons its cherished make-it-yourself approach. Instead, a complicated maze of cross-partnerships is emerging that will reshape the U.S. auto industry.' *Business Week* predicted that, by 1988, American car firms would be buying some 440 000 cars annually from US-based

Japanese plants, plus importing some 900 000 units annually from foreign-based factories.

## Car doubts

As far back as 1984 *Business Week* was having doubts about the scale of the joint ventures. In an editorial to accommodate its cover story, 'The vanishing all-American small car', it noted: 'At first glance, Detroit's decision is hard to quarrel with.' While *Business Week's* editors recognized that joint ventures would enable US car makers 'to share in rather than fight the cost-saving designs and manufacturing processes that have driven the all-American-made small car from the field', they didn't see this as a long-term solution. 'US car manufacturers should not be so quick to surrender on small cars. By failing to deal with the basic problems in that market, they are probably setting the stage for later retreats on larger cars.'

In the 1986 article, 'Downsizing Detroit: the Big Three's strategy for survival', *Business Week* was still making this point: 'Some critics wonder whether giving up on small cars will lead to a lost manufacturing capacity for bigger cars too – and a dangerous reliance on outside car builders. . . . GM's lesson in California carries an ominous message for other domestic companies and for Big Three plants that make larger cars.'

*Business Week* also noted that Toyota's success in building a car in California 'shows all Japanese car makers that they can successfully transplant production techniques to the US'. *Business Week* added that this would be good news to the Japanese, given that the rising yen would shortly be boosting the price of a Japanese-made car by about $1000. Instead, the Japanese chose to shave their margins, not increase their prices in line with the rising yen. The impact of this on the profitability of Japanese cars sold in America, which largely subsidises their makers in Japan, then quickly fed through to falling corporate profits. Suffice to say, the pressure on them to move upmarket in the US is now increasing, especially as other Asian and East European car makers are coming in and undercutting them on price. The Honda–Austin Rover joint effort may thus be the beginning of another round of strategic alliances designed to gain leverages into the top end of the European and American markets. If so, then GM's Saturn project, originally conceived to stem the Japanese small-car onslaught, but now planned to produce slightly bigger cars, may turn out to be a colossal white elephant – and rather squashed at both ends.

In fact, despite the higher labour costs in the US, so many Japanese car companies – Honda, Mazda, Mitsubishi, Nissan, Subaru, and Toyota – are now building, or planning to build, cars in America that observers are predicting that by 1990 their plants will be turning out over 1.5 million vehicles, up from zero in 1982. No wonder critics such as *Business Week* are questioning the wisdom of US firms shifting their own productions overseas. While the main reason for American manufacturers going offshore is to save on labour costs, two reasons for the influx of Japanese car makers, however, are to avoid being disadvantaged by any further import restrictions, and to allow the smaller firms, in particular, to circumvent the existing quota limits which work against them. It must appear somewhat ironical to many that, just as American car firms risk closing down their domestic plants in order to source from overseas, their Japanese rivals face the same situation, but for different reasons. *The Economist*, in a 1986 article, 'Asian car makers: the sun also rises', said that as the Japanese increase their overseas manufacturing this will lead to local overcapacity problems: 'Increasingly, Japanese car makers are waking up to the fact that some of their own plants may be destined to close – not just those in hitherto high-cost America and Europe.'

## Joint logic

In 1984 the most quoted reasons for joint arrangements were cost and efficiency ones. According to *Business Week* in 1984, it cost up to $2 billion to put a new car on the market – and Ford was reported to have spent some $3 billion developing its world car, the Escort. Further, Japanese auto makers were alleged to be able to produce a small car for anything up to $1500 cheaper per car than Detroit – one-third of this stemming from cheaper labour and more efficient operations, and two thirds attributable to the strong dollar and the differences in tax structures between the two countries. The director of automotive services for Data Resources Inc., of Detroit, informed *Business Week* in 'The vanishing all-American small car': 'The automotive companies of the world simply have to pool resources.' He added that Detroit could not risk the massive sums to develop small cars. Moreover, 'it has to reduce costs, and it's doing that [in small cars] by hooking up with the Japanese'. Ford's chairman announced to *Business Week*: 'We will do whatever is necessary to make it possible to compete, and compete profitably.'

To remain in the sector, American manufacturers saw two alternatives: either buy their smaller cars directly from Japan and badge-engineer them – that is, stick a local name on the grill, which is what General Motors-Holden did in Australia – or buy in Japanese designs and major components, and assemble the cars in the US, adding on some made-in-the USA bits in the process – which is what GM arranged with Toyota. According to *Business Week* in 1984:

> Analysts estimate that cloning an auto design saves as much as $1000 per car in development and other preproduction expenses. Using foreign made parts, they add, saves roughly $700 more.... For a US auto company, buying subcompacts from an overseas supplier can mean the difference between breaking even and earning a few hundred dollars on each sale.

## Buying time

In a 1983 assessment of the GM-Toyota joint production deal, *Business Week*, in 'How the GM-Toyota deal buys time', reported:

> For GM, the joint venture is an elegant way to replace its aging Chevrolet Chevette in half the time and for one-tenth the cost of doing the job alone.... American Motors Corp. used the same cost-saving technique last fall to launch production of the Alliance, a subcompact car built by AMC in Kenosha, Wis., but designed by its French partner, Renault.

*Business Week* continued, 'Because of its small investment in the Toyota-designed car, GM should be able to report almost immediate profits on it... while Ford is still struggling to break even with its three-year-old Escort'. *Business Week* also noted the other side of the GM-Toyota deal – the Japanese partner was being offered a low-risk chance to test whether it could build Japanese-quality cars in the US.

## Buying production know-how

American firms needed to know what made Japanese firms perform so well, and collaborative arrangements were a means of buying learning time, especially in the use of the latest production technologies. *Business Week*, in 'Drastic new strategies to keep US multinationals competitive', said that GM viewed its joint ventures as 'temporary and designed to buy time until the No. 1 auto maker learns how to manufacture a small car profitably'.

*Time*, in a 1984 article, 'Green light: the GM-Toyota deal rolls on', reported: 'The prospect of GM's gaining access to Toyota's small-car know-how sent fear into the boardrooms of Ford, Chrysler and American Motors. GM already accounts for 60 per cent of all US sales of American-made cars, while Toyota has 25 per cent of the market for imports.

*Time* also predicted: 'The GM-Toyota deal is expected to force other US car makers to race to make similar arrangements with Japanese firms. Some industry watchers are even predicting that it will not be long before virtually all small cars sold in the US will be either built abroad or made from imported components.' *Business Week* in April 1986 reported that some industry observers believed that Ford, which had yet to decide on how to replace its Escort, was planning to base half the cars it sells in the US with models derived from Mazda – a move that Ford would not 'confirm or deny'.

*Road & Track*, the American motoring magazine, was more forthcoming. It predicted that, 'in the future, most Ford cars from the Tempo Sierra class on down likely will be developed in Japan and use Mazda running gear'. According to *Road & Track* – and most likely the magazine's source was high in the Ford hierarchy – Mazda's front-wheel drive 626 will form the basis for the next US Mustang in 1988, the Australian Telstar in 1991, the US Tempo/Topaz in 1992, and the European Sierra in 1992. The 323 will serve as the base for the next Australian Laser in 1989, and the next US and European Escort in 1990. The 323 will also provide running gear for two Ford cars destined for the US – the Super Sport from Australia, starting in 1988, and the Tracer from Mexico and Taiwan, beginning in 1987. The smallest Mazda car, the Korean-built Festiva, will also be incorporated into the next European Fiesta, due in 1988.

Given Ford and Mazda's world-wide collaborative arrangements, by 1990 Ford in America will be selling cars sourced from nine countries: USA, Canada, West Germany, France, Australia, South Korea, Taiwan, Mexico and Brazil – but, ironically, not from Japan.

*Road & Track* concluded: 'The advantages are several: By tapping

Mazda's resources, Ford can reduce its own engineering and technical staff and take advantage of lower development and production costs on Japanese componentry.' Perhaps, but is it good marketing when Ford may be mortgaging its future? At the time when word of these arrangements were surfacing, news was also coming out that Ford had lost several key design staff from its European operations.

## Buying management know-how

According to Charles Burck, in a 1983 *Fortune* article, 'Will success spoil General Motors?', the provisions of the GM-Toyota joint production deal 'suggest that GM is pursuing not technological advances but rather the subtleties of management style and production efficiencies which give the Japanese so sharp an edge in the small-car market'. Certainly GM need to learn about these subleties if its Saturn project is to succeed. As discussed in chapters five and six, GM's cumbersome R&D process caused, not prevented, problems with quality and cost overruns, and led to too many compromises in the new models that were coming on the market by the late 1970s. With five car divisions, a separate assembly division, plus Fisher Body division, there were too many communication channels to ensure a smooth and speedy flow of information, and too many vested interests to ensure that the essential direction of strategic decisions remained fixed.

This may explain *Business Week's* comment, in a 1986 article, 'Downsizing Detroit: the Big Three's strategy for survival', that: 'GM executives are questioning the basic premise behind Saturn – that a dazzling display of advanced technology is the key to fighting imports.' According to one industry observer, the Toyota joint venture had 'stunned GM by achieving Japanese-like efficiency with careful management rather than exotic automation'.

Some Japanese car companies have shown that buying know-how is a two-way affair. Mazda, which in 1987 began building-up to 240000 cars annually in its new plant in Michigan, selected as its vice-president of manufacturing the former plant manager of GM's Fiero Car Assembly operation. The Fiero, a two-seater, mid-engined sports car launched by Pontiac in 1983, is made by a completely different process from conventional cars – plastic body panels are mounted over a steel 'birdcage' chassis. The system was invented by a Pontiac engineer and was claimed to make assembly cheaper and more precise. It was also giving the GM division important flexible manufacturing/ marketing leverages since the car's style could be changed simply by bolting new body panels onto the same chassis – and by 1986 the Fiero had already been restyled three times.

## Buying customers

Another reason for joint deals with Japanese competitors may have been a 'pre-emptive' buying one. By producing a Toyota-designed car in California, GM was probably hoping to capitalize on the price/ quality reputation of its partner. *Business Week*, in 'How the GM-Toyota deal buys time', suggested that:

> GM is hoping to snare some entry-level buyers who previously shopped for and bought only imports. Volkswagen of America Inc. reported this 'halo' effect when it began building the Rabbit in the US, and AMC says about half its Alliance customers were considering only imports.

Some US car companies are also hoping for some goodwill rub-off at the top end of the market. When GM announced in 1986 it was purchasing into Group Lotus, the elite British sports car maker and one of the world's most technically innovative auto-engineering companies, one European auto expert informed *Fortune*, in 'GM buys Lotus': 'It would also be buying an image of European styling and performance it never had.' Another industry observer told *Time*, in 'Mixed welcome in Lotus land', that GM's deals with Lotus and Pininfarina, and Chrysler's deal with Maserati, signalled that 'all US manufacturers want to associate themselves with a prestige European firm in the hope some of that rubs off on their own customer image'. And one reason given for GM's interest in acquiring Britain's Leyland Trucks and Land Rover in 1986 was to obtain the top-of-the-line Range Rover. The deal, however, was thwarted by the recalcitrant Conservative government.

In a later 1986 article, 'A passion for Italian bodies', *Time* suggested another reason for the joint arrangements between the large mass-market Detroit companies and the specialist European ones, such as Pininfarina and Maserati:

While typical US auto plants are designed for assembling 220 000 cars annually, Italy still has the kind of shops where skilled workers lavish attention on just 5000 or 10 000 cars a year. Detroit auto makers particularly want to produce top-of-the-line vehicles that can compete with pricey imports.

The rationale behind this is clear. As the mass market – whether for cannelloni, cars, or computers – fragments into a multitude of segments the larger players are attempting to fill the smaller, and often more profitable, niches with rebadged products from outside suppliers who have the appropriate design and production skills. They may also possess the speed needed to constantly respond to changing market demands, a trait the larger, bureaucratic companies often lack. *Time* suggested that it was not surprising that GM, Chrysler and Ford – with its attempts to take over Alfa Romeo – wanted to join the upmarket Italians. The US market for luxury cars had grown from 9 per cent to 15 per cent of the total between 1975 and 1986. This already meant some 1.6 million cars in 1986 and, as Cadillac's General Manager pointed out to *Time*: 'The affluent segment of the population is exploding.'

## European alliances

American car firms are not the only ones looking for collaborative deals. In a 1986 article, 'Europe hangs on', *Automotive News* observed that: 'A combination of slow market growth, continued sales gains by Japanese importers, overcapacity and low profit per-unit depict an unattractive prospect for Europe's mass producers.' One industry analyst told *Automotive News* that Europe's car industry was heading for a major structural shake-down. It was likely to become a two-level industry 'comprised of successful specialists with a strong hold on the world's prestige-car markets, and volume producers that will be forced into greater flexibility and collaboration, including ventures with Japanese suppliers'.

*The Economist* has been promoting this message for some years. In a 1979 survey, 'Motoring into the 80's', *The Economist* said that Japanese car firms, such as Toyota and Nissan, do not manufacture cars, rather they assemble them: 'They buy their parts – on occasions even engines and gearboxes as well as the more usual springs, sprockets and electrical bits – from component manufacturers who make them in millions and sell identical goods to rival car firms.' *The Economist* predicted that, to survive in the 1980s, many of Europe's car makers would have to 'face up to three painful (to some) readjustments': handing the production of the major components, such as powertrains (engine, gearbox, transmission), over to the specialist component industry; pooling their research and development resources, particularly when it comes to meeting political and economic requirements or regulations that affect all manufacturers; and teaming up with Japanese competitors, the best producers of low cost, reliable cars, and who eventually are going to start producing in Europe in order to get under any tariff barriers or import quotas.

In 1985 *The Economist* was still promoting this concept, for a different reason. In 'Reassemble Europe's cars' it claimed that the current over-capacity and resulting price-discounting may be:

> good news for car buyers today but could be bad news for taxpayers tomorrow.... For when the competition threatens to put one of the players out of business, governments will be tempted to intervene with subsidies or loan guarantees – as Britain did with British Leyland and the French government is still doing with Renault and even as free-enterprise America has done in the recent past with American Motors and Mr Lee Iacocca's Chrysler.

The solution, stated *The Economist*, 'short of a big merger or a complete withdrawal of one of the main players, is more collaboration between producers. The deal between Japan's Honda and Austin Rover, British Leyland's volume car division, shows the way'. As far as *The Economist* was concerned the Austin Rover–Honda deal made sense. The UK car company hadn't the resources to develop a replacement for its ten-year-old executive car, the Rover; in return Honda was getting a production base in England that would allow it to gain access to the rest of the European market. Both externally and internally they were designed to appear as quite distinctly different cars. The car began selling in the US in early 1986 as a Honda Acura and, by 1987 as a very British sounding Sterling, not as a Rover – the previous Rover had bombed there a few years ago.

## Buying a Trojan horse?

By 1986 *The Economist* began to see a negative side to the arrangement. In 'BL's rejected suitors', *The Economist* noted that the deal gave Honda 'the best of both worlds in its collaboration with Austin Rover: all the benefits of partnership without any of the responsibilities of ownership'. The British government had just abruptly vetoed the sale of Austin Rover to Ford – as it did with the sale of Leyland Trucks and Land Rover to GM – and *The Economist* commented that: 'Prolonging the discussions with Ford would, at the minimum, have forced Honda to declare whether it was willing to put money into Austin Rover, its Trojan horse for the European car market.'

## Collaborative lattice

Whether anyone now has any doubts about the mutual benefits of strategic alliances, the reality is the world's car, truck and van industries have become a lattice of strategic alliances – to a far greater extent than even *The Economist* had foreseen in 1979 (see Figure 7.1).

## New form of R&D process

One implication is that the traditional, sequential approach to the process of internally developing a new car – and many other products as well – has taken a new turn in recent years. In 1979, in *Product Development: New Approaches in the 1980s*, William Sommers was advocating a new addition to the new product development process that was to be a precursor of an even bigger change. He argued: 'Manufacturing expertise is as much a strategic weapon as the product's features' – as was discussed in Chapter 6. Sommers also presented a new product development flowchart that linked the development of the manufacturing process to the development of the new product. His reasoning was that:

> Often today, the product and the manufacturing process are so interrelated that neither the product design nor the production technique and equipment can be determined separately. Their choice must evolve through a closely coupled, interactive process. (3)

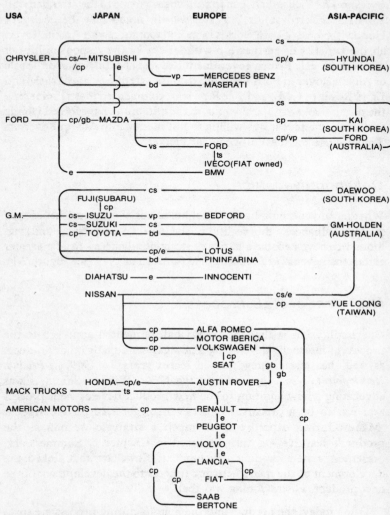

**Figure 7.1  Wheel deals**

*Legend*
cp = car development/production arrangement
cs = car selling/distribution arrangement
bd = car body design/development arrangement
ts = truck selling/distribution arrangement
vp = van development/production arrangement
vs = van selling/distribution arrangement
e = engine production arrangement
gb = gearbox production arrangement

**Figure 7.1 Wheel deals** *(concluded)*

His argument has certainly been borne out by the car firms which have decided to commit the time, money and discipline to internally developing their new models. For some, their efforts are changing the rules of competition. As discussed in Chapters 5 and 6, media interest in GM's new Saturn plant was as intense as the interest in the new car that would eventually emerge. Likewise, even for a smaller Japanese manufacturer, such as Mazda, the ability to develop flexible manufacturing has given it a strategic marketing advantage. For Mazda, the introduction of a new model is now accompanied by the start-up of a completely new or totally refurbished plant as well, to take advantage of the latest production technologies.

What Sommers didn't anticipate was the recent rush by many of the major car companies to form joint development, production and/or distribution arrangements. In other words, just as many companies were agreeing on the need for improving the internal innovation process, the explosion in external collaborative marketing arrangements has now changed the rules of R&D leveraging. The result is that an entirely new aspect of the product development process has emerged, as firms attempt to shorten, or short-circuit, any or all of the stages involved, by going outside for deals. Some of these approaches are shown on the right-hand side of the chart below (see Figure 7.2).

Most major car companies have now adopted at least one of the noted collaborative possibilities – whether it be contracting out the design and early development work of a new model, or buying in engines and other components, or agreeing to produce, distribute and sell the badge-engineered models of a competitor. A couple of car firms have recently managed to arrange just about the whole lot.

Whatever the reasons for these joint deals – to save on development time and costs; to fill out a product line with a host of specialist models; to add sparkle to a jaded image; to get access to superior technical

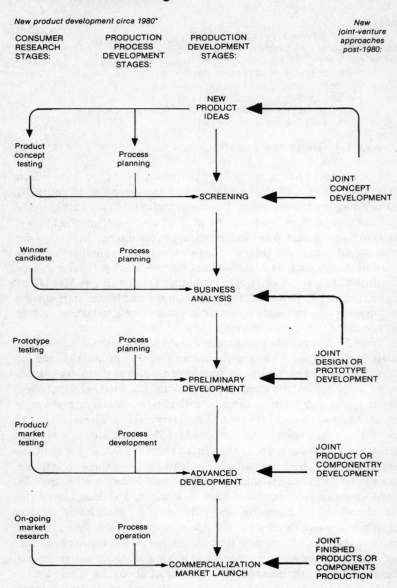

*New product development circa 1980*

CONSUMER RESEARCH STAGES:

PRODUCTION PROCESS DEVELOPMENT STAGES:

PRODUCTION DEVELOPMENT STAGES:

*New joint-venture approaches post-1980:*

NEW PRODUCT IDEAS

Product concept testing

Process planning

SCREENING

JOINT CONCEPT DEVELOPMENT

Winner candidate

Process planning

BUSINESS ANALYSIS

Prototype testing

Process planning

PRELIMINARY DEVELOPMENT

JOINT DESIGN OR PROTOTYPE DEVELOPMENT

Product/ market testing

Process development

ADVANCED DEVELOPMENT

JOINT PRODUCT OR COMPONENTRY DEVELOPMENT

On-going market research

Process operation

COMMERCIALIZATION MARKET LAUNCH

JOINT FINISHED PRODUCTS OR COMPONENTS PRODUCTION

*Based on a simplified version of Sommers.

**Figure 7.2 The changing new car development process**

and/or manufacturing expertise; to obtain the best, or cheapest, components; to plug into someone else's distribution network; to enter a foreign market; to learn someone else's more progressive management practices; or to compensate for past mistakes and/or laxness in one's internal development programme – the number and scope of collaborative arrangements means that the practice of marketing cars has become more complex and unpredictable. And while the short-term benefits may appear compelling, the consequences of ceding one's future prospects to a competitor may take some getting used to – especially when the partnership turns sour.

## Sound marketing?

While collaborative arrangements appear to offer leveraging opportunities at any or all of the stages – from innovation and R&D process to the consumer marketing process – does this necessarily make for sound marketing? As argued in Chapter 6, in the end a company succeeds or fails on the strength, or weakness, of its offering to the market – whether it be a product or service.

If one outcome of collaborative marketing is basically for two companies who have spent years, if not decades, carving out separate identities, to suddenly start sharing the same internal components, and plugging or hanging them together in such a way as to make them look externally different, and giving them individual brand identities via separate cosmetics, badging and theme advertising, will the market automatically accept this sleight? To the generation of Australians who can still remember the last war, can a badge-engineered *Suzuki* Swift really become 'your good old Aussie' *Holden* Barina? If the answer is yes, then the rules of marketing have changed.

The Ford–Mazda arrangement in Australia and New Zealand suggests that it is possible, especially when their external cosmetic differences are quite apparent. Ford currently holds the number one slot in both countries, despite strong competition, with an appeal – and a product mix wider than one based only on Mazda sources – that straddles the entire market. Mazda, in turn, with a smaller product line-up and a separate pricing strategy, has attempted to carve out a more upmarket position for itself. In the process, neither partner acknowledges the connection between them in any of their advertising, though it is fairly common knowledge among new car buyers, and certainly well understood by the motoring press.

Other companies entering into collaborative marketing arrangements may not be so astute, or fortunate, particularly if their respective products and positioning strategies become blurred, leading to confusion in consumers' minds. Firms which have spent years carving out clear-cut identities for themselves, and have built up a loyal base of customers, and then abruptly adopt a smorgasbord approach to their product mix in order to latch onto the latest design, component or process technologies, or to save on R&D costs, may find it difficult to hold their current customers – let alone attract new customers in the long term. This is the very problem that bedevilled GM during the late 1970s and early 1980s, when it adopted common design themes across its various models.

And perhaps an important twist to the Ford–Mazda saga is that, when the yen began to firm against the Australian and New Zealand dollars, and as the price of oil fell, Ford still had enough Australian and European derived models in its mix to offer a wider price and size choice than its main competitors who, over the past few years, had become overly dependent on the one source of supply, i.e. Japan.

## Wide acceptance

In this chapter the car industry has been used to illustrate the wide acceptance of collaborative marketing. This phenomenon is not confined to the car industry. It is increasingly becoming a feature in others as well, from aircraft engines to robots – and especially computers.

In a 1984 special report, 'Reshaping the computer industry', *Business Week* predicted that many of the more than five hundred computer hardware manufacturers, five thousand software companies and more than four hundred makers of telecommunications gear battling it out in the growing information-processing industry would not survive.

One reason was that the traditional boundaries that used to separate the various manufacturers – that is, the makers of mainframes, minicomputers, and communications equipment – were disappearing. Since customers needs were becoming more sophisticated, they were asking for complete solutions to their information-processing needs, and since there was a convergence of increasingly complex and costly computer and communications technologies, manufacturers were having to supply wider-ranging product lines.

According to *Business Week*, the industry will ultimately narrow down to three sectors. At the top will be a few gigantic, vertically integrated, full-range suppliers dominated by IBM, AT&T, 'and perhaps one or two Japanese companies offering soup-to-nuts product lines and low-cost, high-volume hardware manufacturing'. In a 1985 article, 'A threatening telephone call from the computer company', *The Economist* predicted that AT&T could become a formidable competitor to IBM, especially if it should abandon 'its gingerly technology-based thrust and acquire a big computer company to organize its attack (against IBM) around'.

A second, much larger, tier would be those 'systems integrators assembling products from various manufacturers to create customized computer systems for different industry niche markets'. The third tier would be 'a horde of small, specialized suppliers providing the systems integrators with individual pieces of hardware or software tailored to specific markets'.

As a result of this reshuffling, said *Business Week*: 'To survive, once fiercely independent companies – even former competitors – are scrambling to form alliances and partnerships to broaden their range of products.' The catalogue of joint deals involving computer makers is as extensive as the one listing consenting car makers: Honeywell and NEC and Groupe Bull, AT&T with Olivetti, Olivetti with Xerox, Siemens with Fujitsu, to name but a few.

One possible consequence of the rush to strategic alliances is that, in any industry worldwide, there will arise one or two dominant players, each of which forms a core corporation linked to a multitude of smaller, specialist, and dependent satellite companies via a series of joint arrangements and mergers. Many of these firms would once have been major competitors who, in the end, joined the alliance in order to survive, perhaps with the encouragement of their home government. Quite possibly, the core corporation could be a non-producing operation; rather it will act only in a co-ordinating and controlling capacity. These mega-conglomerates will dominate their markets by virtue of their being able to supply virtually every segment. What few areas are not covered will be fought over by mini-conglomerates, each made up of a number of smaller, nimbler, even more specialist companies, many of them with strong local – that is, national – connections. Somewhere on the peripheral could be a number of independent suppliers, offering even more specialist services, components or equipment.

## High divorce rate

Despite this possible future, and what it could hold in store for weak competitors, the need for alliance was put to *Business Week* by a top Olivetti executive in 1986: 'A company's competitive situation no longer depends on itself alone but on the quality of the alliances it's able to form.' Unfortunately, observed *Business Week*, quoting from studies by McKinsey & Co. and Coopers & Lybrand, 'seven out of ten joint ventures fall short of expectations or are disbanded'.

There are many reasons for this:

- Executives put more effort into creating alliances than they do into making them work on a day-to-day basis.
- Partners with different management styles fail to agree in advance on how run the business.
- Managers lower down the hierarchies fail to share a common vision articulated at the top, and often end up in bitter demarcation disputes over control of operations.
- The lack of cooperation among corporate researchers often leads to disputes over the future directions.
- Like marriage, successful alliances require a corporate 'mindset' based on mutuality and trust, not one based on winning vs losing, and most partners find this hard to accept.
- Joint projects may lead partners to venture into new product-market areas that neither are equipped to handle.

As a result, an alliance between a small competitor and a more powerful one sometimes results in the eventual takeover of the former. And when the partnership is between an American and a foreign firm, the problems are even greater. As *Business Week* noted:

> Many naive US companies are still smarting from a painful lesson learned in the 1970s and early 1980s, when they were bushwhacked by Japanese partners that obtained technology through licencing or joint-marketing deals only to use it against their American allies later on.

*Business Week* predicted this would possibly happen to Boeing

Aircraft Co., which early in 1986 signed up with a consortium of Mitsubishi, Fuji, and Kawasaki Heavy Industries to develop, manufacture, and market a small jet. A senior Boeing executive involved in the deal expressed their dilemma: 'We'd rather have the Japanese working with us than with someone else against us.' This statement also suggests another – and rather defensive – reason for many joint ventures.

## Hollow corporations

While collaboration is now an established fact of business life, there are certain possibilities that are causing much concern. The question, 'It may be popular, but is it sound marketing?' only hints at the main issue. If the logic of collaboration is taken to one conclusion, then a country such as the US may find itself with a host of 'hollow corporations'. This was the grim picture painted by *Business Week*, in its 1986 special report, 'The hollow corporation'. *Business Week* warned that:

> From autos to semi conductors, many US manufacturers are turning into marketers for foreign producers. A new type of company is emerging – one that may design or distribute but doesn't actually make anything. A hollow corporation.... What's good for them, however, may not be good for the economy as a whole. If it goes too far, the US could be left without a vibrant manufacturing base. That would leave the nation more dependent than ever on the fewer and lower paying jobs in the service economy.

Defenders of this new approach might argue that they are merely doing what Levitt recommended – thinking and acting in a way that transcends the ordinary, the obvious or the deductive. *Business Week* mentioned Schwinn Bicycle Co. as one company that, having decided it was a design, distribution and merchandising company, now imports most of its bikes from Asia. Schwinn's president told *Business Week* that: 'The leverage of the business was no longer in manufacturing', and a vice-president explained: 'When you are a manufacturing company, your mindset tends to be to sell what you can make. We're market-driven now.' *Business Week* also mentioned Nike Inc., the sports-shoe firm that has manufactured offshore ever since it began in 1964, and which 'thinks of itself not as a manufacturer but as a research, development, and marketing corporation that, like other companies in labour-intensive industries, probably could not compete in any other way'.

There are some who think there is another way – a made-in-the-USA way. In Chapter 6, Allan-Bradley, the Milwaukee-based manufacturer of industrial controls, was mentioned as an example of how flexible manufacturing is transforming American business. Gene Bylinsky, in a 1986 *Fortune* article, 'A breakthrough in automating the assembly line', described how the Allen-Bradley factory can make different versions of a product, in lots as small as a single unit, and do it automatically without slowing down. Bylinsky remarked: 'Neither General Motors nor the Japanese have managed to do that yet.' Apparently Allen-Bradley considered offshore manufacturing, joint ventures and producing under licence before deciding on a local site for its computer-integrated manufacturing, with the objective of becoming the lowest-cost producer. One reason for eschewing production in a low-wage country was that false economies are often the reality in supposedly low-cost offshore operations. Bylinsky concluded: 'For US companies, the Allan-Bradley lesson is that computer-integrated manufacturing provides an alternative to going offshore or going out of business.'

This author's conclusion is that the traditional vertically integrated companies are being supplemented – but not necessarily supplanted – by what *Business Week* termed 'network companies'. While they are not new, 'the network structure is spreading, pushed in part by communication breakthroughs that make it easy to co-ordinate suppliers and customers around the world'. We are in a new era, and collaborative arrangements, whether in the form of joint efforts starting at concept development and ending at the finished product, or in the form of existing products being bought 'off-the-shelf' and 'badge-engineered', are simply the evidence that companies have come to realize there is no longer *one* way to compete successfully in today's 'naked' markets. Likewise they have come to realize that they need to marshall all their resources, and concentrate all their efforts, on their best leveraging opportunities. If it is not sound marketing, then the impact of their own mistakes, fluctuating exchange rates, and the 'naked' marketplace will soon cull them out. And one sector in the 'naked' market place where producers *are* finding the going increasingly tough is the retail trade – as the next chapter will show.

# 8 Leverage in trade marketing

Not so long ago marketing-orientated companies – in particular packaged goods marketers – concentrated their communications budget on 'theme' advertising and made their appeals directly to the consumers through the mass media, in an effort to build a long-term 'brand franchise'. The large number of small – mostly independent – retailers occupied a relatively passive role in the flow of goods between manufacturer and consumer, and were often reliant on the manufacturer's team of regularly calling sales and merchandising reps.

That is now changing. Today's new force of retailers – whether they be an independent operator or a national chain – are now achieving new powers over their suppliers. They can expedite their buying decisions computer-to-computer with manufacturers, thereby eliminating the need to negotiate with reps. They expect their suppliers to earn the right to occupy scarce shelf space according to 'direct product profit' calculations; failure to do so may result in automatic deletion. New products or promotional propositions offered to them by suppliers are assessed in terms of how well they fit in with their own retail positioning strategy, and proof that the product or promotion will be acceptable to the retailer's target market. When it comes to leveraging their goods through retail channels, many manufacturers are now scrambling to learn the new rules of 'trade marketing'.

## Super store

In 1985, with 6200 square feet of selling space, Larry Olson and his wife, Barbara, owners of Shiloh Market, an independent supermarket in Dayton, Ohio, achieved $7.2 million in sales turnover – which worked out at $22.47 per square foot per week, or more than three times the national average of $7 for independent supermarkets and $6.80 for chain stores. When Robert O'Neill, writing in a 1986 *Progressive Grocer* article, 'Is this America's most efficient supermarket?', asked Mr Olson – who had 13 competing supermarkets within a radius of four miles – for the secret of his survival the reply was not the standard, 'location, location, location', but, 'control, control, control'. When then asked, 'How do you maintain control?', Olson answered: 'Through the application of data. If you have good data you have power.' The data comes from scanners, computers and other electronic tools and, explained Olson, 'We couldn't survive without them'.

Besides the usual savings from improved speed and accuracy at the front end of the store, and reduced book-keeping costs, the Olsons' computer helps to keep a regular check on movement and profitability of virtually every item in the store. It also helps to maintain control over advertised features, special discounts and loss leaders. For example, the computer issues a weekly 'zero-movement' report that highlights items that aren't moving off the shelves. These items will be removed by the Shiloh staff, discounted, and placed in the markdown cart of slow sellers. Constantly on the lookout for improved computer applications, Mr Olson also informed *Progressive Grocer* that: 'We're looking forward to going to computer-assisted ordering of all packaged products.' If this store is at the leading edge of what is happening in other outlets across the US – from personal computers to toys – it indicates the growing power that retailers, even the size of Shiloh Market, now have over their suppliers.

## Balance of power

According to Angela Rushton, speaking at the 1982 E.S.O.M.A.R. (European Society for Opinion and Marketing Research) annual conference:

> The nature of a relationship between a manufacturer and retailer, the extent to which it is either harmonious or discordant, largely depends on the power held by each party and the way this power is used. Power relationships also have a direct bearing on the outcomes of negotiations and thus on the

economic and financial fortunes of both manufacturers and retailers. (1)

Rushton said there were 'two archetypal grocery marketing channel configurations' in the UK:

1. Manufacturer — Retailer — Consumer
2. Manufacturer — Wholesaler — Retailer — Consumer

This configuration could equally apply to most developed markets, from Australia to Austria to America. Each participant has a particular obligation and role to play in the flow of goods through the system and, although they need to work together, they also exist as separate businesses with their own objectives, strategies, and constraints. In addition, the parties involved are likely to be unequal in size, strength and ability. Their mutually dependent relationships are therefore built on their negotiating skills. For example, before a grocer agrees to stock a new line, negotiations will take place to agree on matters such as prices, discounts, delivery terms, cooperative promotional support, in-store location, shelf or freezer space allocation and, increasingly, a 'slotting' allowance to enter the item into the retailer's computer.

Rushton argued that:

> The outcome of these negotiations, although they will usually favour one party, must be 'acceptable' to both the manufacturer and the retailer if a trading relationship is to be established. Once a trading relationship is formed, the same ground will be covered again and again in negotiations, the results of which reflecting the balance of power that is perceived to exist by the parties concerned at any one time, as well as the negotiation skills of the individuals involved.

W. Roome, in *Distribution Channels – a Behavioural View,* wrote in 1978 that:

> Power inevitably plays an important part in any negotiating process as each party seeks to further his own interests and obtain the best deal. Morever, with the passage of time, shifts may occur in the relative strengths of channel members, thereby upsetting the balance of power. (2)

## Trade power

There is increasing evidence that the balance of power between manufacturers and retailers is now tipping toward the latter, in particular to the large chains – whether they be supermarkets, toy stores or personal computer outlets. This phenomenon is common to many markets and many countries. Only for the largest and/or strongest manufacturers, totally committed to consumer brand building which is backed up by astute marketing, will there by anything near an equal power-sharing relationship. For the smaller, weaker suppliers not possessing these skills, their relationship with retailers is likely to be one of increasing dependency and vulnerability.

If one word sums up the main force now driving retailing, that word is 'concentration' – which reflects the acquisitions, consolidations and brute-strength growth of the major retailers in many markets. This development may have caught many manufacturers napping. Schultz and Dewar, in a 1983 *Journal of Consumer Marketing* article, 'Retailers in control: the impact of retail concentration' said: 'While manufacturers have long been familiar with increasing concentration in their own fields, that is through purchases, mergers, bankruptcies, and the like, manufacturers selling to the retail trade seem to have been taken by surprise by retail trade concentration.' (3) The authors felt that one reason for this surprise may be that the changes are relatively recent, and the manufacturers have yet to adjust. While the changes may be recent, they are also reshaping the rules of marketing for both retailers and suppliers.

## Wheel of retailing

Jack Kaikati, in a 1985 *Harvard Business Review* article. 'Don't discount off-price retailers', said that:

> The face of retailing is continually being changed by somebody who gets a 'bright new idea'.... The latest alternation comes in this decade from the phenomenal expansion of the off-price retailers, whose promotion of nationally known brand names at low prices has earned them a niche in the industry. (4)

Kaikati argued that the development of off-price retailing is a phenomenon that adheres to the 'wheel of retailing' hypothesis, whereby most retail sectors have been characterized by a series of cyclical changes: small specialty stores eventually get displaced by department stores; these become superseded by discount retailers; and now it is the turn of off-price retailers – 'occupying the gray area between full-service stores and discounters'.

While no new form has succeeded in completely eliminating an earlier form, since there have always been survivors who have developed effective response strategies, Kaikati believed that the remainder of the 1980s would be characterized by stiff competition among the growing number of off-price retailers. This in turn should eventually lead to a 'a shakeout in the off-price arena', he claimed. 'The main casualties are likely to be small, undercapitalized, independent companies.... To survive the shakeout, off-pricers will have to pay close attention to market positioning.' Although he was mostly writing about soft goods retailing, Kaikati's comments also apply to other fields, from consumer electronics to toys.

## Positioning power

Leonard Berry, in a 1982 *Business Horizons* article, 'Retailing positioning strategies for the 1980s', said that, with the maturing of most markets, retailers will be able to grow only at someone else's expense. Inevitably this will lead to cut-throat pricing. Berry suggested that the ways for retailers to avoid losing out in such an environment were first, to carefully define their 'reasons for being' and second, to identify and then occupy an available 'position' in the market:

> Occupying an available position involves 'selling the store', not just merchandise. The company becomes the 'brand', with all marketing variables – merchandise mix, ambience, personnel, advertising, pricing policy – co-ordinated to reinforce what the firm stands for, why it exists.... In a cluttered market place, the well-positioned retailer is distinctive; it is a 'first-choice' outlet. The well-positioned retailer competes on the basis of image, which is harder to imitate than, say, a variable such as price. (5)

The importance of a well-planned positioning strategy was a key point made by Aimée Stern, in a 1986 *Dun's Business Month* article, 'Retailers restructure': 'A vast restructuring is changing the shape of retailing – creating new opportunities for the quick and resourceful, leaving the also-rans by the wayside.' According to Stern there would be three groups of winners:

> The creative specialty chains that have brought unusual merchandising and operational techniques to the business; the innovative department stores that have repositioned themselves with new consumer-driven marketing strategies; and the savvy discounters that have made America a nation of bargain hunters and largely overturned the pricing structure of the industry.

Stern believed that, faced with a low-growth market place, an oversupply of retail outlets, and a mass market that was becoming increasingly polarized – issues which will be examined in Chapter 9 – retailers now recognized they had to select a particular target group based on life-styles and demographic characteristics, and singlemindedly develop a store for them. 'The industry buzzword for this strategy is "focus"', she maintained. 'Through merchandise selection, price level and ambience, a focused store projects a distinctive and consistent image that allows a shopper to decide whether it fits her style and pocketbook.' Stern added that 'focus' meant more than merchandise selection and interior decor. 'The direction starts with top management and goes through buying, distribution and inventory management down to the selling floor. All must contribute to making the store's personality.'

In a 1986 *Advertising Age* special report, 'Grocery marketing: supermarket chains work to fill a tall order', Julie Erickson summed up the recent changes between manufacturers and retailers by quoting the senior vice-president for the Washington-based Food Marketing Institute:

> In the past customer demand was primarily created by manufactures, with retailers the vehicle for that demand. Today, because of the information the retailer has and because the stores have an image with consumers, the retailer has become an important consumer for the manufacturer.

The vice-president for the Food Institute was more direct:

> Today the flow of power is toward the retailer and away from the manufacturer. With overstocked stores and scanning systems, the store has the information and the leverage.

Even stores as small as the Olson's Shiloh market, it seems.

If the manufacturers haven't realized this shift, the retailers certainly have. In their 53rd annual report of the grocery industry, *Progressive Grocer* reported that in their survey of chain and wholesale executives, the percentage who perceived a shift in the industry's balance of power stood at 58 per cent in 1986, an increase of six points over 1985. Of these, about two-thirds felt the retail side was getting relatively stronger, with the largest firms being most in agreement.

What may surprise many manufacturers is just how widespread this power shift has become.

## Toy power

In an earlier issue, *Dun's Business Month* selected Toys 'R' Us as one of the five best-managed companies for 1985, saying the retail chain:

> is in a class by itself. The first retailer to mass merchandise toys at across-the-board discount prices, it is also the first to truly dominate the business. In just seven years, it has captured an unheard-of 14%-to-15% of the highly fractionalized toy market, leaving it with virtually no runner-up in the business.

With more than 230 stores in the chain, and with each nearly identical store occupying some 46 000 square feet and carrying about 18 000 brand-name items, Toys 'R' Us is truly 'a supermarket of toys', as claimed by its chairman. And not only is it big – with 1985 revenues of about $2 billion – it is also profitable. Given its size, Toys has enormous bargaining power with its suppliers and, despite selling brand-name merchandise at prices up to 50 per cent below full retail, it has managed to achieve a return on equity ranging between 21 per cent and 27 per cent during the seven years prior to the fiscal year ended March 1985.

Anthony Ramirez, in a 1985 *Fortune* article, 'Can anyone compete with Toys 'R' Us?', said that the chain sells about $222 per square foot annually vs $125 for its next largest rival, Child World – a 102-store chain – and $134 for Lionel Leisure, the third largest chain, with 52 stores.

Ramirez said Toys' strengths were that it 'is the only national toy supermarket chain; it has the largest, most efficient stores, the best distribution network, and a computerized inventory control system that sends a record of each sale from a cash register to the company's

Rochelle Park, New Jersey, headquarters'. *Dun's* added that: 'This centralized tracking system allows management to project sales for every product on Toys 'R' Us shelves, from dolls and bicycles to computers and video games, and makes possible a unique store-by-store inventory control system.'

*Dun's* noted that 'the company enjoys an unusually good relationship with suppliers'. Not only does it buy in bulk, but it also manages to sell – and therefore buy – on a year-round basis, thereby reducing both party's dependency on the Christmas peak, and cutting down on the risk of not picking the season's 'hot' items. In many respects then, Toys' tracking system allows it to do the market research for its suppliers. This service can be a double-edged sword. If at any time of the year the company is able to spot, and push, the emerging big sellers, by the same process it can quickly spot, and drop, the next line of losers. As the chairman of Toys 'R' Us revealed to *Dun's*: 'It's easy to add a new product line. The trick is knowing when to drop it.'

In Chapter 2, it was noted that in the 1970s many manufacturers were enamoured with the concept of portfolio planning. What the proponents of this approach didn't foresee was that, by the early 1980s, the ultimate decision as to what was a 'star' and what was a 'dog' might wind up in the hands of large retail chains such as Toys 'R' Us, or even small independent stores, such as Shiloh Market. Not surprisingly, this is one strategic decision that any market-oriented manufacturer would still prefer to control.

### Furniture power

The Toy's 'R' Us policy of centralized inventory control is shared by Levitz Furniture Corp., the nation's leading independent furniture retailing chain. Levitz furniture stores are typical of the concept known as 'warehouse' outlets: stores over 100000 square feet stacked with some 30000 items plus 25000 accessories. According to Goodrich and Hoffman, in a 1979 *Business Horizons* article, 'Warehouse retailing: the trend of the future?', the consumer benefits of warehouse retailing come from buying from an enormous selection of furniture at lower prices than conventional furniture stores, and from having immediate delivery. Such stores are not pitched to customers wanting more expensive furniture, the assistance of salespeople, or individual decorating advice. The authors also reported that:

Advantages of the warehouse retailing concept for Levitz are quantity discounts from buying in bulk directly from furniture manufacturers, and profits from high stock turnover. A major disadvantage is the cost of large inventories. (6)

The need for control is obvious.

Started in Pennsylvania, the chain had grown from five stores in 1968 to some eighty stores in 1983, with an emphasis on the sunbelt states, when *Business Week* reported that Levitz had an inventory control system that resembles both the giant Toys 'R' Us and the midget Shiloh Market. 'Computerized inventories now allow store managers to identify the slow-selling items, slash the price, and increase turnover.' *Business Week* continued: 'A centralized, 12-person buying department at Miami headquarters makes restocking, formerly handled by each store manager, a simple matter of checking items off a master list. The reason: "What kind of clout can you have with manufacturers if you have 55 buyers?" (president) Elliott asks rhetorically?'

## Consumer electronics power

Kaikati's earlier 'shakeout' comments also apply to the new retailing of consumer electronics. Alan Radding, in a 1986 *Advertising Age* article, 'Superstores, discounters lead retail revolution', said:

Gone are the days when consumer electronics retailing was dominated by specialized boutiques, intimidating salesmen and high-tech junkies.... In a growing number of markets, super-stores – the market place's newest innovation – and discounters have put out the welcome mat of low prices and wide selection for the casual consumer.

*Business Week*, in a 1985 article, 'Electronic superstores are devouring their rivals', observed:

The proliferation of low-cost consumer electronics products during the past five years has created a new type of retail outlet: the electronics superstore. These stores keep prices low, thanks to volume purchasing through co-ops. They also have huge ad budgets, and they offer the convenience of one-stop shopping.... A bit like Toys 'R' Us for adults, electronics superstores are steadily forcing mom-and-pop competitors to close or sell out. Moreover, they are taking sales away from the

mass-merchant discounters, catalogue showrooms, and department stores.

In a later 1985 article, 'Burned by superstores, Tandy is fighting fire
with fire', *Business Week* reported that superstores had about 10 per
cent of the market and would have about 16 per cent in 1985, possibly
rising to 25 per cent by 1990. *Business Week* also reported that
superstores are big – they average about an acre of selling space – and
they offer a massive selection of audio, video and appliance brand
names. Radding said that it was not uncommon for the largest to stock
'virtually every model of every major mass-market line, including up
to 150 different TVs and 100 videocassette recorders'.

In its earlier article, *Business Week* said that the superstores were
embarking on a rapid-fire national expansion campaign, either by
buying up sites in most major metropolitan areas, or by gobbling up
smaller and weaker competitors. In turn they were funding this
growth through a flurry of stock offerings. In many markets they were
already competing 'head-to-head'. Radding, in his *Advertising Age*,
article described their impact on the Boston market as:

> a harbinger of change for high-tech marketing. In the
> early 1980s, the action was among computer retailers; in
> 1986, the market, like many others around the US is bracing for
> an explosion among broad-based consumer electronics stores.

*Business Week* concluded:

> They are trying to establish position before the market cools. . . .
> The increase in sales and earnings that come with opening more
> stores can hide a multitude of problems. That's why the real test
> for the superstores probably won't come until the expansion
> stops several years from now. Then the chains will have to prove
> they can manage as well as they can grow.

*Business Week* cited Federated Group Inc., a 43-store chain based in
the City of Commerce, California, as 'the prototype of the coming
wave of discount consumer-electronics superstores'. The key to
Federated's success is its product mix – some 9000 name-brands –
aggressively advertised and dramatically merchandised in stores with
over 25000 square feet of selling space. 'We're running a show' said
Federated's vice-president for sales and marketing. The fastest
moving items are sold at close to cost, which means that about 40 per

cent of its goods are generating some 20 per cent of its income.

While this helps build store traffic and repeat business, it calls for astute financial controls somewhere in the mix, and smart centralized buying. *Business Week* reported that in order to boost gross margins, 'which at 29.4 per cent are among the industry's best, Federated links commissions to profits, not sales, and uses a sophisticated point-of-sale computer system to control inventory'.

**Computer power**

In 1982 *Business Week* predicted that a shakeout in personal computers was about to take place. At the time there were some 150 companies with similar products and, argued *Business Week*: 'Companies that do not keep up with technology and those that do not have dealers and proper support will either disappear or be acquired.' *Business Week* warned that personal computer makers needed to master three areas: low-cost production, since hardware was becoming so standardized; a wide choice of software packages, to increase the number of applications; and distribution, since 'retailers have shelf space for just four or five brands; only those makers that keep their products in the customer's line of sight will survive'.

## Shakeout of PC retailers

In the personal computer industry the shakeout of retailers is well underway, spurred on by the faltering of sales growth in early 1985. As far back as 1983 and 1984 *Business Week* and *Fortune* respectively were predicting this shakedown; what neither foresaw was how quickly and comprehensively it would occur. The short history of personal computer marketing illustrates just how volatile and traumatic 'high-speed' marketing has become.

In a 1983 article, 'The chains take over computer retailing', *Business Week* said that some 3000 specialty retail outlets were turning over about $4 billion, which accounted for nearly 50 per cent of the personal computer business. *Business Week* quoted one researcher as predicting that, by 1988, there would be 6500 stores selling 35 per cent of the personal computer business, which in total would be worth $40 billion a year. Since the mass merchandisers were already grabbing the lion's share of the low-priced – under $1000 each – home computer business,

*Business Week* said that the independent specialty shops would have to abandon this low-profit end of the market and concentrate on the more expensive personal computers – at $2000 and up – used mostly for business and professional purposes. Even then their future would not be guaranteed since they would be up against the power of the 'franchises, chains, and manufacturer-owned outlets, such as Tandy Corp's ubiquitous Radio Shack. These national organizations can spread expensive advertising, buying, accounting, and inventory control over a large number of stores'. In this market, 'the name recognition and advertising clout are more important than price', claimed the head of a group of ComputerLand outlets. *Business Week* concluded that, to get the necessary economies of scale in buying and advertising power, the retailers would have to grow fast, whether by internal growth or by acquisition.

*Business Week* gave another reason for the rash of expansions and consolidations. They 'reflect the chains' awareness that manufacturers roll out their hot new products to the largest retailers first'. Joel Dreyfuss, in a 1984 *Fortune* article, 'More power to the PC chains', agreed: 'On the theory that only the biggest will survive, retailers are expanding furiously.' Quoting one owner of a major chain that within a few years there would be from five to ten major competitors, he also predicted that: 'The concentration of retail power will leave computer makers with fewer avenues to the consumer.' Though there were about two hundred manufacturers, most chains carried no more than five brand names. Given the amount of peripheral equipment, including software, there was insufficient shelf space for any more, and besides, that was the limit that salespeople could be expected to understand and demonstrate.

Dreyfuss said that: 'The big personal computer retailers are getting bigger fast. That's terrible news for small computer retailers – and for the scores of manufacturers whose machines aren't proven winners.' They had good cause to be worried:

> The manufacturers of less popular PCs are almost utterly dependent on the smaller retailers – who in turn are dependent on them. Lacking size and therefore clout, small store owners often can't get the best-selling brands, whose manufacturers can afford to be choosy. The dependence of the two weak reeds upon each other will eventually lead to their more-or-less simultaneous demise.

Dreyfuss' prediction was becoming borne out by 1986. In the personal computer industry, many of the weak had disappeared, some of the strong had got weaker, and a few of the strong had got stronger. There have been so many changes that the only safe prediction about the future is that, inevitably, there will be more unpredictable changes. This applies to manufacturers and retailers.

## Watershed year

1985 was a watershed year for the retailing of personal computers. While the growth in personal computer sales slowed to about half the rate in 1984, the number of outlets went from 4400 to 4600 – a far cry from the earlier bullish predictions – and nearly five hundred went out of business. Industry observers were expecting a similar number to fall by the wayside in 1986. 'There are just too many stores chasing too little business', the president of one chain told *Business Week*, in 'Sales are up – but dealers are shutting down'. One reason for this disparity was that cut-throat pricing had turned against the retailers.

By 1986 office-strength and IBM-compatible personal computers had fallen to near the $1000 mark and, Geoff Lewis, in a *Business Week* article, 'Personal computers: just another commodity', said that low price would be a 'mixed blessing' to retailers. While the low price might boost store traffic, the resulting slim profit margins would make it difficult for them to provide the necessary back-up support. 'The computer is a complicated product, and it costs a dealer as much to guide novices through a first purchase today as it did when the machines cost $3500.'

### New retailing forms

Kevin Higgins, in a 1986 *Marketing News* article, 'Computer industry adopts a leaner, market-driven distribution system', concluded that the shakedown would lead to a 'leaner, more marketing-oriented distribution network'. He believed that the retailing of personal computers was undergoing 'fundamental changes' with the decline in 'walk-in trade' and sales to home users. However, nobody seems sure what form the industry will ultimately take. In a mid-1985 assessment, *Business Week*, in 'The computer slump', felt the retailing channel would split into two streams:

The dealers with the financial and marketing wherewithal to cultivate new customers are moving toward a full-service, full-price strategy. They are aping the well-oiled support teams that manufacturers such as IBM use to coddle large customers who are buying more expensive machines. . . . The remaining dealers continue to cut prices and hope that volume will make up the difference.

Higgins considered one complication was the emergence of 'value-added resellers' – or VARS. There were some 6000 of them by 1986 and they operated by buying standard hardware and software components, adding 'value' to them via special services or configurations, and then reselling the 'system' to targeted end-users such as doctors, farmers and specialty retailers. They generally operate out of sales offices which don't have the overhead structure of showrooms. They are biting into the top end of the computer retailing business and, claimed Higgins, they are the 'bane of authorized dealers'. Not surprisingly, this form of retailing can be very profitable since the clients are often less concerned about low price, and more interested in getting an individually-tailored package and supporting back-up service.

The dealers are not giving up this part of the business without a fight and, continued Higgins, 'another noteworthy trend is private labelling of systems, with retailers piecing together a system involving printers, modems, personal computers, and other components manufactured by different vendors, then providing the training and service to make those systems work'. The key to this approach is the retailer's ability to put together a low-cost package and then add value to it. One industry executive informed Higgins: 'Where retailers have the buying clout, you're going to see more of this happening.'

This approach also means a shift in emphasis to 'outbound marketing', with retailers organizing their own sales forces 'according to specialized niches: educational institutions, desk-top publishing, governmental sales, banking, etc'. As another industry executive told Higgins, retailers who successfully target specific niches and provide after-the-sale training, service, and support 'are the only ones surviving'. Inevitably the retailer's reps are finding themselves competing head-to-head with their own suppliers for sales in these niches.

*Mixed fortunes*

*Business Week*, in a 1985 article, 'How to sell computers today – and how not to', compared the fortunes of ComputerLand Corp., the largest chain, with more than eight hundred franchised dealers, with Businessland Inc., a chain of about seventy company-owned outlets. *Business Week* stated: 'The night-and-day difference between ComputerLand and Businessland highlights the sudden changes in computer retailing.' ComputerLand aimed primarily at the walk-in market. Its strategy, and growth, was built around its ability to buy in bulk from suppliers, pass along the discounts to franchises, and collect a 9 per cent combination royalty and advertising fee each month. Businessland targeted business customers and had more than five hundred people in the field. Explained the co-founder: 'Although we look like a retailer, we're not.' The average system sold by Businessland was about $6000 vs about $2000 at ComputerLand. *Business Week* reported ComputerLand's strategy was sound when it was able to 'qualify for maximum discounts on International Business Machines Corp. gear. . . . But that strategy unravelled when other dealers started getting the same volume discounts as ComputerLand'. *Business Week*, in an early 1986 article, 'Sales are up – but dealers are shutting down', claimed that ComputerLand 'has seen 40 outlets close'.

The upshot is that, as one observer told Higgins, 'Computer retailing is dead'. Not quite. It will simply take another form. As Lewis, in 'Personal computers – just another commodity', concluded in March 1986:

> Even if many computer stores aren't ready for a commodity personal computer, consumer electronics stores may be. Federated Group Inc . . . now sells a $1400 Zenith package and is negotiating for the Epson personal computer – made by a subsidiary of the Japanese company that makes Seiko watches. Ironically, the result may be a revival of the flagging home market for computers.

By late 1986 there were even stronger signs, fuelled by news that firms were cutting prices even further – Tandy Corp., for one, was offering a $799 version of a basic IBM PC clone, complete with colour monitor. It's a pity that most of the computer firms around at the time of the first boom won't be present for the second. Those that survive the current shakeout will be ones that can make or buy components for the lowest prices – that is, even more collaborative marketing – and can obtain shelf space and get merchandising support in the new types of outlets now emerging from the next turn of the retailing wheel.

## Car power

There are some twenty-five thousand car dealers – mostly franchised in the US. They sell about ten million cars annually, or about four hundred cars each year per dealer, at an average of one and a half cars per working day. It is not an efficient system. In 1985 *The Economist* argued that:

> The motor industry flouts a basic rule of marketing. It does not make it easy to buy its product. A prospective car buyer has to tramp around several dealers. It would be more convenient to go to one outlet specializing in a particular market niche, but offering the full range of brand names, for example small cars, estate cars or luxury cars.

*The Economist* suggested that a supermarket approach to car retailing would suit buyers who know how much they want to spend but don't have a particular brand in mind. And besides, said *The Economist*, 'customer loyalty to marques is waning'.

That supermarket approach is now starting to take shape. For example, 'auto malls' are now being established which put several dealers on sites of up to fifty acres. Shoppers can thus browse among the various makes in 'much the way shoppers check out designer clothes at department stores', said *Fortune* in a 1986 article, 'Car marketers try the soft-sell approach'. *Fortune* reported that one mall in San Francisco, started in 1983, now turns over six thousand cars a year.

*Business Week*, in a mid-1986 editorial, 'Dealers: kicking carmakers' tires', noted another trend: the growth of super-dealers – 'multistate operations with thirty or more locations, selling upward of a dozen different brands, both domestic and foreign'. *Business Week* claimed that these super-dealers accounted for some 15 per cent of all car sales and the figure could go as high as 30 per cent by 1990. If so they will alter the balance of power that has been in place since Henry Ford first set up a distribution system to sell his mass-produced cars. *Business Week* continued:

> After decades of having the major car makers dictate price, style,

size, and virtually everything else to their franchised dealers, the $260 billion auto-retailing industry has found a dramatic way to reassert control over its business: the formation of megadealerships with the size and clout to start telling auto makers what they and their customers want.

In a follow-up article, 'American super-dealers are moving into the fast lane', in *Business Week*, William Hampton said that while only about two hundred and fifty dealers in the US could be classified as super-dealers, their presence was leading to a 'transformation' of the industry:

The big losers will be the neighbourhood dealers that sell one or two car brands. Industry experts are already comparing them with the corner groceries driven out by the supermarkets after World War II.

Hampton believed that, 'on balance, the shift to megadealers will be good for consumers'. One reason is that, since on average, some 30 per cent of the price of a new car in 1986 was added after the car left the factory, there should be some room to cut this by more efficient retailing. Moreover, super-dealers are more likely to provide better customer servicing, based on factors such as computerized service records, extended hours and the latest in servicing facilities, equipment and training. However, concluded Hampton: 'No auto maker – either domestic or foreign – is happy about one effect of the growing strength of the megadealers: they may soon be able to call the shots on car design and pricing.'

## Grocery power

If there is one arena that typifies all the changes discussed so far, and which illustrates the flow of goods problems faced by manufacturers, it would be the grocery trade. At first glance the power balance between manufacturers and retailers may appear more equal in the US, compared with other countries, which do not have the same antitrust regulations. In Australia the top three chains control about 80 per cent of the grocery trade; in Britain three chains account for about 40 per cent; in the US the top three hold only about 13 per cent. However, the American figure disguises the enormous retail concentrations at regional and local levels, and therefore the fact that as more and more US retail buying points continues to shrink, the fate of more and more suppliers is falling into fewer and fewer hands. In 1983, Schultz and Dewar, in *Retailers in Control: the Impact of Retail Trade Concentrations*, said that in the Miami area in 1980 the top four food trade operators had a 91 per cent share of the market by volume; in Chicago the top four had 83 per cent; in Washington the top four had 80 per cent; and in Dallas the top four had 79 per cent. The authors concluded that: 'If you're a food manufacturer, you have every right to be concerned about these figures.' (3)

*Giant stores*

If Giant Food Inc., of Landover, Maryland, is typical of the strong regional chains then Schultz and Dewar are correct in their assessment. In a 1986 article, 'A Giant among combos', *Progressive Grocer* reported that, with 135 stores, Giant in 1985 ranked as the eleventh largest public supermarket chain in sales ($2.1 billion) and one of the most profitable (after-tax net profit of 2.11 per cent). In Washington, DC, its main area, it is market leader with nearly 40 per cent of the market share, even though its main competitor is Safeway, the nation's largest chain (1995 stores). In its other main area, Baltimore, Giant has some 20 per cent share.

In the US grocery trade, two formats now dominate. One is the warehouse-type with very high volume, very low margins, and minimal service; the other is the combo/superstore, with more selection, more services, and higher margins. Giant has opted for the latter. In 'A Giant among combos', *Progressive Grocer* reported that Giant's food/pharmacy combination stores now average 55 000 square feet vs about 44 000 only a few years ago – the industry average is 27 000:

> The extra space allows Giant to add specialty departments such as gourmet service meat and seafood, expanded service delis, expanded produce, gourmet candy, full-service flower shops and specialty bakers.

Such complexity, combined with razor-thin margins, requires control and, claimed Bill Saporito, in a 1985 *Fortune* article, 'The Giant of the regional food chains': 'Giant dominates its two disparate territories with stylish retailing, iron discipline, and an unparalleled degree of vertical integration.' Saporito pointed out that 'The discipline comes from a sophisticated data-processing network ... and a chipper 72-year-old (chairman) who is one part Mr Whipple and one part Mr Whip.' He added that 'The thread that unifies all Giant operations is electronic.' Giant was the first chain to install computer scanners company-wide, in 1979, and now has a:

> computerized buying system that will analyse such things as current stock and current sales, inventory costs, warehouse space, and promotion schedules to determine, for example, whether a store buyer should stock up on frozen dinners being sold at a discount. . . . Once a decision is made to buy, Giant uses another computer program to execute the order. It is one of the few retailers capable of replenishing its stock electronically.

So much for company reps.

## Divide and rule

When Arthur Lawrence, in 'The Management of Trade Marketing', concluded that: 'The days when the manufacturer could divide and rule among vast numbers of small independent distributors, not acting in concert with one another, have disappeared with the advent of the large multiple operation', he was writing about the UK grocery trade. (7) He could have been referring to any number of industrialized countries.

Lawrence argued that of all the marketing mix elements that must be orchestrated to make a successful brand, 'only the single factor of media advertising is capable of reaching the consumer directly, independently of the intervention of the trade. All the other features which have been so ingeniously planned are totally dependent on the distributive trade performing the functions assumed of it, if they are ever going to influence the consumer'. The other factors, such as whether to accept a new product, the amount of shelf space to allocate to it, the commitment to promotional activities, and the final price to be charged to the consumer are all matters for the trade to decide, not the manufacturer. And, maintained Lawrence, even a media campaign 'must not only be effective in actually persuading consumers; it must convince distributors that it will be so effective'.

In the face of a barrage of new and not-so-new products, and a continuingly high new-product failure rate, a growing number of trade members are becoming increasingly difficult to convince. Julie Franz, in a 1986 *Advertising Age* article, 'Test marketing: travelling through a maze of choices', reported that, in 1985, there were 2206 new products introduced into food and drugstores. A further 2670 line extensions – of flavour, colour or other ingredients – were also introduced. Even allowing for the fact that there were some 15 000 items in an 'average' supermarket in 1984 – vs 9000 in 1974, when supermarkets were much smaller – most will not stay on the shelves for long, if they got there at all. A top research executive at Leo Burnett Inc. told Franz: 'Of the products that make it into national distribution, 70 per cent either are pulled off shelves or never reach their estimated sales potential. . . . This could be the result of a lack of innovation among new products.' Echoes of Chapter 5.

## Retailer resistance

The resistance to the influx of new brands from chain store buyers, combined with the concentration of outlets into fewer hands and the increased use of computer-generated data, has had a major impact on the buyer–seller relationship. Power is now shifting towards the retailers. As a result, many packaged goods companies have come to realize that they can no longer *market* to the end consumer, and *sell* to the trade. Too many retail buyers have seen too many promised advertising and promotional blitzes that have failed to 'pull' me-too brands off the shelves, to continue to accept this traditional marketing approach from their suppliers.

Consumers may also be cooling toward the increase of new products. In 1986 *Marketing News* reported that data culled from purchasing reports from a panel of fifty thousand households revealed that new product introductions since 1982 had generated 15 per cent less trial, and 6 per cent lower repeat purchasing than in the period 1978–82. *Marketing News* claimed that marketers were trying to counter this indifference by introducing line extensions and improvements to existing brands, in order to capitalize on their familiarity – and no doubt to save on the enormous expense of launching an entirely new brand. The president of NPD, the research firm involved in the panel study, informed *Marketing News* that

Procter & Gamble certainly appears to agree with this philosophy. Long the leading proponent of brand image integrity and

clarity, clearly P&G has shifted its strategy toward line extensions. Liquid Tide, Ivory Shampoo, Duncan Hines cookies and
Crest Tartar Control are prime examples.

Coca-Cola and Pepsi-Cola have also come up a host of line
extensions to fight their cola wars. As far back as 1982 *Business Week*
believed that the introduction of Diet Coke and Pepsi Free would put
pressure on supermarkets to reconsider stocking the minor brands.
John Scully, who was then president of PepsiCo's beverage operations, informed *Business Week*: 'The more brands we and Coke bring
out, the harder it will be for smaller companies to get shelf space.They
have no leverage in the stores.' Neither do the big companies always
have this leverage. In April 1986, one year after the introduction of
new Coke, McDonald's announced that it was going back to the
Classic Coke formula. The only consolation for Coke was that
McDonald's, with 7000 fast-food restaurants, didn't switch to Pepsi.
While line extensions may be seen as good for the likes of Coca-Cola
and P&G, the trade aren't always convinced it's good for them.

At the 1984 annual meeting of the Canadian Grocery Distributors
Institute, held in Toronto, much criticism was directed at the
proliferation of me-too brands and line extensions. The representative
of one supermarket chain informed the meeting that, of the 2155 so-
called new products brought to his chain in 1983, only 705 were
accepted. Moreover, an additional 867 items were deleted to release
shelf space. Another delegate told the gathering that pressure for shelf
space was coming from the introduction of new categories that were
beginning to sell well – such as Tetra Pak juices and diet and caffeine-
free beverages. He then added: 'If shelf space is available, particularly
in our larger stores, there are better alternatives for shelf space than the
proliferation of me-toos, line extensions, and reformulations of new
flavours.' Another supermarket representative argued that the traditional departments of US and Canadian super- and super-combo
stores were not being expanded to accommodate new packaged goods
items; rather the added space was being used for higher profit margin
specialty service departments, such as floral departments, bakeries and
delicatessens.

Saporito's analysis of Giant corroborates these statements. He
believed that Giant's strategic emphasis is now on the perimeter of
the combination stores, though the branded packaged goods have an
important function as well. 'Service departments are the exact

opposite of the original supermarket concept – self-service – and they are expensive to operate, tricky to merchandise, and usually can't stand on their own without the traffic-generating power of the grocery aisles.' If the primary role of packaged goods marketers is to provide the means by which the giant combination stores can build traffic volume, then manufacturers *should* be concerned about this latest turn of the wheel of retailing.

## Promotion vs advertising

Brand marketers are faced with a new dilemma in terms of resource allocation: how to build a strong brand franchise long-term through a clear positioning statement, backed up with sufficient theme advertising expenditure to maintain that position in consumers' minds – vs how to grab a precious share of retail shelf or freezer space, and then defend this space from constant attack by competitors, given the trend that consumers are becoming less brand loyal unless provided with constant promotional inducements. For some brand marketers the choice is more urgent: how to grab a few share points today, in order to look good vs how to develop the brand for tomorrow, in order that one's successor might look good.

An additional complicating factor is that, according to the Point-of-Purchase Advertising Institute Inc., an increasing number of store customers now make their final buying decisions in the store, rather than relying on their prepared shopping lists. In a 1986 pilot study, POPAI found that in-store decisions by grocery shoppers have increased sharply for many product categories since their last study in 1977. For example, 90 per cent of consumers decided on their cookie purchases once in the store (vs 85 per cent in 1977), and 67 per cent decided on their soft drinks choices (vs 56 per cent in 1977). No doubt findings such as these will be used by retailers to persuade their suppliers to divert more funds to in-store promotions.

Richard Edel, in a 1985 *Advertising Age* article, 'Trade wars threaten future peace of marketers', added another cause for concern:

> Some say retailers have become as dependent on fattening the bottom line through deals made in the buying office as through sales at the checkout counter. If this is true, trade promotions could be thought of as an institutional form of bribery to gain and keep market share.

The problem, as many marketers see it, is that they don't always know what happens when they offer rebates and other incentives to retailers. One thing they suspect is that much of the discounting doesn't get passed on to consumers. Retailers may 'buy forward', that is, buy enough to last into the next cycle when full prices can be charged; they may 'divert sales', that is, purchase in an area where the discounts are being offered and then ship the goods to another area where full prices can be charged; or they may simply pocket some or all of the money offered.

Such activities are not surprising, given the amount of dealing that prevails, and given the pressures on the buyers. In its 1986 survey of chain store executives, *Progressive Grocer* reported that when asked to state the hardest issues confronting the entire industry, nearly six out of ten replied: 'Difficulty in maintaining current net profit margin' and 'Competition from non-food retailers'. When asked to state what steps they would be taking to come to grips with their problems, *Progressive Grocer* said 'executives plan to do more for – and get more from – suppliers'. No wonder the recent request for 'slotting allowances' by some retailers has riled suppliers, including Procter & Gamble, as mentioned in Chapter 1.

The amounts of money involved are now staggering. In a 1986 *Advertising Age* article, 'Trade price discounts holding hostages', Edel said that trade allowances can add from 1 per cent to 3 per cent to a retailer's bottom line. In the case of A&P, with 1100 stores and some $7 billion in sales in 1985, trade promotions could amount to between $70 million and $210 million. Felix Kessler, in a 1986 *Fortune* article, 'The costly coupon craze', reported one estimate of 1986 expenditure on consumer and trade promotion as above $200 billion, vs an estimate of total advertising expenditure of slightly above $100 billion. Kessler also reported one study which showed that over the past five years the proportion of total marketing expenditures that makers of non-durable goods allocated to consumer promotion had climbed in almost direct opposition to a decline in the proportion spent on advertising. The proportion spent on trade promotion had remained relatively steady, indicating that suppliers were realizing that if they were going to increase their promotional stakes, they should at least attempt to ensure that as much as possible was aimed directly at consumers:

| *Percentage spent on:* | *1980* | *1985* |
|---|---|---|
| Media advertising | 43 | 35 |
| Trade promotions | 34 | 35 |
| Consumer promotions | 23 | 30 |
| | 100% | 100% |

It is difficult to reconcile the traditional concepts of long-term brand building strategies when 70 per cent of the monies now being spent to support a brand are allocated for short-term tactical purposes.

Kessler claimed that as a result of this changing emphasis, 'marketers of consumer products are rewriting the rules of their game'. However, they may not be doing this as part of a grand strategy review. F. Kent Mitchel, in a 1985 'commentary' article, 'Advertising/promotion budgets; how did we get here, and what do we do now?', in *The Journal of Consumer Marketing*, observed:

> A change in the advertising/promotion mix represents a fundamental, strategic decision about how to market the products in your company. But I'm suggesting that many companies have made this change by drifting into it, rather than by a carefully considered strategic analysis. (8)

Mr Mitchel was speaking as a vice-persident of General Foods Corp., a leading marketing company, and before its merger with Philip Morris. His concern should still apply for, whether marketers like it or not, price support schemes to the trade are an essential part of a retailer's marketing mix.

For most outlets the packaged goods sections will still form the core of their business, even though the more profitable areas, such as fresh produce and home bakeries, may be placed around the perimeter. Retailers have little to lose and everything to gain by accepting promotional support from the makers of leading branded goods. Suppliers' specials, the cost of which are largely borne by themselves, help to generate store traffic and boost retailer's profits, and contribute to the enhancement of the store's price/value image. And to make life really tough for the suppliers, scanner-derived information based on the results of past promotions means the retailer can choose the optimum combination of specials from the items constantly being offered.

## Changing times

There are many reasons why this situation has developed. The mass market is splitting apart, and so the traditional mass-media approaches to reaching diffuse target groups are no longer as effective. This issue will be examined in more detail in Chapter 8. The large number of parity products, combined with the rapid countering of one competitive offer by another, has led to consumers becoming increasingly conditioned to buying on price or some other promotional deal. Short-term planning – including the product portfolio syndrome – plus executive pay and bonus schemes that reward short term performance, has forced many marketers to emphasize quick volume and profit gains – for example, the long-term impact of a reduction in advertising expenditure may be tempered by diverting some of the money to trade dealing. With product life–cycles shortening and companies having to aim new products at segments of markets, there are fewer opportunities to create big brands with strong prospects of long and secure futures. These factors have led many packaged goods marketers to adopt a tactical, short-term mentality where consumer and trade promotions are the main weapons, and where theme advertising is no longer considered the most powerful way to build and sustain a strong brand franchise.

Edel, in 1986, claimed that some industry experts now believed that scanning information was also helping to shift the balance of power to retailers. The increased use of grocery scanners means that individual stores can provide an immediate and constant tracking of virtually all lines, and most important, they can get this information before their suppliers. Edel quoted the US chairman of Ogilvy & Mather: 'Scanners show that brand share can fluctuate from 4 per cent to 55 per cent because of various forms of promotion incentive.... The scanner is akin to Eve with a basket full of red apples tempting manufacturers to forgo the world of branded marketing.' As the head of one of the world's biggest advertising agencies he and his colleagues have much to be concerned about.

Mitchel got to the heart of the matter in his commentary:

In my business – packaged goods – the grocery-trade managers are changing from passive distributors of products to aggressive retailers with adequate scale and management ability to be successful in their own right. This grocery trade wants to run its own advertising and promotion to its customers and expects suppliers to tie in with that. Of course, price is their principal competitive thrust. This reversal of practices that have been in place for decades suggests that our business relations with these respected channels of distribution need some rethinking for the 1980s and 1990s. (8)

In a 1986 speech to the American Marketing Association the chairman of Ogilvy & Mather said that advertisers and manufacturers needed to understand how to use scanning data and how to develop 'shelf space management systems'. 'How would you like to be a salesperson confronting a chain buyer who knows more about product movement, shelf space, sizes etc. than you do?' he asked his audience. Revealing an element of self-interest, he added:

Data from scanning should enable manufacturers to bring some much needed discipline to the spending of $25 billion on trade promotion or price discounting. A better knowledge of how promotion works, and what combinations produce optimum sales and profits, should enable manufacturers to spend less trade money for the same effect, permitting the funds saved to be channelled back into higher profits and the development or maintenance of brand franchises ... [Scanning] is a tool that will either completely undermine the concept of branded marketing and consumer franchise building or it will provide the means to better understand the marketing process, leading to a new era of a more balanced marketing, an era that will benefit the manufacturer, the retailer, the consumer and, I hope, Ogilvy & Mather.

All of which may help to explain why, in 1986, O&M announced it was moving into supermarket 'shelf space management consulting', thereby adding another dimension to the 'full service' agency concept.

The growth in sales promotion activities is not limited to grocery retailing. In a 1986 *Advertising Age* article, 'Sales promotion comes into its own', Paul Edwards stated:

Today, sales promotion embraces a wide range of activities, many of them an integral part of a company's marketing plan. Frequent-flier programs have enabled airlines to build a base of loyal customers where none existed before. Sweepstakes and contests are a staple for some direct marketers. Rebates and financing plans sweeten the offer for car dealers. Magazines entice new readers with a seemingly limitless string of premiums. And for marketers of package goods there is an unending flow of freestanding inserts, envelopes stuffed with coupons, game cards and contests.

## Trade marketing era?

If the 1950s through the 1970s can be thought of as the golden era of consumer marketing, then the rest of the century will possibly be known as the period when trade marketing came into its own. Lawrence, in 1983, argued that:

> Getting trade distribution... is an aspect of a company's operations which ranks in importance with its strategies for product marketing, for product development, for manufacturing efficiency and for financial planning. A company should no longer be content to leave to a subordinate 'sales department' the task of achieving the sales throughput for which the market is assumed to be ready to provide a channel.

We are indeed in a new era.

Brian Mitchell, in 'Communicate to become retail smart', in the Australian business magazine *Rydges*, claimed there was an enormous lack of knowledge of the retail trade by marketing people in the packaged goods industry. He felt that one reason for this affair was the separate – nearly independent – lines of communication between the key participants in the marketing process (see Figure 8.1):

'There is a heavy line between marketing and the consumer on the one hand and sales and the retailer on the other, and only intermittent communication across the divisions', noted Mitchell. Often a brand manager gets exposed to the sales force when briefing them on some new programme. In such a situation the marketing person is moving:

> from an ideal world of market shares, brand statistics and marketing objectives into the real world of retailer relationships.... This is a world which the salesforce understand, because they live in it. It is a world where logic doesn't always prevail and where brand loyalty takes a definite backseat to more pragmatic considerations such as immediate profits.

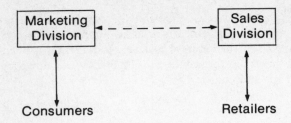

**Figure 8.1   Communication between key participants in the marketing process**

Increasingly, suppliers are realizing that the world of the major groups, or 'accounts', is one where only senior representatives, with real power to make important sales *and* marketing decisions, are gaining entry. This is a world for trade marketers, not salespeople (see Figure 8.2):

The call for a trade marketing group, charged with the responsibilities of marketing to each of the company's major retail accounts, is not a recent one. In 1979 Foy and Pommerening, in a *McKinsey Quarterly* article, 'Brand marketing: fresh thinking needed', suggested that if packaged goods marketers examined all their trade accounts closely they might have found that their largest retail customer generated the same amount of revenue as some of their largest brands. And a closer analysis of discounts, advertising subsidies, sales force efforts and logistics costs for each major account – provided the company *had* the information – would have shown wide variations, and probably some results that were contrary to the company's official policy regarding its dealings with the trade.

The authors concluded that:

Successful marketing in today's trading environment requires more than a national strategy under-pinned by a strong product-management focus.... Today, individual trade customers need to be managed as profit centres of the business, with the same level of management attention that brands have historically enjoyed under the product management system. This implies an integrated sales/marketing concept whereby product and account strategies are coordinated and balanced.

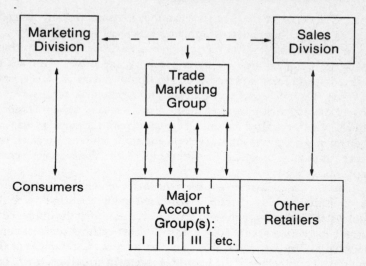

**Figure 8.2 Trade marketing linkages**

They added that what they were asking packaged goods marketers to do was 'basically no different from the approach many industrial manufacturers have adopted for some years now in managing their product range across a spectrum of a few large customers'. (9)

## Trade marketing leverage

Since then the concept of trade marketing leverage has steadily gained acceptance, as manufacturers realize they must increase their level of marketing service to the trade. This service can take many forms: providing retailers with ways to improve their merchandising effectiveness; showing retailers how to measure the real costs of handling products; collaborating with retailers on the use of scanner-based techniques to measure the incremental profit and volume achieved from various promotional efforts; and even involving retailers in the company's new product development programme. Most importantly, by a regular monitoring of trade activities and the use of offers, it can help restore a balance to the relationship, something that is in the best interest of both parties. Unless marketers can impose performance criteria on their trade dealing they will continue to come out second best. Given the increased concentration of retail trade in so many sectors these comments may apply elsewhere as well.

To achieve this level of servicing, companies are setting up trade marketing groups, headed by top-calibre executives with senior marketing and sales experience, and staffed by specialists in a variety of fields. Trade 'clients' may get serviced in much the same way that advertising agencies service their clients – ideally as professional equals. Whether called national, key, or corporate account managers, their main objective is the development and maintenance of an on-going mutually-beneficial relationship with their major chain accounts.

This increased awareness that the achievement of distribution through the trade is a strategic issue, deserving the same degree of priority as marketing to the end consumer, means that the influence of a trade marketing group is likely to cut across existing organizational boundaries. In particular, it is likely to force a reassessment of the traditional dominance of the brand management structure, where one executive may be responsible for the marketing of each brand. One possibility is that, if the concentration of retail trade continues, brand management will become more of a team, or power-sharing function; in other companies it may be reduced to that of a service role. Whatever finally evolves, it appears to be already undergoing a change. Brand strategy decisions appear to be shifting higher up the hierarchy, where the manufacturer, trade and consumer perspectives can each be considered equally. Tactical decisions may become the major focus of attention at the brand management level, where a quick-fire stream of promotions – such as coupons, in-pack prizes, contests, and price-offs etc. – are needed to keep up a brand's momentum and to counter competitive activities.

Arthur Bragg, in a 1982 *Sales and Marketing Management* article, 'National account managers to the rescue', stated that to succeed, a major account programme needed the 'support and active involvement of top management', and to be headed by a 'sales executive who has status within his company'. He was referring to industrial companies, but his comments would equally apply to a consumer goods firm. His last point is essential. The need for horizontal management skills is likely to lead to more firms adopting a 'matrix' management approach, rather than the traditional top-down hierarchies.

Trade marketing executives – who probably will have had senior level sales *and* marketing experience – can effectively carry out their task as equal negotiators with senior buying personnel only if they have commensurate authority within their own companies. If a trade marketer is presenting a packaging change to the buyer in a major account, and the buyer suggests a way to redesign the pack so as to reduce space taken up on a shelf, or to cut down on store handling costs, the last thing the trade marketer should have to say is: 'Good point, but I'll have to raise it with my marketing people back at HQ.' In fact, if a company is serious about the trade marketing concept, such a situation should not even arise. When any packaging is in the process of being redesigned the opinions of both consumers and trade would have been sought. Certainly the trade marketer would expect to be consulted, and perhaps provide equal input to the final decision – and possibly even to overrule the preferences of the brand manager concerned if it came to a stand-off between the consumer research results and the trade's requirements.

Far-fetched? Bill Saporito, in a 1985 *Fortune* article, 'Procter & Gamble's comeback plan', told how retailers now use a technique known as direct product profitability – or DPP – to assess the attractiveness of brands. In a 1986 *Business Week* article, 'At today's supermarket, the computer is doing it all', Gary Geipel reported that: 'The concept was born in the early 1960s, but it wasn't until the cost of mainframe computer power fell in the 1980s that DPP caught on.' Saporito explained that:

Using DPP, retailers can measure the handling costs of a product from the time it reaches the warehouse until a customer takes it out the front door. DPP has revealed that some high-volume products have such high handling costs that they are less appealing – and deserve less shelf space – than retailers once thought.

Saporito also reported that:

after running DPP studies with several retailers, P&G redesigned its Ivory shampoo bottle from a teardrop shape used in test markets to a squarer, barrel-like look. The DPP data indicated that the new shape, which takes up less space, saves distributors 29 cents a case.

Naturally, when P&G finds a superior benefit it tells its customers. Saving the trade some money is no exception. A 1986 ad in *Progressive*

*Grocer* featured Larry Olson of Shiloh Market in one of P&G's favourite formats, the testimonial. Enthused Mr Olson:

> *'P&G must have had customers like me in mind when they came out with new Citrus Hill Select frozen orange juice in a 16-ounce can. It takes up 34 per cent less freezer space – and they pack 15 units in a case as opposed to the industry standard of 24.*
>
> *'Using P&G's Direct Product Profit calculations, my rep showed me that I was actually saving 3c handling cost on every can of Citrus Hill. P&G has redesigned packaging on Downy, Tide, Ivory Shampoo, Pringle's, Always, and many of their other products to help reduce storage and handling costs.*
>
> *'It means a lot when the space is tight to have the more profitable brands.*

As an advertisement it may not be creative, but it sure works hard to demonstrate P&G's new found commitment to the well-being of the trade. It also sums up the importance that consumer-oriented giants such as Procter & Gamble now attach to achieving leverage in their channels of distribution. One chief executive told Saporito: 'Its been a quantum change. There's certainly a greater willingness to pay attention to what we want and need.' Which is exactly what independent Mr Olson is also saying.

However, paying attention to the wants and needs of *consumers* is still a prerequisite for success in the final stage in the flow of goods. The next chapter will examine the problems that marketers are now having in achieving leverage in the consumer market, or more appropriately, the kaleidoscope that is the consumer market.

# 9    The end of the mass market

The US market for many products is breaking up. Income polarization, combined with demographic and lifestyle shifts, are forcing firms to reassess their traditional approaches to mass-marketing. This reassessment was explained by *Business Week*, in 1983: 'A splintered mass market forces companies to target their products.' More recently, a senior planning and research executive at the J Walter Thompson advertising agency told *Dun's Business Month*: 'Everything we do today is targeted to a specific group. Ten years ago, the focus was the young family. Things were much more homogeneous.' Today, things are much more heterogeneous. The 1980 census established that dramatic changes in family, household, and marriage patterns over the 1970s had altered the makeup of American society at the national, state and local levels. Bruce Steinberg correctly identified one shift crucial to marketers when he entitled his 1983 *Fortune* article: 'The mass market is splitting apart'. In a 1985 article, 'Snapshot of a changing America', *Time* identified another important change: 'The US population is growing older and thinking smaller.'

According to some demographers, the most important change is that the US has become a kaleidoscope society. The implication is that no longer can marketers plan on the basis of past population growth rates – their markets have become more complex, more fragmented, and they are constantly shifting. We are in an era of 'composition-driven' change:

## Changing demographics

- In 1970 the US population was 205 million; in 1980 it was 223 million; without immigrants the population is expected to peak at 246 million in the year 2000, and start to decline. With projected fertility and immigration rates, the population is expected to be 260 million by 2000, an increase of 17 per cent over 1980. *Time* predicted that, by 2085, the US population will be 300 million, of whom 10 per cent will be Asian, 16 per cent Hispanic, 16 per cent black, and 'a diminishing majority' of 58 per cent non-Hispanic whites.

- Despite the increase in the number of people, the rate of population growth has slowed considerably since 1960. The total fertility rate declined from 3.7 births per woman in 1960 to 2.5 in 1970 and has fluctuated between 1.7 and 1.9 since 1976. In the late 1970s there was a slight 'baby boomlet' which was largely due to the sheer numbers of women of child-bearing age.
- In 1970 the median age of the US population was 28 years; in 1980 it was 30 years; and it is expected to exceed 36 by the year 2000.
- In 1970 40 per cent of all households were made up of married couples with children; by 1985 this family structure made up only 28 per cent of all households. There are now more households comprised of married couples and no children (30 per cent) than there are with children. The 'typical' American family of mother, father and two children so often portrayed by Madison Avenue in the past in fact made up only 11 per cent of all households in 1985. There were more family households headed by females (12 per cent). And nearly a quarter (23 per cent) of all households had an occupant living alone.
- The number of people under 18 will grow by 7 per cent between 1980 and 2000 (to 69 million); the number of people between 18 and 24, who form the main work-entering group, will decline by 11 per cent (to 25 million), and already the owners of businesses dependent on cheap, young, part-time staff, such as supermarkets and take-away outlets are feeling the pinch; the number of people 25–34 will decline by 3 per cent (to 34 million); the number of people 35–44 will increase by 53 per cent (to 41 million); the number of people between 45–54 will increase by 55 per cent (to 36 million); the number of people between 55–64 will increase by 12 per cent (to 23 million); and the number of people over 65 will increase by 28 per cent (to 32 million).

One demographer summed up the implications of these changes to *Time*: 'By the late 1980s, one-half of our households will be headed by baby boomers. One-fourth of our population will be elderly. These two groups will define our society for a very long time.'

## Two-tier economy

• America is shifting toward a two-tier economy. In 1983 Steinberg reported that the broad middle class – defined as families with incomes between $15000 and $35000 per year in constant US dollars – fell from 51 per cent of total families in 1973 to 44 per cent in 1982. The two groups at either end of this continuum both grew as a percentage. Steinberg argued that:

> Most businessmen don't realize it yet, but the middle class – the principal market for much of what they make – is gradually being pulled apart. Economic forces are propelling one family after another toward the high or low end of the income spectrum. For many marketers, particularly those positioned to sell to the well-to-do, these presage good times. For others used to selling millions of units of their products to middle-income folks, the prospects are altogether darker.

In 1986, Rena Bartos, best-known for her book on the changing role of women, *The Moving Target*, agreed: 'It may be unrealistic to think of American consumers in terms of of mass markets. We are moving to a two-level pattern of luxury and value.' According to Bartos, at the upper end is a growing demand for luxury, whether it be in fashions, restaurants, hotels or automobiles. At the other end there is a new sense of value, as typified by the move away from all-purpose department stores to discount outlets. Bartos also suggested that it may be unwise to stereotype today's consumers; given the many choices before them they may sometimes act in ways that at first appear out of character. 'The same lady may shop at an elegant store as well as a discount store. It is the upscale customers who tried generic brands first.' (1)

## Women at work/men out shopping

• Bartos has said there is another 'simple demographic fact that is the basis of a quiet revolution: the dramatic rise in the number of women in the US who go to work'. In 1985 54 per cent of all women over 16 were working, whereas only 32 per cent could be classified as full-time housewives – with the remainder being made up of women who were students, retired or disabled. As a result, said Bartos: 'Working women are really the majority of all active women in our country. This is a fact that many marketers have not yet absorbed.'

In its 53rd Annual Report of the US grocery trade, in 1986, *Progressive Grocer* observed 'Today's key industry phrase is "niche marketing" and it's hard to imagine that any niche is more important than working women.... The 'superwomen' juggling family, career and household duties such as food shopping put a premium on time.' As a result, continued *Progressive Grocer*, while women working full time visited supermarkets roughly the same number of times per week as non-working women, and spent about the same amount of money, they took less time per trip. They were also more likely to shop on the weekends whereas shoppers without jobs said this was their least favoured time. Working women were also more likely to shop in the evenings. This means that a store's merchandising and promotional efforts, and hours of operation, must allow for these differences if returns are to be maximized.

• If there is a quiet revolution as a result of more women at work, there seems to be an even quieter one resulting from an increasing number of men doing the grocery shopping and other domestic chores. In a 1986 *Business Horizons* article, 'The male queue at the checkout counter', Ronald Michman said: 'Abundant literature deals with the two-income family and the changing roles of women. However, little has been written about the changing roles of men and how marketers can motivate men as purchasers.' (2)

According to Michman, male baby-boomers are more likely than previous generations to accept new values, such as doing the shopping, cooking, child-caring, and other household tasks. While women may still predominate in doing household chores, their outside work and other interests means that the traditional roles of men and women are no longer so distinctly defined. Products formerly aimed at men as the head of household – cars, insurance and banking services, for example – are now also being targeted toward women. And products once aimed only at women – cooking and cleaning, in particular – are now directed at men as well. Michman concluded: 'Instead of appealing to the same old stereotypes, alert marketers will adapt quickly to the changing role of the male consumer.'

Michman cited one recent study that showed men accounting for 40 per cent of grocery shoppers in the US. Like their female counterparts, their time is at a premium, and this has led to some important characteristics of male shoppers, said Michman. They are less likely to pre-plan their shopping trip, such as cutting out coupons, looking at different supermarket ads, or making up a shopping list. They are more likely to impulse buy and to buy convenience foods. As a result, they are more likely to spend more on food shopping than are their female counterparts. According to Michman, they are also more likely to show greater brand loyalty and, if so, then marketers will need to examine demand analysis for their products and services in terms of how men and women buy separately – and how they share decisions.

Not everyone agrees with Michman. In a 1986 *Progressive Grocer* article, 'The myth of the male shopper', Priscilla Donegan pointed out:

Grocery shopping is no longer just 'women's work'. Increasingly, supermarket aisles are being populated by men. But don't alter your merchandising techniques or product mix yet. There's more – or, perhaps, less – to male shoppers than meets the eye.

Donegan argued that, just as there are no longer 'typical' consumers, there are no 'typical' male shoppers. Rather, they span the demographic and socio-economic spectrum just as females do, and therefore, 'it is not surprising to find that male shoppers are inclined to shop the same way and purchase primarily the same items that female shoppers do'. As a result, they are no more likely to impulse buy – except when they first start shopping, and are initially uncertain in a supermarket – and they are no less likely to use shopping lists or price-off coupons. The main determinant of the latter is how much time the shoppers have for this type of pre-trip planning. Further, specific items purchased by men and women – such as national and generic brands – are also likely to be similar.

Donegan said that the main differences in shopping behaviour take place when single male shoppers are compared with married shoppers, male and female. Here they are more likely to fit the male stereotype. At the same time they cannot be ignored since, in 1983 there were some 20 million single males over 18. Older men also constitute an important market, claimed Donegan, and *Progressive Grocer's* 53rd

Annual Report results revealed that men 55 years and over make up half of all male primary shoppers. One result of findings such as this is that some grocery retailers are starting to direct some of their advertising towards men.

However, argued Donegan, more important to retailers is the finding that, in 1983, 43 per cent of all households had two or more wage earners, and nearly three-quarters of all households with income levels over $30000 had two income earners. Many of these couples will share responsibilities, including shopping – whether alone or together. This may help to explain why so many supermarkets have added specialty sectors, from cheese to seafood, and why fine, frozen convenience foods have become so popular.

Donegan concluded that: 'The bottom line for most retailers is that they must know their customers. This means recognizing that there is no longer only one type of shopper. Today's supermarket shoppers come in all sizes, shapes and genders.'

## Kaleidoscope of opportunities

To judge by some of the recent articles on the new segments that are emerging, America is now a constantly shifting kaleidoscope of target market opportunities.

- 'Insurer markets to Hispanics with Spanish sales promotion materials, services, and ads', *Marketing News*, 1984
- 'Asian-Americans targeted by insurance firm', *Marketing News*, 1986
- 'Courting the well-heeled car shopper: In the flourishing $15000-and-up corner of the US auto market, Detroit is trying to regain lost ground, European car makers are thriving, and the Japanese are at the gates', *Fortune*, 1985
- 'Affluent marketing: Fragmentation enriches problems in reaching group', *Advertising Age*, 1986
- 'The decline of first class: On most airlines in the US, flying in the front cabin is no longer worth the price of a full-fare ticket', *Fortune*, 1986
- 'How cosmetics makers are touching up their strategies: Companies used to sell fantasies and dreams. Women now buy reality and value', *Business Week*, 1985

- 'Low-budget banking: To their surprise, banks can make money serving the poor', *Fortune*, 1985
- 'High times for a low-end retailer: Let other retailers upscale. Family Dollar Stores owes its remarkable growth to loyal budget shoppers', *Dun's Business Month*, 1985
- 'Companies target big-spending teens: Teens – with income from part-time jobs – are buying big ticket items and forming brand preferences. Its a $45 billion-plus market', *Dun's Business Month*, 1985
- 'Marketers should target the 51st US state: The college market', *Marketing News*, 1986
- 'Pontiac's ad efforts sport collegiate look for spring', *Advertising Age*, 1986
- 'Prince tries pasta for gourmet market: A product for "aspiring yuppies"', *Advertising Age*, 1986
- 'What the baby-boomers will buy next: The leading edge of this affluent group is about to turn 40 and enter its peak spending years. Boomers want quality goods and champagne to go with them', *Fortune*, 1984
- 'The upwardly mobile downhill slide: Ski biz sets out to get the whole family back on the slopes', *Time*, 1984
- 'Out of breath: Even as Wall Street, the sporting-goods world keeps getting swept by fads. Take jogging, which is lurching into middle age along with the baby boomers', *Forbes*, 1984
- 'Yuppies uncork a boom in fine French wines: US buying power and worldwide speculation are proving a heady combination', *Business Week*, 1985
- 'Financial woes for baby boomers: They're not all yuppies, study finds', *Automotive News*, 1985
- 'Growing pains at 40: As they approach mid-life, Baby Boomers struggle to have it all', *Time*, 1986
- 'Sun, fun and sales meetings: Once for swingers only, Club Med now woos corporate customers', *Time*, 1986
- 'Marketers mine for gold in the old: Households Madison Avenue calls 'mature' are wealthier, more numerous, and more willing to spend than ever. The market will keep growing, yet many companies are unskilled at reaching it', *Fortune*, 1986
- 'The new old: Where the economic action is. It's the over-50 generation that will propel consumer demand in the years ahead', *Business Week*, 1985

- 'Wild to see the world: Senior citizens travel as never before', *The Globe and Mail*, 1984
- 'Chevy woos women: Sports dollars cut for major effort', *Advertising Age*, 1985
- 'The lather wars have shampoo makers hunting for niches: One promising market is the growing number of women over 40', *Business Week*, 1984
- 'Nike pushes upscale women's wear', *Advertising Age*, 1986
- 'High-fashion names knock themselves off: Career women seem to be eschewing mouseburger uniforms for name-designer lines at less than *haute* prices', *Fortune*, 1985

## 'Demassified' media

Marketers are finding it increasingly difficult to reach their chosen targets for, as the mass market is splitting apart, so too is the mass media. Nowhere is the change more apparent than in network television. In 1975 the 3-network share of prime time TV viewing was 89 per cent; by 1985 it was 73 per cent. Yet during the same period household TV viewing per day had increased from 6 hours and 7 minutes to 7 hours and 10 minutes.

This fragmentation of the network TV audience, and the rise in daily viewing time, has come about through the growth of other forms of telecommunications, which have given viewers an ever-increasing choice in what to view, and when. Nearly half of all US homes are hooked up to cable TV – and it is not surprising that the 3-network's share of the total audience in cable households was only around 55 per cent in 1985. About one third of American households have VCRs, and in 1985 some 700 million cassettes were rented. Predictions for VCR penetration range as high as two-thirds of all homes by 1990. And whereas in 1975 there were about 100 independent TV stations, by 1985 there were nearly 250, though consolidations were bringing that number down. Some independents are starting to rival the major networks in size. For example, the Tribune Co. and Rupert Murdoch each have slightly more than 18 per cent penetration of total TV households, compared with just over 19 per cent for NBC, the smallest of the big three. Looming over the horizon is possibly the greatest change to come: international broadcasting via satellite.

After surveying its panel of media executives, *Advertising Age* in

1984 concluded that: 'the growing number of choices in audience availability within (the) mass market is forcing marketers to rethink their strategies'. One top agency official said that: 'Audience segmentation, or 'demassification', is the biggest underlying trend in all major media.' In 1985, Richard Edel, in an *Advertising Age* article, 'Advertisers switch buying functions', said: 'A revolution in consumer reading and viewing habits is threatening to shake up time-honoured traditions of broadcast advertising.'

## Measuring target audiences

One of the biggest shake ups is in the ways audiences are now measured, and how marketers then allocate their media budgets. As with viewing patterns, much of this change is technology-driven.

Leo Bogart, in a 1986 *Journal of Advertising Research* article, 'What forces shape the future of advertising research', concluded that:

Technological changes in the media pose new and different problems of accurate audience measurement. Ingenious attempts are now being made to improve on the established methods of producing the ratings on which the whole structure of broadcasting programming has become dependent. But there will surely be a desire on the part of advertisers to know more about audiences than the revised ratings will tell them. (3)

One thing they want to know is, what are people doing when their TV is turned on? Bogart cited one American study which, with the aid of stop-motion video cameras, recorded household TV patterns. Bogart reported that the researchers found that: 'No one is in the room 15 per cent of the time the TV set is one and . . . when people are in the room, they are actually looking at the set three-fifths of the time.' Bogart concluded: 'This research raises fundamental questions about the meaning of 'audience' statistics.' In particular, results such as these raise fundamental questions about audiences rating figures based on diary records kept by household panels.

## Cross-impact

Two recent trends are having a cross-impact on each other: the mass market that is fragmenting and the proliferation of telecommunications alternatives. Together these two forces are hastening a number of changes in media and buyer behaviour research and applications.

In mid-1986 the E.S.O.M.A.R. (European Society for Opinion and Marketing Research) Conference on 'Marketing, Advertising and Research; are there East and West?' addressed this issue. Arranged in cooperation with the J.M.A. (Japan Marketing Association) and the A.R.F. (Advertising Research Foundation of the USA), the conference was only the second such meeting between three of the world's major associations in the fields of research, marketing and advertising. The A.R.F. session on 'US advertising research today – opportunities from technology and market changes for marketing, advertising and media and research' was probably one of the few public forums where top executives of the major media and consumer research firms in the US have openly discussed their views – and their own company's latest developments – on audience and consumer research.

## New measurement system needed

William McKenna, President and Chief Operating Officer of Scan-America, Inc., Chicago, Illinois, told the delegates that, in the US anyway, television is now:

> the victim of target audience fragmentation. Remote controlled television sets, cable television, multi-set homes, VCRs and direct satellite broadcast are but a few examples of the technological trends that fragment and reduce in size the audience available in any one programme segment for television commercials. (4)

As a result, claimed McKenna, advertisers and marketers are asking for a new measurement system:

> one capable of providing advertisers with a continuous flow of consumer targeting information; and one that is based upon the product consumption and media exposure of the world's consumer populations.

The solution appears to be 'single-source' data – which in the US means a system that combines the continuous measurement of product purchasing and TV viewing in the one household. If the predictions of its proponents come true, single-source data will provide a dramatically improved way by which marketers and advertisers target their advertising and promotional activities, particularly under test-marketing conditions. Single-source data is the result of two developing technologies: data scanning devices, which measure product purchasing patterns, and 'people meter' devices, which monitor household viewing. The two types of separately collected data are linked up in a centralized storage and disseminating facility provided by a number of research firms now operating in the US: (see Figure 9.1)

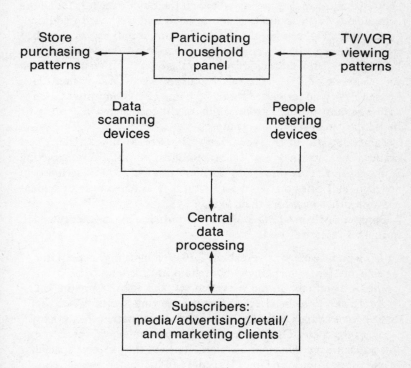

**Figure 9.1 Single-source research**

## 1984 and all that

In each home all participating members are issued with electronic access cards, resembling a credit card, which they use in stores to record their purchases. All supermarkets in the test area are recruited as participants in the study, which may mean that the research company pays for the installation of the scanners. When shopping, the respondent's identity code is typed into the store's computerized register by a cashier who also records all purchases by scanning each item's bar code. The shopping records are then transferred to a centralized processing facility where all the buying records for all the respondents in the household are collated and tracked. In addition, each cable TV set in the home is monitored by an attached microprocessor which records the programmes and commercials being played, and automatically transmits each day's results through the telephone lines to the research company's central computer. Each household is paid for participating by being offered incentives such as cash discounts off their grocery bills, or the chance to win bonus gifts in regular sweepstakes and contests.

Aimée Stern, in a 1985 *Dun's Business Month* article, 'Test marketing enters a new era', said that: 'Electronic mini-test marketing is a science fiction film come to life. Imagine 2500 households in sixteen small cities scattered across the US watched over by a giant computer that monitors their lives.'

Barbara Buell, in a 1985 *Business Week* article, 'Big brother gets a job in market research', said:

It's a bit Orwellian.... At about 2.30 each morning, a computer dials the James C. Sullivan household in Pittsfield, Mass., taps into a black box on the television set, and silently siphons off information on the sleeping family's viewing habits. When the Sullivans shop, a computer at the local supermarket tracks their every purchase. Their cable TV programs don't always carry the regularly scheduled commercials. Instead, they receive special messages from a private TV studio in Pittsfield, a city of more than 50 000 about two hours west of Boston. A lot of personal detail on the Sullivans goes into the computer. It knows what food their cat eats, the favourite cereal of their three children, Bryan, 8, Coleen, 5, and Christine, 4, and even what deodorant Debra, 28 and Jim, 30, use.

One marketing expert, who requested anonymity, jokingly told Stern that: 'The only thing that isn't known about (such) people is how many times they fool around.'

Once the emotional reaction is overcome, it is not difficult to see how Buell could say that this high-tech approach is 'changing the way companies like Procter & Gamble, Campbell Soup, and Gillette try out new products and decide where to broadcast their commercials. These innovative research companies are targeting smaller samples of the public than ever before and testing them more extensively'. Advocates claim that single-source results are more accurate and available faster and more cheaply than traditional test-market methods, three indispensable attributes in today's high-speed marketing.

Various approaches to single-source data collection are being developed and refined, as are the possible ways in which the results can be used. One top advertising executive predicted to *Advertising Age*, in a 1986 article, 'ARF panel projects future role of media', that media planning will become 'market investment planning, combining trade and consumer promotion and media allocation into one unified discipline'. Not everyone agrees. The VP-Research for NBC-TV told *Advertising Age* that the people meter would be defunct by the year 2000, and that a form of the diary methodology would still be the primary form of demographic measurement in TV. *Advertising Age* reported that the networks were displeased with recent people-meter results which showed that, in some cases, audiences had been over-reported by the diary method. Judging by what has already been discovered, there will be more surprises to come.

## BehaviourScan

Gerald Eskin, a former econometrician and associate professor of marketing and now vice-chairman and a founding member of Information Resources, Inc., of Chicago, Illinois, told the E.S.O.M.A.R. audience that his company's system, called BehaviorScan, was originally set up in 1979 in two test markets: Marion, Indiana, and Pittsfield, Massachusetts – where Buell based her 1985 *Business Week* story. At the time of its formation, the concept was so appealing that clients such as Quaker Oats, P&G, Kraft and Coca-Cola signed on for future services. By 1983 IRI's ten biggest clients were

Dart & Kraft, General Foods, General Mills, Campbell Soup, Nabisco Brands, Procter & Gamble, Quaker Oats, Ralston Purina, R.J. Reynolds Industries, and R.T. French. BehaviorScan now monitors more than 3000 households in each of eight small-town markets. By the end of 1986 it expects to operate in 30 small-towns and neighbourhood clusters within larger cities, with over 50000 households being measured.

A feature of the BehaviorScan system is that the TV monitor makes a recording every five seconds, providing very fine measures of household viewing. Eskin presented results showing the proportion of viewers who switched channels either prior to, during, or immediately after commercial breaks, which typically last up to two minutes. His argument was that 'reach' figures tend to overstate the true nature of audience viewing patterns, since some viewers – especially those with remote controllers – briefly flick across to other channels during commercial breaks.

## Leverage index

BehaviorScan can also calculate which TV programmes and dayparts attract the heavier purchasers of any given brand or product group – a critical issue as the mass market splinters and marketers aim new products at more narrowly defined, and harder to reach, target groups. This information allows each client to calculate a 'leverage index' for any given programme. If one programme has a leverage index of 120, this means that viewers of that programme have a 20 per cent higher per capita consumption of the product category than the general viewing population – hence the attraction of single-source data to clients looking for greater efficiencies in their media buying. Using various linear programming techniques, the astute media buyer – by juggling programmes with similar target audience rating points to find those with the highest leverage indices – can optimize a brand's advertising schedule, saving his or her client enormous sums of money, and increasing the chance of the brand's success.

Eskin mentioned the Campbell Soup Company of Camden, New Jersey, as one company which managed to achieve about 10 per cent in leverage across all its advertised brands. Eskin proclaimed:

> What this means is that 10 per cent more impressions were delivered against target buyers, where target buyers were defined by each brand according to its marketing and advertising

objectives. This is equivalent to increasing the ad budget by 10 per cent under the old scheduling system. Another way to interpret this is, with a 10 per cent increase in leverage the advertising spending could be reduced by 10 per cent with no loss of impressions delivered against target buyers. (5)

Eskin also claimed that, with an increasing proportion of a brand's support expenditure being shifted from theme advertising to various forms of trade and consumer promotions – a trend discussed in Chapter 8 – BehaviorScan can provide both the retailer and the marketer with detailed breakdowns of the effect on sales of various forms of price-offs, in-store displays or any combinations of promotional efforts. Since this data is so applicable at the individual store level, this is one reason why retailers are willing to participate in the programme. And a side benefit to marketers is that they can share the single-source data with the retailers, thereby helping to equalize their power relationship.

Eskin also argued that advertising and promotion should no longer be considered as separate issues, with separate data bases or research programmes. One strength of single-source data bases is that the impact of promotional activities can be linked to various media schedules, and the results tracked in terms of purchasing responses. 'Should promotion for a new product start before, at the same time, or after the advertising starts?' he asked rhetorically. On that important score he had no research results to give away.

Felix Kessler, in a 1986 *Fortune* article, 'High-tech shocks in ad research', was able to enlighten us however. He said that the:

sophisticated new techniques of market research are yielding fascinating and sometimes startling facts about how consumers behave and how advertising works – or doesn't. The new methods, introduced a few years ago, have begun to prove their value in an era when familiar brands are dying, new brands are flopping, and all brands are having a tougher time getting on cramped supermarket shelves. On this market research frontier, some of Madison Avenue's most venerable verities are being disproved. Most surprising finding so far: Trying to goose sales by a big increase in a product's TV ad budget often doesn't pay.

Kessler reported that, after studying the results of more than 450 advertising tests, executives of IRI concluded that the number of times a commercial plays on TV is usually less important than its copy or focus matter. The IRI argument was that if a company tests an equivalent $10 million advertising campaign with one panel, and a $5 million campaign with another, and both panels record the same purchasing reaction after a year, 'that raises the possibility that a reduction in spending might be in order'. Kessler added that: 'This notion is understandably spooky to people who work in advertising agencies, which generally get paid a percentage of what their clients spend.'

This high-tech testing is already highlighting one important point – when it comes to understanding what makes advertising work, advertisers still don't have the answers. As one top ad executive admitted to Kessler: 'It's frightening, but brands double their ad budgets in most of these tests, and nothing happens to sales. That says there have to be a lot of other variables out there.' Another added: 'The one thing we have learned is, there is no magic formula that works on everything.'

This in itself is an important step forward in marketing thinking. Kessler concluded that marketers will have to proceed on a case-by-case basis to find out what works in terms of different creative approaches, media mix and expenditure levels. The end result will be less opinion and fancy, and more hard realism, particularly as the various research approaches to single-source data get developed.

## ScanAmerica

ScanAmerica Inc. is a joint venture of Control Data's Arbitron Rating Co., which measures TV viewing, and SAMI (Selling Areas-Marketing Inc.), a Time Inc. subsidiary. William McKenna, President and Chief Operating Officer of ScanAmerica, told the E.S.O.M.A.R. conference that while his company had only set up a 200-household panel in Denver, Colorado, in late 1985, its target was a 5000-household national panel eventually. McKenna also claimed that ScanAmerica had also introduced a few innovations to single-source data collection. One is an on-screen 'prompt' which periodically appears on the top corner of the TV screen, and reminds viewers to confirm their presence in the room by pushing their identity number on their people meter.

Another is a hand-held portable bar scanner issued to each household. Traditionally, in an area where a single-source project was conducted, all the grocery retailers would either agree to install the necessary scanning equipment, or would be willing to modify their own in-store scanner software, to allow their equipment to accept each panelist's identity card before their purchases get recorded. Two limitations of this system are that not all stores are willing to participate, and that some consumers will occasionally make purchases outside the test area. The hand-held scanner, which is a 16k microprocessor, allows panellists to record their purchases to be recorded at home while they unpack their shopping bags. The data is then transmitted through a device attached to participants' TVs.

McKenna announced that:

> The ScanAmerica design has responded directly to the single-source system objectives developed by the advertising industry.... It contains TV viewing and product purchase data obtained from the same source – individuals within the same household. The design can be used in a continuous measurement system and placed in a projectable sample of consumer households in most countries of the world.

The implications are obvious for any marketing company contemplating a global approach to their business.

## TestSight

When you are among the last to enter a market, it pays to have something special to offer. A.C. Nielsen Co., a subsidiary of Dun & Bradstreet, and currently the giant of TV-audience research for the big-three networks, claims it has done just that. In a 1985 *Advertising Age* article, 'Tracking Nielsen's ERIM development', Jack Honomichl explained how the company broke a few of its own operating rules – and spent some $16 million – in setting up its TestSight system to counter BehaviorScan, in particular: 'Nielson was playing catchup, and to be really successful, it had to beat IRI at its own game.'

In 1984 Nielsen introduced its ERIM TestSight system in two test markets involving 2500 households in both Sioux Falls, South Dakota, and Springfield, Missouri. William Gold, vice-president for marketing for Nielsen, claimed that TestSight's main advantage is that it can deliver test commercials to both cable and non-cable households. In this way test markets can be selected without having to worry about whether they have been developed as cable markets. To support his claim that this flexibility is advantageous, Gold presented results showing that the behaviour of cable households is different from non-cable households with respect to television viewing and product purchasing. Not only is cable household viewing higher than non-cable, but so too is the amount of channel switching – which is not surprising, given the greater choice of viewing in cable households, noted Gold. In addition, in most product categories, cable households exhibit higher purchasing rates compared with non-cable. 'The main implication', observed Gold, 'is that test results from a cable only system in the US are biased. This may result in different marketing decisions than would have otherwise been made.'(6)

Whichever system wins the most support – and notable by its absence from the speaker's podium was AGB Television Research, a British-based company which is currently beating out Nielsen in the audience-research wars in Europe, and is now making a bid for the US market – the method of measuring viewing and purchasing behaviour patterns has now dramatically changed. Advertisers, marketers and the media are still trying to adjust to some of these changes.

## Buying time

One such adjustment involves how firms do their media buying – an increasingly important function when mass markets splinter, and marketers aim their products and services to ever-smaller and more narrowly defined target groups. And when a new research technique suggests that heavy buyers of their brand are more likely to watch programme A than programme B, then they are going to sit up and take notice. This is particularly true if they are also informed they may be able to reduce their total advertising budget as well, with no appreciable loss in sales.

The new approach to buying time may already be taking effect. In 1985 network advertising budgets declined 2.5 per cent from 1984, although the networks argued that 1984 was an unseasonally high year due to the Olympics and the election. By contrast, spending on alternative media, such as direct mail, cable and syndicated TV was up by proportionately much more, which may have reflected the attempts by marketers to target their advertising more efficiently for less expense.

All of this is putting pressure on the networks. In 1987 The *Wall Street Journal* reported that, as a result of initial people-meter tests by Nielsen, fewer viewers were watching many programmes than diaries were indicating – in one test all top ten shows were claimed to be overstated by the diary method. Not surprisingly, the *Wall Street Journal* reported that: 'Advertising agencies, which place about $8 billion in advertising on network television annually, want to base new ad rates on people-meter ratings alone – and, they hope, wring price cuts from the networks.' Equally unsurprisingly, the head of research at one of the big three reported: 'We would be fools to accept a number that's lower just because the measurement changed – the audience is the same.'

Whatever the cause and effect, 'efficiency' and 'effectiveness' are the current hot buzzwords of TV broadcast buyers, according to *Advertising Age*, and the major networks are feeling the impact in a variety of ways. Christine Dugas, in a 1985 *Business Week* article, 'A harder sell for Madison Avenue', argued that as more of the total support expenditures of packaged goods companies, in particular, go to promotional purposes, the tendency will be to take money away from advertising. As a result they are putting pressure on their advertising agencies to reduce the costs of producing commercials and to increase their effectiveness in buying media space and time.

Some companies have already set up specialist task forces to find more economical ways to buy media. In 1984 P&G set up a twelve-member group, each responsible for a specific advertising medium. Verne Gay, in a 1984 *Advertising Age* article, 'P&G cuts new media pie', claimed that, according to one source, the presence of the taskforce 'has resulted in a whole new way of looking at the media world from P&G headquarters'. Gay explained that:

Each media expert will ascertain gross ratings point buying levels for each brand and then map the best and most efficient route for advertising.... All this activity adds up to a revolutionary media thinking at a nation's No. 1 advertiser, a company long known for staunch conservatism and ability to notch greater media efficiencies than its competitors.

It is not difficult to imagine single-source data being an integral part of this new drive for efficiency and effectiveness. It is not a trend that will please the nation's advertising agencies.

Some large companies have discovered another effective way to reduce their advertising costs; they are taking media buying responsibilities away from their advertising agencies and forming their own in-house units, often to buy in conjunction with specialist media buying services. This is not surprising. Some of the recent mergers – Procter & Gamble with Richardson Vicks, Philip Morris with General Foods, and R.J. Reynolds with Nabisco – have created packaged goods giants, each of which now spends more than one billion dollars annually on media. This gives them enormous buying clout, both with the networks and the agencies who do their buying. Should they all decide to set up in-house media buying units, the impact on Madison Avenue would be momentous. Even if they don't, their buying power with the networks gives them enormous leverage. One media buying executive informed *Business Week* in a 1985 article, 'New? Improved? The brand name merger', that these new giants should be able to negotiate as much as 10 per cent discount with the networks. A marketing consultant said that the bigger companies would also get priority rights to the most sought-after time slots. As GM's chairman, Roger Smith, said in chapter one: 'Use your weight to your advantage.'

## Selecting targets

Even as demographic, economic and social forces are leading to a splintering of the mass markets, American marketers are finding new ways to pinpoint their target groups. Product bar coding, point-of-sale and in-home scanners, plastic credit cards and people meters are making it possible for marketers to measure and monitor critical information – who is buying and watching what, when and where. The new technologies also provide the means by which marketers can conduct precision product and commercial testing in a near real-world environment – all at an affordable cost and in double-quick time.

The new technologies will continually develop, and will be expanded to cover a host of media offerings, since advertisers also need to precisely target their advertising budgets. Network TV is under increasing pressure from specialist TV, radio and print media. Direct response advertising is one of the fastest growing sectors. As reported in *The Economist* in 1985: 'Businesses want forms of advertising that are targeted more accurately on the consumers they are after – and they are getting them . . . the blunt instrument of mass media is becoming more pointed.'

As was noted in Chapter 1, consumer goods companies such as Campbell Soup Co. have already recognized that traditional mass marketing – and mass media – approaches are no longer appropriate. Instead, many are adopting a more 'regionalized' approach. For Campbell this means a Creole soup for Southern markets, a red-bean soup for Hispanic areas in Texas and California, a soured pickle for the north-west, and a spicier pinto bean for the south-west.

In a 1987 article, 'Marketing's new look', *Business Week* observed:

> As the regionalization trend spreads, it will have broad implications for marketing and for the US media. It will mean increased fragmentation of product lines, with numerous products custom-made by national manufacturers for local tastes and fashions. Even when the product itself remains the same, regionalization will mean less national advertising and more local targeting – bad news for network TV and national magazines but good news for local media such as newspapers and radio. Finally, regionalization will mean greater use of coupons, sales promotions, and co-operative programs with retailers.

Regionalization will also probably mean that manufacturers will locate certain categories of marketing people closer to their markets. As was discussed in Chapter 8, there is already pressure on companies to adopt a more matrix-like approach to their marketing structure, in order to extend horizontal communications and decision making. *Business Week* reported that Campbell has:

> carved the US into 22 regions. There is a combined sales and marketing force in each one, which no longer operates merely as an extension of the corporate office. Every regional staff studies marketing strategies and media buying and gets an ad and trade-promotion budget. .... Campbell, in effect, is converting some of its local sales staff into autonomous marketers.

*Business Week* offered another reason for regionalization. It 'may give consumer-goods companies a way to get on a nearly equally footing with increasingly powerful supermarket and grocery chains. The regional marketing staff will allow them to store up-to-date information on individual stores'.

Echoing the comments made by the chairman of Ogilvy & Mather in Chapter 8, that creating 'shelf space management systems' was a new development in the agency's 'full service', agenda, *Business Week* stated that Campbell had used its computer systems to help the Grand Union Co. supermarket chain to 'create a detailed diagram of the most profitable way to arrange the shelves of its soup section'. While this move was praised by Grand Union's vice-president for merchandising operations, *Business Week* pointed out: 'Campbell's efforts to co-operate with the retailers may win the company something much more important than plaudits. They could ease the relentless, profit-paring pressure to offer concessions to the trade.'

It is quite possible that a combination of research technologies, splintered target markets, and a regionalized sales and marketing structure will mean more balancing of power between manufacturers and retailers – many of whom are also adopting a more localized approach to their business strategies. The eventual losers will probably be the network media suppliers and the now more assailable regional brand manufacturers.

## New media forms

Should marketers substantially alter their traditional approaches to reflect the splintering of mass markets and the growing power of retailers, then new media formats are likely to follow close behind. A top ad agency executive informed *Marketing News* in a 1984 article, 'Ads in year 2000: agency executives forecast their appearance and delivery', that one of the biggest advances over the next twenty years will be in the ways in which advertisements are aimed at selected target groups. He predicted that, by the year 2000, almost every interest group – 'consumer, commercial, religious, political, sports, entertainment, intellectual, social, activist, passivist, and hobbyist' – will have their own TV channel, access cable or satellite transmitter. Newspapers and magazines will be satellite-transmitted to printing facilities, with opportunities for spectacular advertising effects – three-dimensional, holography and possible pre-programmed sound or optical chips ready for activation by the reader. Digital signal processing will result in more effects and higher-quality sound and image broadcasting, including holography transmission and reception in the home. Instant communications between listeners and broad-casters for polling, opinions and purchasing will be feasible.

Market researchers will also keep pace with these changes, suggested Laurence Gold to the 1986 E.S.O.M.A.R. conference:

The operative word will be sensors, devices that may be carried, worn or even implanted just under the skin, if we can persuade people to accept them. ... The sensors will 'read' the wearer and identify not only who it is, but his or her physiological state, perhaps in response to stimuli created by television programs or advertising messages.

And therein lies the rub. As the senior agency executive announced to *Marketing News*:

One of the secrets of successful advertising in any age is to stand out from the crowd, whether we're talking about 1884, 1984 or 2084. Advertising may be getting more sophisticated, with better production values, but the job an ad has to do has always been and will always be the same – to select its audience, separate itself from the competition, and sell.

In this respect, at least, marketing has not entered a new era.

In the next chapter another issue that will always be the same – marketing 'value' to the consumer – will be explored. What has changed is how marketers add superior value to their products and services, and how they must now out-execute their competitors with respect to *all* the tasks involved.

# 10    Leverage by marketing 'value'

As discussed in Chapter 3, US marketers are realizing that their biggest challenge is not to develop strategies and plans, but to make them work. In particular, they need to make them work better than their competitors. Out-executing the competition is a prerequisite for any sort of success in the many turbulent markets that now characterize much of US industry.

## Out-executing the competition

Collectively, a great number of external and internal forces have turned many formerly stable and secure domestic markets into veritable battle zones, and in the process they have led to a rethinking of the ways in which firms should compete. The chairman and CEO of Wendy's International Inc. explained to Business Week in 1983 that: 'The main thrust today is taking business away from the competition, and that fact, more than any other, is modifying our business. . . . You have to out-execute the competition, and that's why marketing is more important than ever before.'

For many companies, out-executing the competition is easier said than done. In Chapter 2, Thomas Bonoma was quoted as saying, in his 1984 *Harvard Business Review* article, that most firms and many managers had real difficulty with what he termed 'low-level execution tasks'. In his 1985 book, *The Marketing Edge*, Bonoma offered one reason why: 'Business school training, it seems, has bred too much of an armchair general's skill at commanding an army from the safety of the rear lines and too little of the master sergeant's ability to take a platoon up a hill under heavy fire.' (1)

According to Bonoma, marketing execution takes place at four structural levels in the corporation:

- *Policies:* the directives issued by management that determine either the firm's marketing identity, such as its shared culture and purpose, or its basic *directions,* for example, as formulated in its marketing strategy.

  - *Systems:* the marketing tasks that are routine to a firm's ongoing operations, and which attempt to allocate resources and control marketing practices, for example, its sales force reporting and control procedures.

    - *Programs:* the firm's guidelines for integrating low-level actions in order to maximize sales of a product line, or penetration of a target segment, for example, the tactics by which its key accounts are managed.

      - *Actions:* the low-level 'blocking and tackling' tasks by which the essentials of the marketing job get executed, for example, advertising, pricing, sales force management, trade promotions, etc.

## Adding value

While Bonoma felt that managers have the most difficulties with the low-level actions, he also argued that:

Programs are the most natural 'unit of analysis' to the marketer. It is with these formally or informally tailored combinations of product, promotion and distribution that the marketer hopes to add unique value to his firm's offerings and differential satisfaction to the customer.

The concept of added value has become an important issue for US marketers. In their bellwether 1981 article in *Business Horizons*, 'The misuse of marketing: an American tragedy', Bennett and Cooper argued that the failure to deliver product value was the main factor contributing to America's lack of international competitiveness:

The marketing concept has diverted our attention from the product and its manufacture; instead we have focused our strategy on responses to market wants and have become preoccupied with advertising, selling, and promotion. And in the process, product value has suffered. (2)

According to the authors, the American task was clear:

> We must go beyond the marketing concept. The answer lies not just in satisfying customer needs but in providing a product of superior value to the market place. We must adopt a product value concept.... The product value concept is a business orientation that recognizes that product value is the key to profits. It stresses competing on the basis of customer need satisfaction with superior, high-value products. Value depends on the customer's perception of the product attributes, which are largely a function of the firm's technological, design, and manufacturing strengths and skills.

In other words, the emphasis on marketing programmes and actions may lead to too much reliance on the traditional marketing activities. To add value, a firm needs to think in terms of *all* the processes – R&D, production and operations, trade and consumer marketing – involved in bringing products to the market place. Bennett and Cooper said there should be no limit to a firm's focus:

> Above all, the firm must recognize what it does well. It must be aware of its distinctive competencies and unique resources. Having identified these areas of excellence, the firm should use these in its task of producing a product of superior value.

Schultz and Dewar, in their 1983 *Journal of Consumer Marketing* article, 'Retailers in control', agreed. They argued that one of the important ways for manufacturers to ensure their brands survived was to look for ways to differentiate their products from competitors:

> Build in some value that your competition can't or won't be able to offer. Your absolute goal should always be to try to move from price competition to brand competition, for that is the only way brands will survive in the concentrated market place. Often, that means changing your outlook from volume to profit or margin. And, it is always easier to justify a price differential for a product that is significantly better. (3)

Peters and Austin, in *A Passion for Excellence*, also agreed:

To test our point, we stopped in early 1983 at a local co-operatively owned grocery store in Palo Alto, California, and priced what any fool (any engineer at least) would believe was clearly a commodity – one-ply toilet paper. The *generic* type, in a four-roll pack, was going for 79c at the time. Then we travelled just two blocks to the nearest 7–11. There we priced Procter & Gamble's Charmin entrant into the one-ply sweepstakes; the tag was fully $1.99. Within two blocks, an 'upscale' service-delivery vehicle (7–11) and P&G's long-term devotion to product quality (and squeezability) had added $1.20 (value) to the price of a four-roll package of one-ply toilet paper! Needless to say, the returns to P&G and Southland (owners of 7–11) exceed those of most co-op stores and generic producers by a tidy sum. (4)

## Expectations of value

Theodore Levitt, in *The Marketing Imagination*, said:

There is no such thing as a commodity. All goods and services can be differentiated.... A product is, to the potential buyer, a complex cluster of value satisfactions. The generic 'thing' or 'essence' is not itself the product.... Expectations are what people buy, not things. (5)

As Bennett and Cooper claimed: 'Value depends on the customer's perception of the product's attributes, which are largely a function of the firm's technological, design, and manufacturing strengths and skills.' Cognitive buyer theory suggests that consumers seek information in order to make a rational assessment of a product's attributes and benefits before making a conscious decision to buy or not to buy. Other theories suggest that consumers respond, perhaps unconsciously, to cues which attract their attention and affect their buying behaviour – with only a limited cognitive process. Consider the following:

One of the ladies stood up and she said, 'I'll tell you what I don't like.' She said, 'I don't like your fish', and we said, 'What do you mean, you don't like our fish?' She said, 'Well, it's not fresh. I like to go to a fish market and buy fresh fish.' The fish guy was there, and he stood up and said, 'What do you mean it's not fresh? We get it fresh every morning from Fulton Fish Market, and we get it fresh from the Boston piers every morning.' He said, 'I guarantee you it's fresh!' She said, 'But it's packaged. It's in a [plastic wrapped] supermarket package.' So what we did was to set up a fish bar with ice in it. And we did that right after the meeting. Now there's wrapped fish in one place, but some people like to buy it fresh right off the ice, so it's available across the aisle at the same price off the ice. Our packaged fish sales didn't decrease at all, but we doubled our total fish sales.

From: *A Passion for Excellence*: Stew Leonard Jr, a retailer, recounting an incident during a customer focus group meeting, as shown in the PBS film, *In Search of Excellence*.

This argument for added value raises the question: what *is* the advantage to the marketer for adding value? For most marketers, the concept of added value is predicated on the belief that consumers will pay more, for more. The search for added profits through added value is thus seen as a viable goal by many marketers trying to avoid cut-throat price competition in over-crowded markets. The converse may also be viable. Marketers may achieve added profits if they can persuade consumers to pay less, for less, and still receive satisfaction. It all depends on how firms create expectations of value in the first place, through their positioning strategies, and whether these expectations can then be met.

## Premium position for an ice cream

Products aimed at the affluent must continually reinforce or enhance the premium image of the product, said Charles Kanan, the president of Haagen-Dazs Shoppe Co. Inc., makers of the top-of-line ice cream, to delegates at the 1986 Promotion Marketing Association of America's Education Conference:

The mystique that surrounds premium products is fragile. One error in how the product is presented to consumers can destroy that image with a single blow. The wrong promotion, even the wrong execution of the right promotion, can shatter what has been built forever.

The Haagen-Dazs firm believes that consumers will trade up for real quality, and has striven to maintain its 'reputation for excellence, for perfection, for a premium product well worth the price', explained Kanan. As a result, the company will not run promotions solely to achieve a short-term boost in sales: 'There's nothing wrong with aggressive promotion, but remember that the affluent resent being "sold at"; they prefer being "presented to".'

Barry Feig, in a 1986 *Advertising Age* article, 'Products need share of heart', said that Haagen-Dazs succeeds because it wins the hearts of consumers, not just their minds. 'Achieve a share of heart and share of mind will follow', he said, 'yet companies insist on separating the product benefit from the emotion feel.' The trouble is, continued Feig, marketers 'over-intellectualize' their product benefits, and ignore 'the quirks of human personality that really make or break any product. . . . A purchased product is a manifestation of how consumers want to feel about themselves, how they want others to see and react to them. It's up to the marketer to make everything about the product contribute to a positive self-concept.'

'Haagen-Dazs won the war of hearts with a product that should fail by most contemporary standards,' persisted Feig. Yet:

> people stand in lines to pay $2 for a Haagen-Dazs ice cream cone that's loaded with extra butterfat, calories and cholesterol. . . . So why should it succeed in a health and body-conscious society like ours? Because enjoying Haagen-Dazs makes people feel good about themselves. They can give in to temptation. And they rationalize it by leaving off the potato for dinner.

## Jaguar's value

By 1980 Americans had stopped feeling good about buying Jaguar cars, and no amount of rationalization could get *them* behind a wheel of what once represented the epitome of British style, engineering and refinement in a luxury automobile.

Rena Bartos claimed in 1986 that: 'Brand and company images are built on trust. Once that trust has been eroded, it is very difficult to recapture it. An organization's reputation is a very precious commodity. It warrants very careful cultivation and protection.' By 1980, when compared with BMW, Mercedes-Benz and the rest of Europe's élite, Jaguar had lost its premium reputation, and was fast becoming a marque with no value.

That Jaguar regained the trust of American buyers of luxury motor cars, with a product that was essentially more than a decade old, was an epic achievement. Jaguar managed to claw its way back into the American market – and profitability – by a renewed commitment to the basics of automobile manufacturing and marketing. In three of the four stages in the flow of goods process – manufacturing, dealer (trade) and consumer marketing – Jaguar gained new leveraging strengths in a surprisingly short time. Through a combination of sheer hard work and sacrifice on the part of both its labour force and management, a strict quality control programme worked out with its suppliers, an invigorated American dealer network, and a new deal struck with potential buyers, Jaguar achieved more than a sevenfold increase in sales to the US in the years 1980 to 1986. There was also an element of luck – a long boom in the American economy and a rise in the US dollar occurred just when required. Most important, perhaps, the company brought in a new chairman who was under no illusions: there would be no government bail-out. Jaguar *had* to succeed on its own, or be shut down.

## The cat comes back

Writing in a special supplement on Jaguar in the British journal, *Motor*, Anthony Curtis in 1983 observed:

> There's material enough for a novel or two, as well as a clutch of business management case-histories, in both the speed and the completeness of Jaguar's remarkable return to health. Only three years ago the company was facing ruin.

1980 was indeed a nadir for Jaguar. Output had sunk from 26 500 cars in 1978 to a low of 14 000, of which 3000 were shipped to the US, Jaguar's largest foreign market. In 1976 some 7000 had gone there. Productivity was so bad that only 1.4 cars per employee were coming off the line. An expensive new paint plant, finally commissioned in 1978, was having so many teething problems that virtually every car had a major defect. In a 1984 story *Time* pointed out: 'In 1980 Jaguar was losing $1.5 million a week, and its sleek models had acquired a well-deserved reputation for shoddy workmanship and unreliability.' This comment was typical of the time – expressed admiration for what the products had once represented, tempered by criticism for what was termed the British 'disease'.

Even the sleek models were beginning to show their age. Jaguar's newest model, the XJS sports car, had been on the market for some five years, while its mainstay, the XJ sedan, was first introduced in 1968. That was the year Jaguar's parent company, British Leyland, was formed out of the merger between the Standard-Triumph and Leyland concerns, and British Motor Holdings, which itself had been formed only two years earlier by a joining of Jaguar with BMC, a company made up of the Austin, Morris, MG, Riley and Wolsely brand names. It was a merger that ultimately failed. There were too many overlapping models, too many scattered plants, and too little cooperation between managers of what in effect were competing divisions, and not enough direction from the top, for a coherent and profitable new car programme to be developed and implemented. Many of the plants were virtually under the control of militant shop stewards, and product quality and reliability were among the worst in the industry. Most models introduced in the early to mid-1970s were market failures. As with many unmanageable companies, the tragedy was that there were many excellent designers, engineers, managers and workers who were trying to do their best, despite the circumstances. Almost inevitably by 1975 the company had turned to the government for a financial bail-out and, through a series of unexpected circumstances, the energetic (Sir) Michael Edwardes was appointed chairman in 1977.

In his 1983 book, *Back from the Brink*, Edwardes admitted that Jaguar had been a difficult issue:

> In the case of Jaguar we failed to solve its many problems at the first go; the product was not reliable, the paint finish was well below par, and productivity was abysmal. Losses were enormous, but the structure of the total (BL) cars business was such that it was impossible to pull out separate results for individual operations.... Some managers were more concerned with producing new models and reaching new standards of engineering excellence than with managing the business. It proved difficult to get across to them the simple fact that Jaguar was not being managed – despite the fact that warranty costs were too high; that dissatisfied customers wrote or telephoned us from as far afield as the west coast of the United States; and that failure of components, particularly electric, was putting the reputation of the car at great risk. (6)

Edwardes half jokingly said that Jaguar's problems of quality and reliability in the US were so great that, even the most enthusiastic owners would say: 'It's better to have two, if you want to be sure one stays on the road.' Another joke, out of Germany, was that the company should provide every new Jaguar owner with a free Mini, to be carried in the trunk – the Mini could then be used to get home when the Jaguar broke down.

The task of turning Jaguar around was entrusted to John Egan who, in 1980, was the European marketing director for Canada's farm-equipment maker, Massey-Ferguson, but was persuaded to come to Jaguar as chief executive. Egan was quite familiar with the automobile industry, having worked with the AC-Delco parts operation of General Motors in the UK, and with the Unipart operation of BL, before joining Massey-Ferguson in the mid-1970s. That Egan had such a sound background in parts operations was possibly an important factor in how he set about restoring Jaguar to health.

Even though he believed that behind the poor quality and dismal sales there were some basic strengths to Jaguar, such as its strong design tradition and basic excellence of the product, Egan revealed to David Fairlamb, in a 1985 *Dun's Business Month* interview, that his mandate from Edwardes was 'to make it work or close it down'. In his book, Edwardes said that:

> John Egan believed what other Jaguar executives would not; that mounting losses made Jaguar's demise a certainty, unless the turn-around could be accomplished so quickly that the 1981 plan would show a vast improvement and the company would project a break-even, or better still a profit for 1982.

## Quality through manufacturing leverage

Curtis said that one of Egan's most important insights was 'to recognize quality as being the factor that mattered above all else.' Egan commented: 'I knew I didn't have a saleable product until the quality was right.' In a 1986 interview with *Business Week*, Egan explained: 'Improving quality was the No. 1 problem on our hit list.' He added that when he arrived at the company, Jaguar was '41st on a list of 40 cars' rated for quality by J.D. Power & Associates Inc., a US research firm that tracks new car buyers' satisfaction levels. Egan was only half joking. Michael Dale, senior vice-president for sales and marketing at

Jaguar Cars Inc. in the US, revealed in a 1986 *Fortune* article: 'How we rebuilt Jaguar in the US', that at the time of Egan's joining, Power did not include Jaguar in its survey, 'because so few of our customers were willing even to discuss the ownership of their cars'.

To find out just how bad the quality was, the company undertook its own research programme. Curtis reported that close inspection of typical cars being produced at the time showed up to 150 'significant' faults were occurring in each, ranging from paintwork to steering, for which urgent action was required. To rectify the situation, Curtis disclosed that:

> individual members of the board of directors were charged with the task of solving 12 especially vital problems; Japanese-style 'quality circles' were set up in the workforce; a dialogue with customers was established to identify particular causes of dissatisfaction; and a rather more forceful dialogue with suppliers begun.

This last point was something of an understatement. Fairlamb reported that the management taskforces found that while many of the faults were the result of in-house inefficiencies, at least 60 per cent could be traced to components bought from outside suppliers. As a result, explained Fairlamb: 'Egan called in the suppliers and threatened to buy abroad unless they shaped up. Most did; those that didn't were dropped.'

Edwardes was more expansive. He revealed that Egan's team tackled Jaguar's reliability problem:

> methodically by first ascertaining the failure rate of Jaguar components versus those of our major competitors and then by debating the facts with each supplier – usually by inviting the whole board of the supplier company to visit Jaguar's Brown Lane factory for a full discussion. Although improvements were literally demanded of suppliers, the aim was usually to go to those meetings armed with positive suggestions and solutions. Seemingly intractable problems were solved by setting up joint taskforces; to provide the right sense of urgency, the approach to warranty costs was modified when the full cost was charged to the supplier. Those suppliers who could not meet our requirements lost the business.

On the production lines a quality index system was installed to monitor each feature of every car, to allow for immediate corrective action.

Egan also set out to improve Jaguar's abysmal productivity. In 1980 some 14500 cars were being produced by about 10500 workers. This was eventually trimmed to 7200 though, as output has increased, so too has the workforce. While Jaguar invested heavily in advanced production technologies, productivity bonuses were also introduced, and all employees were issued with shares when Jaguar went public in 1984. Millions of pounds were spent on unscrambling Jaguar's shambolic system of 'jobbing' that had developed as a result of the poorly assembled vehicles coming off the lines, and which somehow had to be corrected before delivery. The situation had become so bad that there were delays of up to three months before customers received their new cars.

What Jaguar discovered was that successful cost cutting *and* improved product quality can go hand in hand, something that many other manufacturers are now also realizing. In a 1986 *Fortune* article, 'Cutting costs without killing the business', Maggie McComas argued that: 'Cost cutting is the new religion of business.' And many managers practising this religion have found that, often the biggest problem is not cost per se, but poor product quality. McComas pointed out that, in their efforts to improve their products, some companies have recently:

> adopted the 'cost of quality' measure proposed by celebrated quality expert Philip B. Crosby (*Fortune*, August 18). Essentially Crosby's measure shows the cost of doing things wrong – sending back materials that aren't up to standard, pulling defective parts off an assembly line, employing quality checkers to catch workers' mistakes, and placating disgruntled customers through warranty work. As more things come to be done right the first time, those costs shrink.

And as the product's quality goes up, companies hope that so too does customer satisfaction.

## Dealer leverage

Dale revealed that soon after taking up his post Egan made another crucial decision. He 'realized that if he was going to save Jaguar it would have to be done in the US. No other market was big enough to provide the volume he needed to bring the production line alive'. As a result, Egan held a series of meeting with the American dealers in order to explain to them what was being done to rectify the quality and delivery problems. Dale noted: 'Hearing for the first time an English auto executive really grappling with the quality problem, the dealers left the meeting feeling that there was now hope of survival.' They also left agreeing to raise their sales levels by 50 per cent in 1981.

Egan struck a bargain with the dealers that helped them through the low period of 1980–81. BL was in the process of eliminating the loss-making Triumph and MG marques from its lineup, the very cars that had previously provided the bulk of sales for the US dealers. However Egan believed there was a clear conflict of interest when Jaguar cars were sold alongside non-luxury cars, and was determined to have his US dealers sell exclusively in the top end of the market. As the President of Jaguar Cars Inc. told Peter Dron, in a 1983 *Motor* interview, the dealers who can sell small sports cars are not necessarily the same as those who can sell luxury cars: 'The sort of people who buy our cars have nice houses, they wear expensive clothes, and they live in style. The sort of showroom that will attract them must match that style.' (Three years later Honda used a similar argument when it decided to sell its new entrant, the Legend, into the luxury car sector by setting up a new dealer network.)

Dale explained how, in 1980, the dealers who were not deserting were struggling to move their backlog of unsold vehicles. At the same time they were under pressure to do so from BL, which itself was in cash flow difficulties in the UK. To meet BL's demands would have required a professional liquidator and that, claimed Dale 'would have made the dealers instantly uncompetitive, and among the victims would have been most of the 250 Jaguar dealers, who also carried MG, Triumph, or both'.

In order to ease the transition to luxury cars, the parent company agreed to buy back – on a type of sale-or-return arrangement – excess Rover, Triumph and MG parts over a two-year period. As Dron pointed out this was 'an expensive gesture, but one that not only rescued some dealers from disaster but also one that expressed a belief in the future for an organization that would now sell only Jaguars'.

By 1982 Jaguar was beginning to show positive results in the US. The reasons for this turn-around, said Fairlamb, were that:

the company was making quality cars again, and they were

being delivered on time following a strict discipline imposed by Egan. That boosted dealers' morale dramatically, especially in the US, and they once again began putting time and effort into persuading customers to buy Jaguars and giving more floor space to the car.

So much so that sales in the US had gone from just under 5000 in 1981 to slightly over 10 000 in 1982. Dale explained: 'It was heady stuff for a company that was in ruins only 24 months before, and we started to dream in quite a different way about our future.'

However, while the dealers were successful in selling the cars, there remained the question, could they service them to a sufficient standard to maintain buyer loyalty and goodwill? Dale revealed that: 'Some dealers, it was clear, did not know the meaning of good service.' He believed that one problem was partly to do with numbers. While the number of dealers had shrunk to under 200 from 250 two years earlier, in 1982 Jaguar were selling only 49 cars per dealer, against 161 for Mercedes-Benz. A problem was that many dealers couldn't afford the facilities, equipment or skilled mechanics and management to compete in the luxury end of the market.

These fears were being borne out by customer tracking surveys, carried out by J.D. Power and begun in 1982. Each month about one hundred new Jaguar buyers were contacted, and telephone interviews then took place over a three-stage period: after they had their car for 35 days, 8 months, and 18 months. In this way information was gained about their purchasing process, their initial reactions to the car and dealer, and their later experiences and problems with both car and servicing. Similar interviews were also carried out with drivers of other makes, for comparative purposes.

The early results confirmed their worse fears. Dale explained:

> The Power interviewers taped some of their conversations, and the chorus of complaints we heard gave us an all too clear picture of what it meant to own a Jaguar: dirty service-department waiting rooms, incompetent mechanics, indifferent dealers.... Hearing the customers' own words energized everybody.... The message started to reach down right from the top of Jaguar: 'You'd better satisfy the customer, because we are not going to be content with anything else.'

By early 1984 Jaguar's top management concluded they had to shrink their dealer network by about 20 per cent in order to raise its overall quality and effectiveness. Since federal and state laws were in force to prevent manufacturers from arbitrarily terminating a franchise without acknowledgement of the dealer's investment, a buyout package was offered. Each outgoing dealer was offered $5000 goodwill for every car sold in the past twelve months, plus a negotiated price for parts. The total cost to Jaguar was some $10 million, or nearly a year's profit. Egan admitted: 'It's bold, and generally when we've been bold we've been right.' Dale reported that in one country, where three dealers were eliminated and a new one appointed, Jaguar's market share went up tenfold.

## Customer leverage

While Jaguar was steadily improving its car quality, delivery scheduling and dealer performance, it still had to convince a critical market that the car was worth buying. Certainly price was working in Jaguar's favour, given the relationship of the dollar to the pound. In 1983 Dron pointed out: 'The cheapest Mercedes-Benz gas car is close to 50000 dollars, and the BMW 733 is around 41000 and very austere and teutonic inside. The only other rival is the Cadillac Seville, at 27000 dollars, and that isn't even worth discussing. At 35000 dollars, the Vanden Plas is a steal.' However, buyers in the Jaguar sector don't need to look for bargains. Dale said that Jaguar wanted to broadcast the improved quality, but in such a way that didn't simply draw attention to the poor results in the past. As a result, 'we stuck to Jaguar's traditional advertising strength, showing the elegance and beauty of the car – but we doubled the warranty length to two years and told the customer so loud and clear'. By 1986 the warranty had been extended to three years. A 1986 ad for the XJ6 in the New Yorker featured a left-hand drive car parked in a typically 'quaint' English village street – with obligatory pub in the background – and promised:

*THE BEST JAGUAR EVER BUILT*
*The fluid lines of a celebrated shape.*
*The reliability of proven engineering.*
*The security of a 3-year, 36000 mile warranty. . . .*
*JAGUAR: A blending of art and machine*

The results of this approach, said Dale, have been 'electrifying'. Hyperbole aside, the turn-around of Jaguar has been impressive by any standards. 1985 was the best year in Jaguar's history. Output was up 15 per cent on 1984, to 38 500 cars, of which approximately 20 500 were shipped to the US. In 1986 Jaguar sold nearly 29 000 cars in the US, even though the old XJ6 was in the final stage of its life cycle, and it was common knowledge that a new model was in the offing. By 1986, profits of nearly $139 million were made on total sales of almost $1.3 billion, compared with a loss of $44 million on sales of $270 million six years previously. In early 1987 Jaguar's workforce was increased by 700, to 12 000, and Egan announced that total output for 1987 was expected to increase to 47 000, up from 41 400 in 1986 and 38 500 in 1985. And while output was up, so was productivity. As noted earlier, in 1980, 1.4 cars per worker were produced annually; by 1985 that figure stood at 3.8.

One of the most satisfactory results has probably been the Power customer satisfaction score. By mid-1983 Jaguar was scoring slightly above average, and had tied with Nissan in 13th place out of 27 marques. In 1984 Jaguar had made the biggest leap in the study's history, and had jumped into sixth place. In 1985 it moved into fifth place and was ahead of all but Mercedes in the luxury car sector. Dale concluded: 'We have plenty to do, and not all our customers are satisfied. But our recovery has convinced us that people with conviction can overcome just about any obstacle.'

## Why Jaguar succeeded

It was probably Dron who got closest to accounting for Jaguar's turn-around when he said in 1983: 'The actual people involved in the operation have not changed radically, but the whole operation . . . has been held upside down and shaken hard and then put back together again.' Starting with a product that was basically a design of the 1960s, Egan and his group found the ways to achieve new leverages into the harsh American market of the 1980s. That is the measure of their success. In the process, they also laid the groundwork for the replacement XJ series that will take them towards the next century. The new XJ6 was introduced in the UK in late 1986, and was to go on sale in the US in the spring of 1987. Like the new 7-series BMW, the new Jaguar retains a strong link with its predecessor. One senior executive said of the Jaguar design philosophy: 'It is most unusual for a luxury car manufacturer to develop a radically different car. . . . If we have to put our name on it, we've failed.' It is hard to believe that not long ago discriminating buyers were reluctant to purchase *any* car with the name *Jaguar* on it.

Another reason for buyers wanting to purchase the new XJ6 may be its price – about $40 000 in the US, as opposed to the $45 000 to $68 000 for the top-of-line BMW and Mercedes models. Besides a more advantageous exchange rate – which may not last – the British Jaguar has another factor working in its favour. In 'A big leap for Jaguar', *The Economist* reported that, like the BMW, the Jaguar is 'mostly new under the bonnet', and sports 'a host of gadgets'. Further, 'the designs of both cars allows them to be manufactured more quickly (and cheaply) than the models they replace'. It is quite likely the same manufacturing processes that will help to keep Jaguar's costs down, will also help to keep its quality up.

Peter Dormer and John Thackara, writing in the British magazine *Design* in 1984, also tried to explain the success of companies such as Jaguar. They said there was a growing demand for the added value of well-made, expensive goods, since low prices were no longer the main purchasing criteria:

> Just when the production ideal of a standard, automatically assembled 'world car' has become practicable, problems of marketing them have arisen. . . . Consumer demand for the qualities of leather seats, walnut fascias and assorted accessories has given renewed importance to the very craft skills which mass production had in theory made obsolete.
>
> Flexible manufacturing and computer controlled assembly can, it is true, adapt to the demand for variety. And no doubt robots can be taught to sew leather and to work wood. But the economic value of full automation – quite apart from issues of employment – is not self-evident.
>
> The consumer's stubborn affection for 'good workmanship' is a singular contradiction. For it implies that there are elements of industrial production where the cost advantages of automation may be outweighed by the diminished value perceived in these products by consumers. People may, in other words, be willing to pay *more* for products incorporating human skills.
>
> For years, priority was given to reducing costs, first by controlling wages and inflation, latterly by the introduction of new technology and automation. But just when new technology has made it feasible to match the low retail prices of overseas

competitors, the rules of the game have changed. Consumers have switched the emphasis of their priorities from price to quality and value.

## Yugo's value?

Not all consumers are at this end of the spectrum. Some consumers still place an emphasis on price. The crucial question for manufacturers is, what trade-off in quality and value should they accept in return? The case of the no-frills Yugoslavian-built Yugo GV suggests that there are limits, even when the price tag of a new car is only $3990. Introduced into the US market in mid-1985, the Yugo is a minicar based on a licensed Fiat design. It sold more than 8000 cars in less than two months, and the company talked about an initial annual volume of 70000 units. *Dun's Business Month* said that: 'Probably General Motors has little to worry about from tiny Yugo, but its pride has been hurt. Complains one GM executive, 'I'm tired of people asking why we don't make a cheap car, like the Yugo.''

That was in late 1985. Since providing 'products and services of such quality that our customers will receive superior value' is at the very heart of GM's mission statement, by mid-1986 that same executive was probably quite pleased GM wasn't making cheap cars like the Yugo. Less than a year after the Yugo's launch, *Advertising Age* said: 'Customer dissatisfaction is sinking the Yugo despite its $3990 price tag.' The latest survey by J.D. Power & Associates showed the Yugo scoring the lowest of any car, with 80 per cent of buyers reporting a problem with their new vehicle. Mr Power told the Detroit Auto Writers Group: 'A certain minimum level of reliability and dependability is the price of being in the marketplace. If you don't have [reliability], you're out of the marketplace, like the Yugo will be.'

Whether the makers of the Yugo will be able to create a turn-around in the same way that Jaguar has done, is open to question. Still, it wasn't too many years ago that the Japanese were being criticized for making cars unsuitable for the American public. In today's high-speed markets, anything is possible.

What the Jaguar experience has shown is that it is possible for a nearly moribund company to restore its competitive health, not by staking everything on a grand strategic plan, but by securing total commitment to the low-level programmes that are essential for everyday successes, and then executing *all* of them well. Out of these everyday successes the long-term planning, built around an 'added value' philosophy, can start to take shape.

Other companies which have reached a similar conclusion have also discovered something else – the inadequacies of traditional corporate structures and ways of running a business. The founder and chief executive of ANALOG Devices Inc., a Massachusetts company specializing in systems and components that link sophisticated measuring instruments to computers, told *Fortune* in 1987 that, like many other high-tech firms, his company's most worrisome weakness was its own management system. 'While the technologies we develop and market are quite new, our management practices and policies are archaic. We've been managing through vertical, departmental structures that seemed to work well. But we've done a miserable job of linking the disciplines across the organization – engineering, manufacturing, and marketing – in a way that yields the best product for the customer.' In fact, this same issue formed a common theme through Chapters 5 and 6. He added that the necessary corrective measures were neither simple nor quick – as GM is discovering with its Saturn project. 'Once you awaken to that challenge and decide to do something about it', he said, 'you may face a five- to ten-year correction exercise. And you may wind up replacing a whole generation of people in one discipline before you're through.'

Peter Nulty, writing in the same *Fortune* special report, explained how companies which are currently 'flattening the pyramid' are doing so by slashing layers and layers of 'number-crunching minions and report-writing middle managers', and for a specific purpose: 'Most of the managers who survive downsizing will be those who tangibly improve the company's products – and profits.'

Said the vice-president of human resources at a major US finance house: 'Managing used to mean getting things done through others. Now it means getting value added, and that's a revolution.' Nulty added:

The rise of the value-added manager has already begun. In lively new industries and perky old ones alike, middle managers' responsibilities are becoming less bound up in the bureaucratic tasks of writing reports and filling out forms, and more concerned with exercising the craft they started with, be it sales, engineering, or accounting. As their numbers dwindle, middle

236 The New Marketing

managers will act more as coaches to the troops below and as coordinators who exchange information horizontally with other middle managers rather than relaying it between upper and lower ranks.

While Nulty said that value-adding managers in their slimmed-down corporations will find their jobs 'riskier and more demanding' – which is not surprising, since there will be fewer places to hide and fewer people to blame – he also believed that their jobs would be 'more purposeful and rewarding' than those of the traditional bureaucratic structure. Given Jaguar's performance between 1980 and 1986, there shouldn't be too many middle managers remaining in that venerable company who would disagree.

While the emphasis in this chapter has been on the importance of adding value to products as a way to adding profits – and value – to companies, it is quite likely that there may be many consumers wanting to pay much less, and willing to receive much less in return – that is, the antithesis of the value-added approach. To meet the needs of this special group – and still make a profit – may mean rewriting some of the rules of marketing warfare. This notion will be discussed in Chapter 11, when marketing's fifth 'P': *Customer Servicing*, is the topic.

# 11 Customer servicing: The fifth 'P'

By the early 1980s, most so-called 'marketing-oriented' companies, with their MBA-trained executives, had learned the conventional 'rules' of marketing warfare, if not the requisite buzzwords – from 'learning curves' to 'positioning strategies'. So much so that there had developed a sameness to their competitive activities, to the point that any one firm's action quickly became negated by another's. The resulting stalemates saw many companies left struggling, and bereft of fresh ideas. The continuing high failure rate among new products also suggested that many companies were still not very good even at the basic tasks of marketing.

As we saw in Chapter 10, Thomas Bonoma, in *The Marketing Edge*, in 1985, expressed surprise that his research showed how often marketers had problems executing the low-level 'blocking and tackling' tasks. Bonoma believed a contributing factor was what he termed 'global mediocracy', by which managers pick no one task for particular emphasis. Rather, they try to do an adequate job with each task. Bonoma concluded that such 'democratic even-handedness' would inevitably ensure 'the mediocracy of all'.

By contrast, he argued, in the firms that are best at low-level execution:

> there is a real facility for handling one or two marketing functions with greatness or at least flair, and competence at the remainder. No marketers are good at everything, but the most able concentrate on doing an outstanding job at a few marketing subfunctions and an adequate job with the remainder.

By concentrating on a select number of tasks, Bonoma said: 'The result is what the consultants call "enduring competitive advantage." ' (1)

In today's high-speed markets not everyone shares this view about what leads to an enduring competitive advantage. Many retailers, faced with the twin forces of low population growth and a fragmented market, are finding the going especially tough. In a 1986 article, 'There are two kinds of supermarkets: the quick and the dead', *Business Week* observed:

> Fewer new customers means fiercer competition. These days most retailers have been forced to fight for market share. But it's a real slugfest in the supermarket business, where net profits average a penny for every dollar in sales. Says one executive: 'You can't do a couple of things well. You have to do everything well.'

Manufacturers are sharing this view. E.&J. Gallo Winery, of Modesto California, totally dominates the $8 billion-plus US wine industry. In 1985 it shipped more than 150 million gallons of wine, and grabbed more than 25 per cent market share. Astute marketing companies, such as Coca-Cola – with its purchase of Taylor California Cellars – have tried to take on Gallo, and one by one they've had to quit the field.

Jaclyn Fierman, in a 1986 *Fortune* article, 'How Gallo crushes the competition', asked Ernest Gallo, the elder brother, and chief marketer, for the secret of their success. His reply was: 'A constant striving for perfection in every aspect of our business ... unlike our major competition, wine is our only business.' Fierman concluded: 'Plainly put, [the Gallos] are better at the nuts and bolts of the wine business than anyone else in the world. They are more resourceful, more thorough, more exacting. And they are not afraid to exercise their power over grape growers, distributors, or anyone else.'

Just how powerful they can be is shown by their Bartles & Jaymes wine cooler brand, which is now the leader in what has become one of the few growth sectors in the wine industry. The previous leader, California Cooler, was displaced within a couple of years after Gallo entered the fray. A top executive who helped set up California Cooler explained: 'They aim all their guns at once.'

## More guns needed

In mature markets, especially, all 'products' – whether tangible goods or intangible services – must contain the seeds of continuous repeat business from satisfied customers. In 1985 the president and CEO of Mack Trucks Inc. told *Dun's Business Month* that in the flat truck market anyway, holding onto customers is crucial: 'You lose a customer today, a traditional Mack customer, and you do not get another crack at the guy for six or seven years.'

As a result, companies are looking for new ways to both capture and hold customers. Increasingly, they are finding new ways to expand on the traditional four elements of the marketing 'mix' – *product, price, place* and *promotion* – in order to achieve these dual objectives. In the process, some of them have discovered a new 'P': *customer servicing.* Successful marketers who are already well versed in the function would argue it should never have been left out of the mix in the first place.

In a 1987 cover story, 'Pul-eeze! Will somebody help me?', *Time* claimed that: 'Personal service has become a maddening rare commodity in the American marketplace.' *Time* blamed the demise of servicing on the 'economic upheaval' of the past decade or so:

> First came the great inflation of the 1970s, which forced businesses to slash service to keep prices from skyrocketing. Then came deregulation, which fostered more price wars and further cutbacks. Meanwhile, service workers became increasingly difficult to hire because of labour shortages in many areas. At the same time, managers found they could cut costs by replacing human workers with computers and self-service schemes.

*Time* also said that fewer workers were often over-worked workers, and therefore they had less time to spend on generating goodwill with their customers. As one airline union official noted: 'If today's jumbo jets were staffed at the levels of a decade ago, the planes would carry 20 flight attendants instead of twelve or 14.' *Time* also mentioned the increased use of computers to monitor the performance of various service staff, such as reservation clerks who take bookings over the telephone. Said one industry observer: 'These assembly-line methods increase profits by boosting productivity, but there is a long-term hidden cost – the decline in service.'

Customers are now beginning to react against this decline, argued *Time*: 'Americans tolerated, and even welcomed, self-service during an era of rising prices, but now a backlash is beginning. Result: some companies are scrambling to make amends, and "quality of service" is on its way to becoming the next business buzz phrase.'

## Customer servicing

In 1984, the chairman and CEO of AmEx's Travel Related Services Co., which was then the company's most profitable division, informed *Business Week* that: 'Service is our most strategic marketing weapon.... It's the only way we can differentiate our product in the marketplace.' Even though the American Express Co. may be considered as competing in a 'service' industry, this statement is not a reflection of convoluted semantics. Rather, as was pointed out to *Business Week*, this particular division of AmEx had elevated the service function to full marketing status, where it is used as the central contact with customers. Even for this type of business however, claimed *Business Week*: 'Using service as an active marketing tool is still a rare phenomenon.'

Rather than treating customer service as synonymous with handling customer complaints, 'relegated to a back room and staffed with low-paid, indifferent clerks', other companies, such as IBM, General Electric, General Motors and Procter & Gamble, have recently begun to expand their customer service departments. The main reason, as *Business Week* noted, was that: 'growing numbers of businesses are beginning to perceive buyers' views as integral to the design, manufacture, and sale of products and services'.

Another reason for companies actively soliciting feedback from their current or potential customers is that, by taking advantage of relatively low-cost toll-free numbers and marrying it to the power of minicomputers, companies are finding that 'the close interaction with customers provides them with enormous amounts of market information that helps them increase profits'. These companies are finding that callers ring in not only to complain, but also to obtain advice and information, and even to make constructive suggestions. As a result, stated *Business Week*, companies with properly trained customer service staff can discover from their callers a wealth of information:

- Demographic and other details, such as usage – and mis-usage.
- The impact of advertising and other promotional efforts.
- The competence of the original sales personnel.
- Identification of specific faulty merchandise, which can then be quickly fed back to manufacturing operations.
- Details of customer concerns.
- Clues to the life-expectancy of products.

- What aspects of the product can be repaired at home by the do-it-yourself customers.
- Ideas for improvements, and even potential new products and services.

The most important payback is that satisfied customers are more likely to remain loyal to the manufacturer or supplier, and that means dollar sales and profits. *Business Week* cited one study which showed that companies need to handle carefully those buyers who experience a serious problem – defined as costing $142 or more – with a consumer-durable product. Fewer than one in six complained directly to the manufacturer, largely because they believed their complaints would not be adequately acted upon. And about 90 per cent of dissatisfied buyers did not repurchase, compared with nearly 55 per cent who stayed loyal when their complaints were satisfactorily handled. The study also put a dollar value to each loyal customer. For example, adjusted for inflation since 1979, in 1984 auto makers could look foward to $142000 over a satisfied customer's lifetime.

## Adding value with servicing

As argued, customer services – or 'servicing' – can be thought of as a marketing function that encompasses more than merely fielding customer enquiries and complaints. Adding customer servicing to a product helps to increase the level of customer satisfaction, both expected (pre-sale) and actual (post-sale). Servicing can therefore be regarded as a function that both differentiates a product from competitors and adds value to a product, and thereby helps a company to increase the probability of a new sale and of a repurchase.

According to Theodore Levitt, in *The Marketing Imagination*, a product is more than a tangible thing, and from the buyer's point of view, 'the product is a promise, a cluster of value expectations of which its non-tangible parts are as integral as its tangible parts'. As a result, said Levitt, 'companies that market tangible products invariably promise more than the tangible products themselves'. (2) A car firm and its dealers may provide extra customer-servicing features – ranging from special financial terms at the time of purchase, to above-the-norm post-purchase servicing contracts. With respect to the former, in 1986 Detroit's car makers were all heavily committed, as they attempted to sell more cars by offering low-interest auto-loans. In the process they have turned their credit subsidiaries into broader financial companies, a move that is causing much anguish among traditional lenders, such as banks.

## Building relationships

While some critics might argue that offering cheap loans detracts from the perceived value of a new car, many companies are adding extra servicing items in order to escape competing on price, and because they are finding it increasingly difficult to win on product terms alone. In high-speed mature markets a technological edge is often a fleeting occurrence. As a result, companies are turning to other means – customer servicing in particular – in order to gain and/or hold loyal customers. The following matrix shows some options that are available to build enduring customer relationships: (see Figure 11.1)

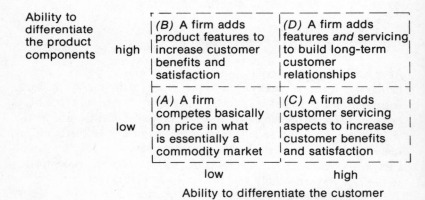

Figure 11.1 Building customer relationships

*Price-oriented company*

In quadrant (A) a company finds it has no product or customer servicing advantages: by default it is forced to compete primarily on price in order to win and hold customer loyalty. Under these conditions, unless a company can sustain its lowest cost of production advantages, long-term success is questionable.

*Product-oriented company*

In quadrant (B) a company seeks out technological superiority in order to deliver superior benefits and greater levels of satisfaction to the buyer, and thereby to win and hold customer loyalty. In certain instances the buyer may tolerate some inadequacies in customer servicing so long as the product performance remains superior. For example, buyers of luxury, high-performance cars may accept the high cost of spares and the inconvenience of few servicing outlets, in order to experience superb driving pleasure and enjoy the status of a scarce marque name.

This may be a difficult strategy to maintain if customers have a limit to the servicing difficulties they will tolerate. As Time said in 1987:

> Customers show a reasonable level of satisfaction with the merchandise they buy, thanks largely to technological advances. But the harsh world of the service economy intrudes once again on their contentment when a modern product suffers a breakdown. In a sense, consumers are victims of high-tech bounty. . . . Autos has become such sophisticated machines by and large that only dealers with space-age diagnostic devices can fix them.

Time could have added: 'and at out-of-this-world prices'.

*Servicing-oriented company*

In quadrant (C), having recognized the difficulty of sustaining a product performance edge based on long-term technological superiority, a company may assiduously provide extra customer servicing features to give it a competitive advantage. Under these conditions, some car buyers may be perfectly happy with a model that has only average performance characteristics, so long as they can obtain the peace of mind that comes with a guaranteed warranty backed up by a dealer they know and trust.

The weakness of this strategy is that technically superior products, sold price-competitively and supported by generous warranty and servicing terms, may eventually erode the loyalty of buyers of service-oriented companies – even those with the stature of IBM. In a 1987

*Fortune* article, IBM's big blues: a legend tries to remake itself', Carol
Loomis argued:

> Customers are not as deeply in IBM's thrall as they once
> were. The executives who run information services in major
> corporations have typically gained experience and confidence,
> and perceive themselves as having lost the need for a seeing eye
> dog provided by IBM. . . . At lower managerial levels, moreover,
> the proliferation of both minicomputers and personal com-
> puters, or micros, has created squads of new buyers whose
> allegiance to IBM may be weak, or may never have formed at all.
> In progress is the gradual disintegration of the FUD factor – the
> fear, uncertainty, and doubt that once gripped customers
> thinking of buying from vendors other than IBM.

The new adage may be that 'No one ever gets promoted for buying
IBM.'

### Relationship-building company

In quadrant (D) a company attempts to provide a total 'package',
based on superior product and customer servicing performance. In
this situation the company doesn't just win and hold satisfied
customers; rather, it systematically develops a binding customer
relationship based on the buyers' expectations and trust that they will
not be let down on *any* count.

Levitt had a strong view on relationship building:

> With increasing interdependence, more and more of the world's
> economic work gets done through long-term relationships
> between sellers and buyers. It is not just that once you get a
> customer you want to keep him. It is more a matter of what the
> buyer wants. He wants a vendor who keeps his promises, who'll
> keep supplying and stand behind what he promises.

According to Levitt, the buyer may initially make a purchase
principally for the technology of the product being supplied. Over
time that technology may become less important relative to:

> the system of benefits in which the technology is embedded.
> More important than technology will be the other benefits and
> interactions, like services, delivery, reliability, responsiveness,

and the quality of the human and organizational interactions between seller and buyer over time.

Not all buyer-seller situations can expect long term customer relationships, warned Barbara Jackson in a 1985 *Harvard Business Review* article, 'Build customer relationships that last'. She was primarily referring to industrial marketing, and said that in some situations, such as the marketing of shipping services, it may be too costly for a supplier to attempt to stay close to each and every customer. While the buyer may appreciate the benefit of a close servicing relationship with a particular supplier, there will be many instances where the advantages of shopping around, or having several suppliers on hand, outweigh that benefit. This is a reality that many suppliers must recognize and live with. Under these circumstances, said Jackson, the seller should practice 'transaction marketing', not 'relationship marketing'. (3)

According to Jackson, relationship marketing is appropriate when the buyer of certain products or services selects a particular vendor and 'generally expects to continue with that supplier for an extended period. In short, it expects a relationship'. Jackson cited the customer for medium-size or large computer systems as the type requiring this type of relationship. She added that:

> Because commitments from their customers usually last a long time, mainframe computer vendors have been able to take a long view of their customers' relationships. They have sensibly invested up-front resources to win commitments, helped customers with long-term planning for computers, and generally acted as if their customer relationships would continue. For them, relationship marketing has been a sound choice.

This was also the type of situation referred to by Levitt.

## Broken relationships

With respect to consumer goods, the US car industry was one where long-term customer relationships had broken down. It used to be that the Detroit car makers attempted to capture first-time buyers with base-line models, in order to move them up through the ranks as family life cycle and economic circumstances changed. For GM, the ideal customer was one who began their new car buying life with a Chevrolet Biscayne and ended it with a Cadillac Fleetwood Brougham. However, that sort of progression broke down when the Japanese, in particular, began to offer the best value for first-time buyers, and the European luxury car makers offered the best quality and status for mature buyers. In other words, Detroit's manufacturers lost their product advantages through poor quality, and as far as many Detroit-car buyers were concerned, the poor customer servicing they had tolerated for so long finally provided an added incentive to switch. It is perhaps ironical that in 1986 GM, which has the provision of 'products and services of such quality that our customers will receive superior value' written into its mission statement, had to resort to a continuous stream of price discounting and cheap loans as the only short-term way to stem its slipping market share. And even that failed.

## Customer expectations

In a 1983 *Harvard Business Review* article, 'Good product support is smart marketing', Lele and Karmarker also said that when making purchases, customers are likely to believe they are buying something more than the physical product – they also have expectations about the type and amount of post-purchase support. According to Lele and Karmarkar:

> Product support encompasses everything that can help maximize the customer's after-sales satisfaction – parts, service, and warranty plus operator training, maintenance training, parts delivery, reliability engineering, serviceability engineering, and even product design. (4)

In other words, product support, like customer servicing, is anything that helps cement an ongoing customer relationship.

Unfortunately, argued the authors, in most companies product support is thought of as a function that is not an integral part of the firm's comprehensive marketing strategy. Where this is the case, the product support function may have any or all of the following characteristics:

- Product support is merely a collective of individual tasks – from the handling of customer enquiries at the head office to the training of service personnel out in the field – all performed in the absence of an ultimate 'integrating theme'.

- Companies do not centralize responsibility for product support. Rather, individual departments carry out their own tasks and, as a result, top management may receive a disjointed picture of total product support, and its impact on customer experiences and satisfaction. Equally important, feedback from the various departments may not get fed into product design decisions.

- The lack of central co-ordination may lead to individual departments adopting support or servicing approaches that are in conflict with each another – a local parts depot attempts to keep spares to a minimum to reduce costs, while the servicing engineers try to carry as wide a range of spares as possible to meet all possible contingencies. When the customer servicing concept is extended to cover both pre- and post-sale servicing functions, then the potential for this conflict is even greater.

  For example, sales representatives may promise certain post-purchase services in order to close a sale – such as the promise of immediate delivery of spare parts – that neither the local parts depot nor the servicing engineers can possibly fulfil. The result may be unsatisfied customers who eventually transfer their business elsewhere, and the real cause of this breakdown in the customer relationship may never get traced.

- Where there is diffusion of servicing responsibilities, top management may focus their attention on internal departmental issues of efficiency and cost control, and not on external 'customer-oriented measures', such as the amount of 'downtime' the customer has suffered – and the cost of this downtime to the customer – as a result of the failure of each machine, vehicle or piece of equipment supplied by a particular company.

A cyclical effect may emerge: product breakdowns occur and are not rectified to the customers' satisfaction. Customers complain. The supplying company confuses symptoms with cause. Money and resources get thrown at selected symptoms. The breakdowns persist. Customer complaints continue and intensify. Managers get shuffled or bounced. The cycle repeats.

## New segments

To break a cycle such as this, Lele and Karmarkar suggested that managers examine 'how customer expectations can affect support and marketing strategies and then learn how to use these expectations constructively'. One way is to segment the market on 'the basis of customers' support expectations', not just on the basis of product benefit expectations. In other words, on the basis of quadrants (*C*) and (*D*) requirements, not just on (*B*).

The authors offered word processors as an example. One target group could be the *one-machine office*, where a machine breakdown means a serious disruption to the flow of work. 'The customer therefore expects both a low failure rate and minimum downtime per failure. Support costs or maintenance expenses are of secondary importance.' Under these conditions the target may be less price-sensitive to the new machine cost.

Another target group could be *multimachine offices*, where replacement machines may be readily available if one machine fails. As a result, 'assuming that both the failure rate and downtime per failure are reasonably low, the customer is likely to be more interested in keeping maintenance and repair costs low over the life of the product'. Under these conditions, the target market may be more price-sensitive as well – the decision may be to purchase 20 low-priced clones of the market leader, when only 18 are needed, and for perhaps the price of 12 from the leader. The total cost difference can be spent elsewhere, and the two spares can be used in case of breakdown.

'To meet customers' needs in each segment', argued the authors, 'management can choose a variety of strategies. For the word processor market, a company could do the following:

- design for higher reliability (and charge a premium);
- provide parts and service support as needed without a fixed-fee service contract;
- develop a monthly service contract; or
- use a spare machine on-site and incorporate its cost in the maintenance contract.

Each of these support strategies affects such major elements of marketing as product design and development, production and delivery, sales, and pricing'.

## Paper cup servicing

One reason why the Fort Howard Paper Co. bought the Maryland Cup Corp. in 1983 was not just to expand its product line and increase sales, but also to acquire Maryland's marketing skills, which included renowned customer servicing. As *Business Week* commented in 1983:

> Savvy Maryland Cup made its name by turning what is essentially a commodity business into a service business. The company not only supplies cups and plates to restaurants and food service companies, but also jumps in with special promotions and new products. It even offers suggestions on store layout.

A spokesperson for McDonald's said of Maryland: 'Our relationship goes beyond that of an average supplier affiliation. We work as partners.'

In a 1978 article, 'Maryland Cup sells more than just paper cups', *Business Week* observed: 'A paper cup is a paper cup, after all, and a manufacturer without something extra to offer could easily succumb in a low-technology, highly competitive business.' Instead, what Maryland offered was a 'system', or packages of equipment and merchandising assistance. In other words, it was the 'aggressive backup service' that kept Maryland out of cut-throat price wars with its competitors. That could mean advising ball parks on how to keep their beer cool and frothy, or how restaurants should offer three sizes of soft drinks in order to boost total beverage revenues, or how institutions such as hospitals could save operating costs by switching to disposables, without downgrading the presentation of meals. The president of Maryland informed *Business Week* that their customers looked upon the company not as suppliers but as 'experts in their business', a comment echoed by the McDonald's spokesperson several years later. Maryland's top sales administrator added: 'We don't talk about cups. Sometimes we don't even mention price. We talk about a concept, such as "How would you like to have more customers, bring them back more often, and increase their check size?" '

## Carpet servicing

One company providing superior value to customers by offering both product and servicing benefits is Feltex New Zealand Limited, the largest maker of woollen carpets in the world, and the biggest maker of synthetic carpets in Australia. In 1985 it established a new division, Feltex Modular Carpets, and a factory in Sydney to manufacture and market high-technology modular carpets for contract clients in Australia, New Zealand and South-east Asia. Feltex produces carpet modules, or squares, under licence to Milliken and Company of the United States, the second largest textile company in the world, and No. 1 in the commercial modular carpet market.

New technologies are used in both the selling and production processes, and these give Feltex the chance to gain important leverages into its targeted commercial markets. In the process Feltex has changed the rules of marketing carpets in the Australasian region.

The new carpets reflect two important changes in office construction and use – the development of movable flat electrical cabling which can run under carpets, and the fact that constantly changing office space and usage requirements involve frequent shifting of partitions, people and equipment – such as computers, photocopiers and word processors. These changes have put new demands on floor coverings.

In terms of product benefits, Feltex claims its modular carpets offer significant advantages, particularly in terms of design detail and flexibility, expected wear life, 'dimensional stability', ease of under-floor access, portability, handling and storage costs, and cleaning properties. By means of product 'life-cycle costing' arguments, Feltex says that while the initial price of its modular carpets is comparatively higher than average commercial broadloom carpet, the total 'system' cost is comparatively lower when measured over the lifetime of its use.

However, the key to the success of the Feltex system is unlikely to be its product cost-customer value argument. Rather, it is the way the concept is sold to prospective clients. The method employed by Feltex, and Milliken, shows the marketing imagination at its most creative level – the use of one technological breakthrough (computer-assisted carpet design) to market another (computer-controlled modular carpet production) in order to build a long-term customer relationship.

Prospective clients, whether from Perth, Auckland or Singapore, can fly to Sydney and immediately begin planning the carpet design required, using the design computer facilities Feltex has installed. These clients – such as architects or interior design consultants – have some 16 million colours and 3500 standard designs to choose from, or they can create a unique design for their respective clients. The computer screen displays the carpet design and allows the client to modify colours, scale and detail. It will also display the final carpet design, in perspective and complete with fixtures and fittings, in a three-dimensional screen replica of the office, corridor, or other room setting. The clients can see the end result before the samples are even made. What previously took weeks can be achieved in a few hours. Feltex's clients can also return to their own clients with a hard-copy colour printout of the selected design, or designs, in the simulated room that has been drawn. Finally, since the so called computer-aided 'aesthetics system' is hooked up to its dyeing machine, Feltex can print out carpet samples in the new patterns in a relatively short time, for final approval.

Peter Petre, in a 1985 *Fortune* article, 'How to keep customers happy captives', called this type of approach to selling 'channel systems'. He said it was given this name:

> because they're meant to cure headaches for people in a company's distribution channels – for example, commercial customers and key middlemen. Some channel systems enable customers to order instantly and better manage their inventories. Customers use others to analyse costs, control quality, lay marketing plans, and electronically seek advice. In all cases, by helping the customer solve a problem the company supplying the channel systems stands to increase sales or otherwise benefit ... When the systems work well, they are enough to make a marketing manager's mouth water.

Given the level of personal customer attention and servicing, one cannot help but conclude that Feltex's presentation-to-sale ratio probably approaches 1 : 1. That would indeed make any marketing manager's mouth water!

## Computer servicing

One bright spot in the personal computer industry during the slump of 1985–6 was Compaq Computer Corp. of Houston, Texas. It is one of the very few companies to master the dangerous game of marketing IBM-compatible personal computers. Compaq – which stands for

*Compa*tible *Q*uality – was founded in early 1982 by three senior executives from Texas Instruments who wanted to go into business for themselves. The story is that the three executives first sketched out the layout of their basic computer on the back of a place mat in a coffee shop in Houston. According to John Stackhouse, writing in the Australian business weekly, *The Bulletin*, their requirements were that their computer 'had to be compatible with the industry standard, which they correctly foresaw as being set by IBM. It had to be smaller and faster than the opposition. And it had to offer better value'.

Compaq's success goes deeper than that, and shows their sound grasp of the flow-of-goods concept of marketing. No matter how good the machines are, Compaq would possibly be just another IBM clone maker if it hadn't latched on to a key ingredient for success in the marketing of personal computers – the trade. In fact Compaq computers are as much designed, and priced, for the benefit of its dealers as they are for its end users. By changing a few rules, and introducing a new level of customer servicing – for the dealers – Compaq set out to position itself as one of the few credible challengers to IBM. According to *The Economist*, in 1985, 'better than anyone else, Compaq has mastered the art of competing in the IBM-compatible market'.

In a 1986 *Business Week* article, 'Will Compaq be dethroned as king of the compatibles?', Jo Ellen Davis reported that: 'The Compaq formula is to price its machines at the same level as IBM's but incorporate a few key features the originals don't have.' It has also tried to make sure that its computers run all the popular software programmes considerably faster than IBM's PC. For example, its portable computer is more powerful and versatile than IBM's, and this has helped to make it the No. 1 seller worldwide. It is this approach to product development that has helped Compaq to become known as the quality alternative to IBM, and preferred by 'computer literate' buyers.

Compaq set out to aim its products at the business market, and to stick to this one objective and do it better than anyone else. As with any mass market for consumer goods, distribution and shelf space are essential pre-conditions for success. Of the hundred or so makers of personal computers, Compaq is one of the few firms to gain wide distribution in terms of the number of outlets stocking. In fact, with some 2900 stores worldwide, it has a larger number stocking than even IBM, according to Davis.

There are a number of reasons for this. To reach the business market, Compaq sells only through authorized dealers, rather than through a conglomeration of sales people, agents and independent distributors. By concentrating on retailers such as ComputerLand and Sears Roebuck – which in 1986 decided to drop Apple from its Sears Business Systems Centers, and sell only IBM, AT&T and Compaq machines – the company avoids the ill-feeling that is caused when a computer maker's direct sales force skims off business with large corporations by undercutting its retailers. Each dealer acts as the only point of contact with the consumer, and offers all pre- and post-sale support, training, installation of extra features and warranty services.

Compaq knew that it would always be smaller than IBM, and therefore would have no hope of matching the Big Blue's production costs – but it could compete on price terms by living with slimmer margins. Its machines were originally priced so that dealers could gross 36 per cent on sales made at the suggested retail price, vs 33 per cent on IBM sales. Compaq also gives its dealers generous discounts and liberal return policies, as well as offering them an attractive advertising programme which, unlike standard co-op advertising arrangements, allows dealers to choose where to spend the money.

Compaq, then, deliberately set out to woo the independent dealers, in the belief that assured, limited and committed distribution is better than a grab-bag assortment of channels – or worse, no assured distribution – a tactic most other personal computer makers have failed to match.

Further, Compaq set out to reinforce its dealers' loyalty by constantly involving them in its market research and product development programmes. As one major dealer principal commented to Brian O'Reilly in a 1985 *Fortune* article, 'Compaq's grip on IBM's slippery tail': 'Compaq's success isn't from the latest technology or a lot of razzle-dazzle, but with coming out with what dealers want.' In the same year the chairman of another chain told Mark Ivy, in a *Business Week* article, 'Compaq must try harder to stay No. 2': 'They have established themselves as the retailers' company.' If Compaq can hold this position, it will be because it fully understands what is required to deliver superior 'customer servicing' as the fifth 'P' of its marketing mix.

What Compaq has demonstrated – just as IBM did when it introduced its PC – is that to manage the market it decides to enter, a firm needs to carefully orchestrate, and tightly control, a marketing strategy which breaks a few of the prevailing rules of competitive practice. In doing so, it is more likely to realize the crucial leveraging opportunities that are present in the flow-of-goods approach to marketing – even if its main rival might be as swift and powerful as IBM.

Can Compaq maintain its leverages? Davis was uncertain. Early competitors hadn't the managerial and financial resources to slug it out when IBM finally caught up with its backlog of demand for the PC in 1984. However, by 1986 the market had a new set of competitors – industrial giants from South Korea and Japan, and powerful electronic retail chains in the US. While Compaq's original game-plan was to produce superior products to IBM, and sell them at IBM prices, Davis explained that: 'New cloners are taking the Compaq formula a step further. They add features such as faster microprocessors and higher-capacity disks – and then undercut the IBM and Compaq price.' David concluded: 'They've all watched Compaq – and learned how to do it right. . . . Compaq could find itself squeezed between a pack of cheaper clones and a more aggressive IBM.' If this happens then Compaq may find it has to rewrite its original formula, and give superior servicing an added dimension.

## People Express servicing

People Express Airlines Inc. of Newark, New Jersey, had also shown what could be achieved when firms reached 'imaginatively beyond the obvious or merely deductive', to requote Levitt, in order to realize new leveraging opportunities. Formed in 1981, in response to deregulation of the airline industry in 1978, People Express proved that a great many air travellers were willing to pay less, for less, even if it meant flying out of the dingy – not to say chaotic – Newark Airport.

In order to provide this new level of value, and customer servicing, People Express – and in particular its chairman and co-founder, Donald Burr – had to rethink the concept of what makes an airline competitive, given the changed operating conditions.

In 1980 a top advertising agency executive informed *Business Week*: 'Deregulation has pushed the airline industry overnight into a new era of mass marketing.' *Business Week* said: 'Forced to compete as they never competed before, the airlines are examining advertising and marketing approaches that are old-hat to other industries but are new to them – and are proving to be controversial as well.' Whereas airlines traditionally competed on appeals such as convenient schedules, friendly service, silver cutlery, roomy seats, plane safety, and occasional discounts, the 'mass marketing' approaches encouraged them to offer new attractions: coupons good for future flights at half price, wholesaling seats to travel agents and other major distributors, giveaways, contests and, when all else had failed, price cutting. The problems were that these approaches weren't attracting new air travellers and besides, any one offer by one airline was quickly matched by a competitor. Such was the nature of mass marketing. Another top agency executive complained to *Business Week* that price competition had become so fierce that some companies faced operating at a loss. 'It worries me to get so far away from the ideas of confidence and image that we've promoted for so long', he added. What he thinks today is anybody's guess.

If mass marketing techniques had some airlines confused, the techniques introduced by People Express must have caused them apoplexy. In terms of service People offered only the basics, in order to get its fare structure down. The company hired independent firms to handle services such as maintenance work and taking telephone reservations. And while reservations were taken by phone all tickets were sold on the plane. Customers bought their snacks and beverages in flight, or brought their own. Passengers also paid to have their luggage checked, and they had to pick up their bags if they connected with other flights.

People also was creative in its employment policies. While employees were lower paid than other airline employees, and did not belong to a union, they took part in a profit-sharing scheme and were required to buy some stock in the company at a substantial discount from the market price.

Aside from a small group of senior managers, People had only three classes of employees – flight managers (pilots), customer service managers and maintenance supervisors. All workers took part in a 'cross-utilization' scheme. For example, on their days off flying pilots might spend time in jobs such as accounting, sales, recruiting, training or flight dispatch. There were no secretaries, even for Burr. Managers did their own typing and answered their own phones.

People looked everywhere to save costs. On a 727 there were 185 seats, about 40 more than on competitive airlines. Planes were generally leased, not bought. These policies paid off. In 1981 People's average cost per seat per mile was 6.66c, compared with 8.63c for

TWA and 8.15c for Pan Am, according to Peter Nulty in a 1982 *Fortune* article, 'A champ of cheap airlines'. As People's general manager informed Nulty: 'You don't keep costs down by counting pencils and paper clips. You have to squeeze massive productivity out of people and planes.'

And the company passed its economies on to passengers. Its fares were both cheap and simple. On each route there were two basic fares: peak – mostly daytime and early evening flights on week-days – and off-peak – mostly late nights and week-ends. Nulty said that People's pricing strategy was originally designed not to take passengers off competing airlines, but to 'lure them from the roads and rails on routes where there is a lot of ground traffic and not much airline service'. Thus its fares from Newark to West Palm Beach, Florida, were $89 peak and $69 off-peak, compared with about $130 for a bus or train. Nulty concluded: 'Two kinds of travellers like People's fares: those with little money and those with plenty of money who would like to keep it.'

It was this approach to pricing that led *Time*, in a 1986 cover story, 'Fare games: flying has never been cheaper', to proclaim: 'People Express has become the Greyhound of the skies.' People's fare structures certainly increased air traffic. When it began to fly to Boston in 1981, airlines on the New York-Boston run carried 1.4 million passengers a year. Three years later 3.8 million passengers were flying the route.

People was also prepared to carry its fare wars into the heart of its competitors' territories, and this may have been the start of its undoing. When it first began flying the Newark-Chicago route in 1984 it charged $79 for peak and $59 for off-peak fares – about 70 per cent below coach fares on the full service routes. When it started its non-stop flights between Newark and Los Angeles, also in 1984, its one-way peak fare was $149 and off-peak $119. The previous low fare on the route had been $199 for an advance purchase ticket.

*Time* commented: 'To offer such fares, People Express had to come up with a revolutionary method of operation. It is like no other airline, from the way it handles baggage to the duties its pilots perform. Its unorthodox style has forced carriers to re-evaluate almost everything they do.' To paraphrase Davis, some of them have watched People – and learned how to do it right, quickly.

# Air pockets

By mid-1986 People had grown from a three-aircraft fleet serving by-way destinations into a 117-plane network covering 107 North American cities, plus London and Brussels. The number of passengers carried had risen from one million in 1981 to twelve million in 1985. And People was so successful in driving down overheads that in 1985 it cost it 5.28c to fly a passenger one mile compared with 8.5c for the industry average. However, claimed George Russell, in a mid-1986 article, 'Air pocket in the revolution', in *Time*: 'People gained size but it failed to gain strength.' The reason for this was that: 'the company had strayed seriously from the keep-it-simple formulas that had made People a case study at business schools across the US'. Such is the adaptability of business professors that no doubt it will remain a case study, but now for quite different teaching purposes.

In the first six months of 1986 People lost nearly $103 million and in order to stay aloft began to sell off some of its assets, notably Frontier Airlines, the Denver-based, full service, fully unionized carrier which it purchased in late 1985 for nearly $310 million. Some industry observers were even predicting the eventual fall of People. *The Economist* concluded: 'Icarus-like Mr Donald Burr – the man who revolutionized America's airline industry – is being humbled by his own ambition.' *Fortune* noted: 'It cost People Express many millions and eight painful months to learn that its new shoes were too big.'

*The Economist* argued that the flaw in People's original formula was that: 'for profits to grow from low-cost tickets, the airline has to grow – and the more it grows, the more it exposes the weaknesses of an inexperienced staff and an inadequate reservations system. Morever, the established airlines have learnt to fight back'.

Russell said that People might have stayed out of financial trouble had it not purchased Frontier. This was part of Burr's programme to install a nation-wide network of carriers, with the subsidiaries feeding passengers on to the planned full-service People flights operating long-haul flights out of key airports – the hub-and-spoke system that now characterizes the US airline industry. Instead, observed *The Economist*: 'The reality is a mismash of management methods and a crippling burden of debt.'

People first tried to retain Frontier as a full-service carrier. However, it was already making losses and facing stiff price competition from its competitors and so, in early 1986, it was changed to a no-frills airline. That move alienated Frontier's traditional customers, and by mid-1986 Burr tried to turn it back into a full-service airline. Frontier's losses continued and its sell off became inevitable if People was to survive.

People itself lost its own way in the turmoil. In June, 1986, Burr announced that People was going the full-service way in order to tap the business traveller sector. As one industry observer informed Russell, it was a 'major strategic error'. Business travellers constituted only a small sector of the market – and one hotly pursued by other carriers who could offer more reliable and comfortable services. This flip-flop approach to marketing had another side effect – the departure of key staff, disillusioned with People's recent progress and Burr's autocratic leadership style.

The trouble was, claimed Russell: 'Burr's Denver foray violated one of the initial ingredients in People's formula for success – offer no-frills travel in areas away from heavy competition.' What Burr didn't anticipate was just how successful his new-found rivals would be in attacking People on price terms. And in order to do that, said Russell: 'They had on their side a powerful weapon that People lacked: the sophisticated, highly computerized reservation systems linking them with at least 20 000 US travel agents.' People's competitors used their reservation system quite selectively, noted *The Economist*: 'Rather than offering all their seats at People's prices, they have been offering merely enough to lure some passengers away and so stop Mr Burr's airline from filling its aircraft – which is the only way a low-fare operator such as People can make a profit.' In other words, People's competitors had an operations leverage that it couldn't match, or outfox.

## People's servicing breakdown

The summer of 1986 was a period when the US air travel industry reached its upper limits. Under deregulation, a horde of upstart airlines, unprecedented bargain fares and an American public that decided to stay in the USA, bookings had increased from 319 million passengers in 1984 to 410 million in 1986. In 'Unfriendly skies', *Time* remarked: 'What was long an elitist and expensive but comfortable means of transportation has been transformed into a democratic, cut-rate mass-transit system that is straining to serve the hordes of new passengers.' At People the straining was near to breaking point. In a *Fortune* article, 'The US air travel mess', Jeremy Main said that in 1986 there was a growing number of written and telephone complaints from passengers to the Department of Transport about the poor service. Here People topped the list: 10.38 complaints per 100000 passengers vs 4.86 for the number two, Pan American. *Time* reported that Newark Airport had an average of 146 delays for every 1000 take-offs or landings. This was 40 per cent up on the previous year, and the highest in the nation. It is not surprising that People Express became known as People Distress. The summer of 1986 could not come at a worse time for People – it planned to have its new terminal at Newark, and the nation's largest, completed in 1987.

In the end, People was forced into a merger with Texas Air, another large low-cost airline, by massive losses and cash flow difficulties, and by over-comitting itself to an expansion programme which it was unable to sustain in the face of some rather brutal competition.

The lessons from People seem clear. Having reached 'imaginatively beyond the obvious or merely deductive', and rewritten the rules of marketing an airline service in a deregulated environment, People appears to have then departed from them without having a clear idea of what its new set of rules should be. In addition, it seems to have failed to foresee just how quickly and effectively its big national competitors, in particular, would learn how to counter its price discounting by introducing some new rules of their own. If People falls, warned *The Economist*, 'those who thought the deregulation of America's airline industry would let a thousand airlines compete must resign themselves to a rivalry of oligarchs'. If that occurs, then an era of airline marketing epitomized by People's rise and fall will quickly have passed, and another will begin. One thing is for certain, however: it will not be a return to the days of mass marketing. We will be in a new era.

The examples in this chapter have shown that in a wide variety of industries it is possible for companies to rewrite the strategies for success. For each company examined, part of this rewriting has included a new definition of what constitutes customer servicing, in order to achieve some additional marketing leverage.

However, strategies by themselves are insufficient. What is also required is mastery of what Bonoma termed the low-level 'blocking and tackling' tasks. While this is not to deny the importance of strategic planning, each company analysed in this chapter has demonstrated that it is at the execution level, not the grand strategy

level, that day-by-day marketing advantages are gained and
sustained – or lost.

# Conclusion

The main argument in this book has been that the classical approach to marketing in America is coming to an end. This fundamental shift is not surprising. For the past several years US firms have had to make wrenching adjustments as a result of the many forces now shaping the way they operate: the maturing of many markets, plus income polarization combined with other demographic and life-style shifts, are forcing firms to change from mass-marketing to precision segmentation strategies; technology-led competitors are playing by different rules from market-led companies; shortened product life cycles are a fact of life in this time of 'high-speed' marketing, and besides, anything that looks like succeeding is immediately 'cloned'; product launch costs continue to climb, yet failure rates remain as high as they were twenty years ago; retailers are challenging the manufacturer's right to 'channel management'; deregulation is forcing companies in the banking, financial services, telecommunications and airline industries to turn to marketing techniques – as have the suppliers of other services, from leisure centres to legal practices – just when the established marketing firms are changing their own ways; collaborative alliances are reshaping how competitors now compete; exchange rate fluctuations are making it more difficult for firms to decide when and where to locate their offshore production facilities in order to reduce their labour costs; exciting new flexible manufacturing techniques are causing them to rethink the necessity of such a move anyway – particularly when they are discovering that, just when many of them have decided to move their plants out of America, their Japanese rivals are moving theirs in.

In response to these changes and challenges, many companies have pursued – with varying degrees of success so far – courses of action never before attempted. As was examined in Chapter 3, many are finding that the least risky course of action is the one that changes the prevailing rules of moving goods and services from producer to consumer.

In 1987 many of those companies looked at in this book were still rewriting their rules:

- Apple Computer celebrated its tenth anniversary, and 3000 guests were invited to Los Angeles to witness another example of John Scully's 'event marketing' galas. The launch of two new Mackintosh computers was accompanied by the announcement that the machines could do something that, under the irreconcilable Steven Jobs, the company's ex-chairman, no Apple had ever been allowed to do – they could run some programs written for IBM's PC. The unthinkable had become the possible and, as noted by *The Economist*, the move was purely commercial: 'Mr John Scully reckons that such abilities are needed to steal the hearts of corporations now wedded to all sorts of IBM machines.'

- IBM also announced that it was not going to give up its grip on the PC market, business or otherwise. Four new models were introduced and, said the *Financial Times*: 'At a stroke IBM has raised the stakes in personal computing, just as it did when it entered the market in 1981.'

Back in 1981 IBM had rewritten many industry rules when it launched its first PC, as discussed earlier in this book. In 1987 IBM was prepared to do it again. The new range was seen by analysts as double-edged – the bottom end of the range was priced low enough to compete more directly with the clones than its predecessor was, and it was made to a new standard which would be technically more difficult to copy. Gone was the 'open architecture' break-through of 1981. Instead, IBM's new range had a new computer architecture and operating system that was designed to give better graphics, speed and the potential for much larger memory than its existing range of PCs. Indeed, one model incorporated Itel's powerful 32-bit chip, and IBM was confident that, with its range being hard to copy, it was gaining some much needed breathing space, as competitors would be forced back to their VDU drawing-boards. Another important element in IBM's strategy was that, with its new manufacturing facilities, the models were more compact, reliable and quicker and cheaper to build, thereby giving it additional leverages into the market.

IBM also pulled what was becoming a common trick – it announced that not all its new models would be available immediately, thereby hoping to forestall corporate purchasers from committing themselves to the clones, or Apples, before IBM's full range became available for consideration. It is doubtful whether any other competitor could pull this one so often, but as Roger Smith of GM has said: 'Use your weight to your advantage.'

•   Coca-Cola USA decided to capitalize on the momentum that had regained it the number one cola position in 1986, got it to the No. 1 lemon-lime spot – by displacing 7-UP – and helped it achieve a whopping 39 per cent corporate market share. On 5 March it introduced a range of commercials under a 'new feeling' umbrella by staging an advertising first – a 'verticle roadblock'. On that night, during NBC's top-rated Thursday line-up, Coca-Cola bought a total of three minutes of advertising time and slotted a new commercial in each of five of America's most popular programmes. In doing so, Coca-Cola was also following Smith's advice.

•   *Advertising Age* announced that in 1986, Procter & Gamble, perennially the nation's biggest TV advertiser, had cut its prime time network spending by 20 per cent over the previous year, and reduced its total network budget by 8 per cent in its largest-ever network cutback.

One industry source told *Advertising Age* that P&G's spending went in cycles, depending on the number of new product launches, and therefore 'any overall drop in P&G's network TV spending shouldn't be viewed as the beginning of a trend away from network TV advertising'.

Perhaps. Verne Gay of *Advertising Age* reported from other sources that since 1985 P&G had been shifting additional network dollars into syndicated TV programmes and independent stations. Gay also reported that network TV dollars were being channelled into 'P&G's burgeoning customer promotion programs' – such as the inclusion of real gems into selected packages of its products, something the company began in 1984. If P&G really is diverting monies to its promotional activities, this is further recognition that leverage through the trade is of growing importance in the continuing battle for the consumer's mind via the retailer's overcrowded shelf and freezer space.

•   Chrysler announced it would spend some $1.5 billion to buy out the shares held in American Motors by Renault, the struggling French car maker, pending approval by the various government authorities.

The deal would make sense for both parties, it was claimed. The state-owned Renault lost nearly $2.4 billion during 1985-6, and would receive a much-needed injection of cash, plus an agreement that it would be able to continue to sell its cars through AMC's existing dealer network.

Chrysler also had much to gain: about two share points in its combined 12 per cent share of the car and light truck market; a new distribution network (about 1600 AMC dealers to add to its existing 4300 outlets); three additional operational plants, plus the state-of-the-art factory in Ontario, Canada; and the bonus of supplementing its model line-up with one of America's most veneral marques – Jeep, which had accounted for two-thirds of AMC's sales in 1986.

Some industry observers were also speculating that Chrysler, having sold off its European subsidiary to Peugeot in 1978 to stave off bankruptcy, could once again gain entry into Europe if Renault agreed to sell Chrysler's models through its European dealer network.

The risks for Chrysler would be enormous. Some critics immediately and correctly questioned the wisdom of adding another third to Chrysler's productive capacity in North America. However, observed *Business Week*: 'While the acquisition is heralded as a good fit, its success ultimately will hinge on Iacocca's ability to impose on ailing AMC the stay-lean philosophy that turned Chrysler around.' Regardless of whether the deal obtained all the necessary approvals, the fact that Chrysler, virtually bankrupt six years earlier, should be thinking of expanding at a time when GM, the supposed heavy-weight force in the market, was shutting down some of its own factories, shows how in today's fiercely contested markets, only the quick and totally committed will survive.

As illustrated throughout this book, the relentless scrambling for a competitive advantage is a feature of today's mature market places. Companies cannot afford to stop; they may not even have the time to pause and take stock. As Iacocca said in 1987, after announcing the AMC deal: 'You either go forward, or you go backward.'

How ironical then, that while in 1985 General Motors was being lauded for its 'bold bid to reinvent the wheel', only two years on its market share was sliding, its profits were down, factories were shutting, and there was speculation that even the much-vaunted Saturn project might be moth-balled. Some observers, including *Business Week*, questioned the company's ability to compete: 'Even if Smith can solve his company's myriad other ailments, he faces a day of reckoning with one that is GM's very essence: its size. The basic question nagging this biggest, most diverse, and most integrated of car companies is whether it is just too big to compete in today's fast-changing car market.' Smith's comments regarding the power of size, was perhaps coming back to torment him.

*Business Week* posted a litany of factors bedevilling GM:

- A failure to differentiate its family of products, even from each other. Where was the added value for the customer when a Cadillac Seville costing $26 326 didn't look all that different from a Pontiac Calais costing $9 741?
- A failure to achieve higher quality standards and lower unit costs through automation. Where were the advantages of ranks of robots when GM's most efficient plant, producing its best quality car, was one that GM had set up as a stop-gap measure with its rival Toyota?
- A failure to achieve the spirit of innovation and risk taking that is now so necessary to stay ahead of an ever-changing market, despite the most comprehensive reorganization in over half a century. Where is the critical flexibility of thinking and action going to come from when there are as many as 14 management layers in the organization, compared with only five at Toyota? And where are the advantages of continuing with inflexible vertical integration when GM's domestic competitors source their main components from outside suppliers who guarantee faster delivery, lower prices and higher quality, or they lose the business?
- A failure to stop even its American competition from taking sales away from it. Where are the advantages of all the expensive efforts to overhaul its plants, people and products when it still has the highest unit costs – and break-even point – in North America? As one Chrysler executive remarked in 1987: 'They have failed to comprehend that their market share is gone forever, forever, forever – even if they do everything right.'

No one is writing GM off yet, and certainly not its competitors. As one senior Ford executive commented in 1987: 'When the perception is so strong that GM blew it, that probably means they've already got things turned around.' He then added, rather equivocally: 'They must.'

The point of all this is that, unlike many other companies examined in this book, General Motors had failed to gain leveraging control over all four key processes involved in the flow of goods and services concept of marketing. As stated early in this book, this is not a new concept. What is new are the many ways it is now being interpreted and implemented by many of America's once traditional marketing-oriented companies.

Central to the argument that the classical, or traditional approach, to marketing is coming to an end is the suggestion that it has been replaced by an approach that involves a complete reassessment of every function or process to do with the flow of goods or services. There is no textbook approach that guarantees success; most companies are proceeding on a DIY basis. There is no grand strategy that is the universal panacea; most companies are finding that an emphasis on doing the thousand small things very well is what more often leads to success – an argument strenuously put forward by Tom Peters and Nancy Austin in *A Passion for Excellence*.

This striving for excellence in the 'blocking and tackling' tasks identified by Thomas Bonoma revolves around four important processes that provide companies with their best leveraging opportunities. The first is the incessant search for, and development of, a constant flow of new products and services, no matter how disruptive this is to the organizational status quo. The Japanese have aptly labelled this flow their 'pipeline of technologies'. Without it they would not be able to keep up with, let alone get ahead of, the ever-changing needs of their markets.

In a 1987 *Fortune* article on how companies are 'speeding new ideas to market', Bro Uttal said that the traditional phased approach to product development will no longer suffice. In fact it is a sure way to commit 'corporate suicide', he argued. In its place, the Japanese have come up with a 'so-called parallel approach ... more akin to a rugby match than a relay race'. In effect, it is a speedier approach because, like the forwards and backs in rugby, the functions of 'design, manufacturing, and marketing rush a new line downfield together.'

If 'new-product rugby' is the catch-phrase for describing the latest approach to the process of new product development, then it may be appropriate to remember that rugby has been described as 'a thug's game played by gentlemen'. It may also be worth noting that, in 1987, the game of women's rugby was played at Twickenham, the 'home' of international rugby. And if managers wish to observe the spectacle of all 15 players rushing a new line downfield together, they should view a video of New Zealand's national team, the All Blacks, arguably the most consistently successful rugby team in the world. What they will see is a team that plays a hard, direct running, passing and kicking game, where a sudden attacking move can be fashioned from any situation and position on the field. It is an uncompromising brand of rugby, and nearly always played to the constantly changing pace and plan as set by the All Blacks.

The second process is the establishment of a truly flexible manufacturing system, with more complex machines, and more electronics, in order to produce an ever-changing range of models that will meet the ever-shifting needs of today's fragmented consumer market place. This means that companies are having to commit increased investment dollars to product development and production. What is the point of a successful 'pipeline of technologies' if a company hasn't the manufacturing speed and flexibility to realize the market opportunities offered by these technologies?

The third process is a new set of organizational structures and marketing strategies that will allow the manufacturer to operate on a more-or-less equal footing with the increasingly powerful retail channels that now characterize most consumer markets. What is the point of a constant flow of new products through a highly sophisticated plant if the company hasn't a trade marketing strategy designed to meet the requirements of this intermediary set of customers?

The fourth and final process is a set of marketing mix elements, including the fifth 'P' – customer servicing – that ensures that the designated target market knows it will receive greater value than can be provided by the competition. What is the point of a flow of goods and services approach to marketing if the customer cannot be gained and held in a mutually beneficial exchange relationship?

To repeat, we have moved into a new era of marketing, and the search for leverages has become of paramount importance. The companies examined in these chapters show no sign of letting up, which is as it should be, and it is my hope that readers of this book will feel inspired to continue with their own search.

# References

## Chapter 1: references

1 Robert Heller, *The Naked Market*, Sidgwick & Jackson, London, 1984
2 Arthur Lawrence, *The Management of Trade Marketing*, Gower, 1983

### Other references

'The new breed of strategic planner', *Business Week*, September 17, 1984, pp 52–7

David Whiteside, 'GM's bold bid to reinvent the wheel', *Business Week*, January 21, 1985, pp 32–3

Jesse Snyder, 'GM's visionary: Roger Smith steers drive to market-oriented future', *Advertising Age*, December 30, 1985, pp 1, 28–9

'Auto bankers: the Big Three financial giants', *Time*, May 26, 1986, p 40

Anne Fisher, 'Ford is back on the track', *Fortune*, December 23, 1985, pp 12–18

'Taurus-Sable send GM back to drawing board', *Automotive News*, December 30, 1985, pp 1–2

Russell Mitchell, 'How Ford hit the bulls-eye with the Taurus', *Business Week*, June 30, 1986, pp 47–8, and editorial: 'Ford sets an example for Detroit', p 68

'New look takes hold at No. 1', *Advertising Age*, May 16, 1983, pp 3, 56

Bob Garfield, 'Bates gives brush-up to Colgate spots', *Advertising Age*, March 3, 1986, p 64

S. Alter and N. Giges, 'P&G, Colgate strike back', *Advertising Age*, June 2, 1986, p 1, 90

Christine Dugas, 'How adversity is reshaping Madison Avenue', *Business Week*, September 15, 1986, pp 94, 98

'Marketing's new look', *Business Week*, January 26, 1987, pp 48–53

Jaclyn Fierman, 'How Coke decided a new taste was it', *Fortune*, May 27, 1985, p 54

'Old Coke is it', *Fortune*, August 5, 1985, p 6

Bill Saporito, 'IBM's no-hands assembly line', *Fortune*, September 15, 1986, pp 85–7

'John Scully: Marketing methods bring Apple back', *Advertising Age*, December 31, 1984, pp 1, 22

Carrie Dolan, 'Apple faces challenge selling new computer for home use', *The Wall Street Journal*, May 3, 1984, p 35

Bro Uttal, 'Behind the fall of Steve Jobs', *Fortune*, August 5, 1985, pp 12–16

'Shaken to the very core', *Time*, September 30, 1985, pp 62–3

'Rebuilding to survive', *Time* special report on corporate restructuring, February 16, 1987, pp 28–32

'Manufacturing is in flower', *Time*, March 26, 1984, pp 48–50

'Kroger's new items get a "placement allowance" ', *Supermarket News*, May 28, 1984, pp 1, 28. See also 'Distributor demand sharpens for new product incentives', *Supermarket News*, August 27, 1984, pp 1, 22

'Carmakers at the crossroads', *Time*, November 4, 1985, pp 36–47

'Europe hangs on', *Automotive News*, January 13, 1986, p 26

'Europe's cars are leaving Detroit in the dust', *Business Week*, April 15, 1985, pp 42–4

'Reassemble Europe's cars', *The Economist*, April 20, 1985, pp 12–13

'Managing America's Business', *The Economist*, December 22, 1984, pp 91–104

'The new corporate elite', *Business Week*, January 21, 1985, pp 58–73

'Marketing: the new priority', *Business Week*, November 21, 1983, pp 66–73

Richard Kirkland Jr, 'America on top again', *Fortune*, April 15, 1985, pp 12–17

Anne Fisher, 'GM's unlikely revolutionist', *Fortune*, March 19, 1984, pp 107–112

'Lulu is home now', *Time*, June 17, 1985, pp 42–5

## Chapter 2: references

1 'Marketing: the new priority', *Business Week*, November 21, 1983, pp 66–73

2 Philip Kotler, *Marketing Management: Analysis, Planning and Control*, 5th. ed., Prentice-Hall Inc, New Jersey, 1984, p 4

3 George S. Day and Robin Wensley, 'Marketing theory with a strategic orientation', *Journal of Marketing*, vol. 47, Fall, 1983, pp 78–89

4 William K. Hall, 'SBUs: hot new topic in the management of diversification', *Business Horizons*, February, 1978, pp 17–25

5 Bruce D. Henderson, *Henderson on Corporate Strategy*, A Mentor Book: New American Library, New York, 1979

6 R. Hayes and W. Abernathy, 'Managing our way to economic decline', *Harvard Business Review*, July–August 1980, pp 67–77

7 C. Don Burnett, Dennis P. Yeskey and David Richardson, 'New roles for corporate planners in the 1980s', *The Journal of Business Strategy*, vol. 4, no. 4, Spring 1984, pp 64–8

8 Robin Wensley, 'Strategic marketing: betas, boxes, or basics', *Journal of Marketing*, vol. 45, Summer 1981, pp 173–182

9 Kenichi Ohmae, *The Mind of the Strategist*, McGraw-Hill Inc., New York, 1982

10 Lee Iacocca, *Iacocca: an Autobiography*, Bantam Books Inc., New York, 1984

11 Thomas J. Peters and Robert H. Waterman Jr, *In Search of Excellence*, Warner Books Inc., New York, 1982

12 Thomas Bonoma, 'Making your marketing strategy work', *Harvard Business Review*, March–April 1984, pp 69–76
13 Tom Peters and Nancy Austin, *A Passion for Excellence*, Collins, London, 1985
14 Milton Lauenstein, 'The strategy audit', *The Journal of Business Strategy*, vol. 4, no. 3, Winter 1984, pp 87–91

## Other references

Robert Heller, 'The five-point fightback strategy', *Marketing*, October 18, 1984, p 7

'Pepsi's marketing magic: why nobody does it better', *Business Week*, February 10, 1986, pp 54–7

Walter Kiechel III, 'Oh where, oh where has my little dog gone? Or my cash cow? Or my star?', *Fortune*, November 2, 1981, pp 148–154

'Picking the winners', *The Financial Times*, January 6, 1976

'The opposites: GE grows while Westinghouse shrinks', *Business Week*, January 31, 1977, pp 60–66

'Wanted: a manager to fit each strategy', *Business Week*, February 25, 1980, pp 166, 168, 173

'General Electric: the financial wizards switch back to technology', *Business Week*, March 16, 1981, pp 74–9

Walter Kiechel III, 'Corporate strategists under fire', *Fortune*, December 27, 1982, pp 34–9

'The new breed of strategic planner', *Business Week*, September 17, 1984, pp 52–7

'The new planning', *Business Week*, December 18, 1978, pp 62–8

'Now that it's cruising, can Ford keep its foot on the gas?', *Business Week*, February 11, 1985, pp 42–4

Robert L. Shook, collaborator, *The IBM Way*, 'Readers Report', *Business Week*, February 10, 1986, p 5

Erwin Okun, Walt Disney Productions, 'Readers Report', *Business Week*, February 17, 1986, p 5

'ITT's personal computer may be too little, too late', *Business Week*, October 22, 1984, p 55

Linda Daly, 'Coaching helps revitalize distribution system', *Marketing News*, April 11, 1986, p 6

## Chapter 3: references

1 Robert Heller, *The Naked Market*, Sidgwick & Jackson, London, 1984

## Other references

'Carmakers at the crossroads', *Time*, November 4, 1985, pp 36–47

'The big peep', *The Economist*, February 1, 1986, pp 64–5

'Procter takes aggressive stance', *Globe and Mail*, July 4, 1984, p B7

'Soft drink wars: the next battle', *Fortune*, June 24, 1985, pp 52–4

'Pepsi's marketing magic: why nobody does it better', *Business Week*, February 10, 1986, pp 54–7

'America's most wanted managers', *Fortune*, February 3, 1986, pp 26–33

'Look who's vexing the real thing now', *Maclean's*, March 9, 1981, pp 57–9

'Coke strikes back', *Fortune*, June 1, 1981, pp 30–36

'Fiddling with the real thing', *Time*, May 6, 1985, pp 44–6

'Coke's brand loyalty lemon', *Fortune*, August 5, 1985, pp 40–42

'Products of the year', *Fortune*, December 9, 1985, pp 68–73

'Coke's switch a classic', *Advertising Age*, July 15, 1985, pp 1, 182

'Marketers find bad news does some good', *Advertising Age*, July 22, 1985, p 6

'New but not necessarily improved', *Time* essay, July 22, 1985, p 68

'IBM is homeward bound', *Time*, August 24, 1981, pp 66-7 (The President's name was A.C. Markkula)

'Using yesterday to sell tomorrow', *Advertising Age*, April 11, 1983, pp M-4, M-5, M-48

'IBM joins the race in personal computers', *Business Week*, August 24, 1981, pp 24-5

'The coming shakedown in personal computers', *Business Week*, November 22, 1982, pp 72-83

'Personal computers: and the winner is IBM', *Business Week*, October 3, 1983, pp 38-45

'At home with IBM', *Maclean's*, November 14, 1983, pp 40-45

'Meet the lean, mean new IBM', *Fortune*, June 13, 1983, pp 68-82

'How IBM made "Junior" an underachiever', *Business Week*, June 25, 1984, pp 106-7

'The change in marketing style at a chastened IBM', *Business Week*, August 27, 1984, p 22

'Risc strategy', *The Economist*, January 25, 1986, pp 64-5

'The workstation sweepstake: it's IBM coming up on the outside', *Business Week*, February 3, 1986, pp 56-7

'Now Big Blue is making waves in shallower water', *Business Week*, September 30, 1985, pp 61-2

'Is IBM playing too tough?', *Fortune*, December 10, 1984, pp 82-5

'Cut-rate computers, get 'em here', *Time*, July 21, 1986, p 54

'The PC wars: IBM vs the clones', *Business Week* cover story, July 28, 1986, pp 48-54

Carol Loomis, 'IBM's big blues: a legend tries to remake itself', *Fortune*, January 19, 1987, pp 34-41

Bill Saporito, 'IBM's no-hands assembly line', *Fortune*, September 15, 1986, pp 85-7

## Chapter 4: references

1 Keith K. Cox, 'Marketing in the 1980s – back to basics', *Business Horizons*, May–June, 1980, pp 19–23

2 Benson P Shapiro, 'Making money through marketing', *Harvard Business Review*, July–August, 1979, pp 136–142

3 Benson P. Shapiro, 'Rejuvenating the marketing mix', *Harvard Business Review*, September–October, 1985, pp 28–34

4 Theodore Levitt, 'Marketing success through differentiation – of anything', *Harvard Business Review*, January–February, 1980, pp 83–91

5 Thomas Bonoma, 'Making your marketing strategy work', *Harvard Business Review*, March–April, 1984, pp 69–76

## *Other references*

'It's Coke vs Pepsi – again', *Business Week*, August 2, 1982, pp 48–49

Walter Kiechel III, 'Corporate strategists under fire', *Fortune*, December 27, 1982, pp 34–9

'Washday blues', *Time*, August 19, 1985, p 48

'Wounded lion? Trail of mistakes mars P&G record', *Advertising Age*, July 21, 1985, pp 1, 50–51

Faye Rice, 'Trouble at Procter & Gamble', *Fortune*, March 5, 1984, p 70

'Why Procter & Gamble is playing it even tougher', *Business Week*, July 18, 1983, pp 134–7

Bill Saporito, 'Procter & Gamble's comeback plan', *Fortune*, February 4, 1985, pp 24–8

'P&G's rusty marketing machine', *Business Week*, October 21, 1985, pp 78, 80

Carol Loomis, 'P&G up against the wall', *Fortune*, February 23, 1981, pp 48–54

'P&G acts fast on pain reliever', *Advertising Age*, May 10, 1984, pp 1, 5

'P&G fills its medicine chest', *Fortune*, December 9, 1985, p 17

'A bite at the biscuit', *Marketing*, October 18, 1984, pp 32–6

'Procter takes aggressive stance', *The Globe and Mail*, July 4, 1984, p B7

Faye Rice, 'The king of suds reigns again', *Fortune*, August 4, 1986, pp 130–132

'Procter & Gamble banks on a new baby: Ultra Pampers', *Business Week*, February 24, 1986, pp 36–7

'P&G's brands shift gear', *Advertising Age*, October 1, 1984, pp 1, 85

L Freeman & J Pendleton, 'P&G takes lead with high-tech detergent', *Advertising Age*, April 14, 1986, pp 3, 115

Laurie Freeman, 'P&G back on track as earnings rocket', *Advertising Age*, July 14, 1986, pp 3, 77

'Testing time for test marketing', *Fortune*, October 29, 1984, pp 57–8

'New look takes hold at No. 1', *Advertising Age*, May 16, 1983, pp 3, 56

'P&G cuts new media pie', *Advertising Age*, December 3, 1984, pp 1, 92

'America's most admired corporations', *Fortune*, January 6, 1986, pp 32–43

# Chapter 5: references

1 Lee Iacocca, *Iacocca: an Autobiography*, Bantam Books Inc., New York, 1984, p 328
2 Edward Warren, 'The interface between R&D, marketing, and marketing research in new product development', *The Journal of Consumer Marketing*, vol. 1, 1983, pp 80–90
3 John Rockwell and Marc Particelli, 'New product strategy: how the pros do it', *Industrial Marketing*, May, 1982, pp 49–60
4 William Sommers, 'Product development: new approaches in the 1980s', in: M Tushman and W Moore, *Readings in the Management of Innovation*, Pitman, 1982, p 59, and originally in: *Product Development: New Approaches in the 1980s*, Booz, Allen & Hamilton Inc., 1979

5 Peter Riesz, 'Revenge of the marketing concept', *Business Horizons*, June, 1980, pp 49–53

6 Edward Tauber, 'How market research discourages major innovation', *Business Horizons*, June, 1979, pp 22–6. See also: 'Market researchers: investigate why new products succeed, not why they fail', in *Marketing News*, September 18, 1981, p 13

7 Roger Bennett and Robert Cooper, 'The misuse of marketing: an American tragedy', *Business Horizons*, November-December, 1981, pp 51–60

8 Daniel Roos and Alan Altshuler, co-directors, *The Future of the Automobile: The report of MIT's international automobile program*, George Allen & Unwin Ltd., London, 1984

9 Robert Heller, *The Naked Market*, Sidgwick & Jackson, London, 1984, p 49

10 James Quinn, 'Managing innovation: controlled chaos', *Harvard Business Review*, May-June, 1985, pp 73–84

11 Roland Schmitt, 'Successful corporate R&D', *Harvard Business Review*, May-June, 1985, pp 124–8

12 William Shanklin and John Ryans Jr, 'Organizing for high-tech marketing', *Harvard Business Review*, November-December, 1984, pp 164–171

13 Harry Gray, 'Research and manufacturing should be partners', *Research Management*, November-December, 1985, pp 6–8

## Other references

'Detroit's uphill battle', *Time*, September 8, 1980, pp 56–62

'Listening to the voice of the market place', *Business Week*, February 21, 1983, pp 58–9

'Marketing: the new priority', *Business Week*, November 21, 1983, pp 66–73

Anne Fisher, 'Courting the well-heeled car shopper', *Fortune*, August 5, 1985, pp 46–52

'US autos: losing a big segment of the market – forever', *Business Week*, March 24, 1980, pp 78–88

'Ford shortens new-product cycle', *Automotive News*, June 3, 1985, p. 20

Russell Mitchell, 'How Ford hit the bull's-eye with Taurus', *Business Week*, June 30, 1986, pp 47–8

'Detroit's new sales pitch', *Business Week*, September 22, 1980, pp 78–88

'The downsizing of Detroit', *The Economist*, August 15, 1981, pp 70–71

'GM's luxury cars: why they're not selling', *Business Week*, January 19, 1987, pp 58–9

Charles Burck, 'Will success spoil General Motors?', *Fortune*, August 22, 1983, pp 94–104

'GM moves into a new era', *Business Week*, July 16, 1984, pp 70–75

'Mr Smith shakes up Detroit', *Time*, January 16, 1984, p 53

Charles Burck, 'A comeback decade for the American car', *Fortune*, June 2, 1980, pp 52–65

'Can GM solve its identity crisis?', *Business Week*, January 23, 1984, pp 32–3

'General Motors: survival of the fattest', *The Economist*, October 12, 1985, pp 45–8

'Buick eyes '88 for "distinction"', *Automotive News*, December 23, 1985, p 25

Anne Fisher, 'GM's unlikely revolutionist', *Fortune*, March 19, 1984, pp 107–112

Charles Burck, 'How GM stays ahead', *Fortune*, March 9, 1981, pp 48–56

Michael Brody, 'Can GM manage it all?' *Fortune*, July 8, 1985, pp 14–20

David Whiteside, 'Roger Smith's campaign to change the GM culture', *Business Week*, April 7, 1986, pp 54–5

'GM picks the winner', *Time*, August 5, 1985 (pages not numbered)

William Hampton, 'Downsizing Detroit: the big three's strategy for survival', *Business Week*, April 14, 1986, pp 56–8

'Ross Perot's crusade', *Business Week*, October 6, 1986, pp 58–63

'GM hasn't bought much peace', *Business Week*, December 15, 1986, pp 22–4. See also editorial: 'Paying "hush mail" won't cure GM's ills', p 72

'Peace for a price at GM', *Time*, December 15, 1986, pp 38–40

'GM's visionary: Roger Smith steers drive to market-oriented future', *Advertising Age*, December 30, 1985, p 1, 28–9

Steven Flax, 'Can Chrysler keep rolling along?', *Fortune*, January 7, 1985, pp 44–9

Susan Fraker, 'High-speed management for the high-tech age', *Fortune*, March 5, 1984, pp 62–8

'The Honda way', *Time*, September 8, 1986, pp 66–72

'Max troubles for Betamax', *Time*, January 16, 1984, p 54

A. Beam & O. Port, 'The filmless camera is here, but will it sell?', *Business Week*, April 15, 1985, pp 79–80

Otis Port, 'Filmless cameras: pictures on a floppy disk', *Business Week*, June 30, 1986, pp 48–9. See also 'A threat to the darkroom', *Time*, June 30, 1986, p 42

'The economy of the 1990s', *Fortune* special report, February 2, 1987, pp 16–53

Jeremy Main, 'Detroit's cars really are getting better', *Fortune*, February 2, 1987, pp 74–82

Penny Sparke, 'In the land of the pink microwave', *Design*, July, 1984, pp 48–9

'Car-makers out to catch the Europeans', *The Bulletin*, January 14, 1986, pp 76–8

'A look into the crystal ball', *Time*, November 11, 1985, p 70

## Chapter 6: references

1  John Schwarz and Thomas Volgy, 'The myth of America's decline', *Harvard Business Review*, September-October, 1985, pp 98–107
2  Robert Lawrence, *Can America compete?*, The Bookings Institute, Washington, D.C., 1984, p 7

## Other references

Richard Kirkland Jr, 'America on top again', *Fortune*, April 15, 1985, pp 13–17

'Now, R&D is corporate America's answer to Japan Inc.', *Business Week*, June 23, 1986, pp 78–82

'Where the big research money will come from in 1986', *Business Week*, January 13, 1986, p 91

'America can beat anyone in high tech. Just ask Bruce Merrifield', *Business Week*, April 7, 1986, pp 44–5. See also: 'A fuzzy picture of the economy', *Business Week*, April 14, 1986, p 92

'America manufactures still', *The Economist*, April 19, 1986, p 81. See also: 'A puzzingly poorly productive America', *The Economist*, March 29, 1986, p 53

'Are America's manufacturers finally back on the map?', *Business Week*, November 17, 1986, pp 58–9

Jeremy Main, 'Detroit's cars really are getting better', *Fortune*, February, 1987, pp 74–82

'Fighting back: it can work', *Business Week*, August 26, 1985, pp 42–8. See also: 'Winners against tough odds', *Time*, December 9, 1985, p 41

'The titans of high technology: Japan and America', *The Economist*, August 23, 1986, special survey section, pp 1–20

Charles Burck, 'How GM stays ahead', *Fortune*, March 9, 1981, pp 48–56

'Detroit's merry-go-round', *Business Week*, September 12, 1983, pp 70–75

'How GM's Saturn could run rings around old-style carmakers', *Business Week*, January 28, 1985, pp 43, 46

'GM's bold bid to reinvent the wheel', *Business Week*, January 21, 1985, pp 32–3

'Saturnalia', *The Economist*, January 12, 1985, p 50

Gene Bylinsky, 'The race to the automatic factory', *Fortune*, February 21, 1983, pp 52–64

Gene Bylinsky, 'A new industrial revolution is on the way', *Fortune*, October 5, 1981, pp 106–114

'What comes after quality circles?', *The Economist*, July 6, 1985, pp 62–3

P. Bolwijn and T. Kumpe, 'Toward the factory of the future', *The McKinsey Quarterly*, Spring 1986, pp 40–49

'The fully automated factory rewards an early dreamer', *Business Week*, March 17, 1986, p 77

Toyo Kogyo Co., Ltd (now Mazda) Annual Report 1982. Plus other *Mazda Marketing News* reports published by the company

'The Honda way', *Time*. September 8, 1986, pp 66–72

Walter McQuade, 'The shape of cars to come', *Fortune*, May 17, 1982, pp 68–78

Nicola Crea, 'Styling and design', *Auto & Design*, October, 1985, pp 11–12

Susan Fraker, 'High-speed management for the high-tech age', *Fortune*, March 5, 1984, pp 62–8

Peter Nulty, 'Ford's fragile recovery', *Fortune*, April, 2, 1984, pp 42–8

Anne Fisher, 'Behind the hype at GM's Saturn', *Fortune*, November 11, 1985, pp 34–42. See also: 'GM's bold bid to reinvent the wheel', *Business Week*, January 21, 1985, pp 32–3

William Hampton, 'Reality has hit General Motors – hard', *Business Week*, November 24, 1986, p 35

'What Mr Fiat learned', *The Economist*, August 30, 1986, pp 9–10; plus 'Agnelli and Fiat: dove va il Numero Uno?', pp 54–6

Gene Bylinsky, 'GM's road map to automated plants', *Fortune*, October 28, 1985, pp 73–8

'General Motors – the Toyota touch', *The Economist*, December 13, 1986, pp 70–71

David Whiteside, 'Roger Smith's campaign to change GM's culture', *Business Week*, April 7, 1986, pp 54–5

'The sweet colors of success', *Time*, January 13, 1986, p 39

'How high-tech tailors are saving a stitch in time', *Business Week*, April 14, 1986, p 83

'Manufacturing is in flower', *Time*, March 26, 1984, pp 48–50

## Chapter 7: references

1 Theodore Levitt, *The Marketing Imagination*, The Free Press, New York, 1983
2 Lee Iacocca, *Iacocca: an Autobiography*, Bantam Books Inc., New York, 1984
3 William Sommers, 'Product development: new approaches in the 1980s', in M Tushman and W Moore, *Readings in the Management of Innovation*, Pitman, New York, 1982; originally in *Product Development: New Approaches in the 1980s*, Booz, Allen & Hamilton Inc., 1979

## *Other references*

'Detroit's merry-go-round', *Business Week*, September 12, 1983, pp 70–75

'Corporate odd couples: beware the wrong partner', *Business Week*, July 21, 1986, pp 98–103

'Drastic new strategies to keep US multinationals competitive', *Business Week*, October 8, 1984, pp 96–9

'The hollow corporation', special report, *Business Week*, March 3, 1986, pp 52–92

'Downsizing Detroit: the big three's strategy for survival', *Business Week*, April 14, 1986, pp 56–8

'US auto makers reshape for world competition', *Business Week*, June 2, 1982, pp 58–63

'Autos: distress that won't go away', *Business Week*, January 12, 1981, pp 38–9

'GM moves into a new era', *Business Week*, July 16, 1984, pp 70–75

'America's car makers: labour's love regained', *The Economist*, July 7, 1984, pp 69–70

Peter Nulty, 'Ford's fragile recovery', *Fortune*, April 2, 1984, pp 42–8

'The vanishing all-American small car', *Business Week*, March 12, 1984, pp 88–95, 142

'Ford's better idea south of the border', *Business Week*, January 23, 1984, pp 26–8

'Asian car makers: the sun also sets', *The Economist*, May 24, 1986, pp 66–7

'How the GM-Toyota deal buys time', *Business Week*, February 28, 1983, pp 22–3

'Green light: the GM Toyota deal rolls on', *Time*, January 2, 1984, p 49

'Ford thinks Japanese', *Road & Track*, July 1986, pp 110–11

Charles Burck, 'Will success spoil General Motors?', *Fortune*, August 22, 1983, pp 94–104

'GM buys Lotus', *Fortune*, February 17, 1986, p 6

'Mixed welcome in Lotus land', *Time*, April 7, 1986, p 35

'A passion for Italian bodies', *Time*, September 15, 1986, p 56

'Europe hangs on', *Automotive News*, January 13, 1986, p 23

'Motoring into the 80s', *The Economist*, special survey, March 16, 1979, pp 1–32

'Reassemble Europe's cars', *The Economist*, April 20, 1985, pp 12–13

'BL's rejected suitors', *The Economist*, March 29, 1986, pp 16–17

'Reshaping the computer industry', *Business Week*, July 16, 1984, pp 48–68

'A threatening telephone call from the computer company', *The Economist*, June 29, 1985, pp 61–2

Gene Bylinsky, 'A breakthrough in automating the assembly line', *Fortune*, May 26, 1986, pp 60–62

# Chapter 8: references

1 Angela Rushton, 'The balance of power in a marketing channel', in E.S.O.M.A.R. conference on: 'Profitable cooperation of manufacturers and retailers', published by E.S.O.M.A.R., Amsterdam, 1982, pp 17–38

2 W.B. Roome, 'Distribution channels: a behavioural view', *Insight: Journal of the Institute of Marketing Management*, 3(10), 1978, pp 22–5

3 D. Schultz and R. Dewar, 'Retailers in control: the impact of retail trade concentration', *The Journal of Consumer Marketing*, vol. 1, no. 2, 1983, pp 81–9

4 Jack Kaikati, 'Don't discount off-price retailers', *Harvard Business Review*, May–June, 1985, pp 85–92

5 Leonard Berry, 'Retail positioning strategies for the 1980s', *Business Horizons*, November–December, 1982, pp 45–50

6 J.N. Goodrich and J.A. Hoffman, 'Warehouse retailing: the trend of the future?', *Business Horizons*, April 1979, pp 45–50

7 Arthur Lawrence, *The Management of Trade Marketing*, Gower, UK, 1983

8 F. Kent Mitchel, 'Advertising/promotion budgets: how did we get here, and what do we do now?', *The Journal of Consumer Marketing*, vol. 2, no. 4, Fall 1985, pp 45–7

9 P. Foy and D. Pommerening, 'Brand marketing: fresh thinking needed', *The McKinsey Quarterly*, Spring 1979, pp 49–58

## Other references

'Is this America's most efficient supermarket?' *Progressive Grocer*, March 1986, pp 109–116

Aimée Stern, 'Retailers restructure', *Dun's Business Month*, February, 1986, pp 28–32

Julie Erickson, 'Grocery marketing: supermarket chains work to fill tall order', *Advertising Age* special report, April 28, 1986, pp S-1 – S-35

'53rd annual report of the grocery industry', *Progressive Grocer*, April, 1986

'The 5 best-managed companies', *Dun's Business Month*, December, 1985, pp 31–43

Anthony Ramirez, 'Can anyone compete with Toys 'R' Us?' *Fortune*, October 28, 1985, pp 67–71

'Levitz Furniture: sitting pretty as it waits for the recovery', *Business Week*, February 7, 1983, p 66

Alan Radding, 'Superstores, discounters lead retail revolution', *Advertising Age*, January 9, 1986, p 15

'Electronics superstores are devouring their rivals', *Business Week*, June 24, 1985, pp 40–41

'Burned by superstores, Tandy is fighting fire with fire', *Business Week*, October 28, 1985, pp 54–5

'The coming shakeout in personal computers', *Business Week*, November 22, 1982, pp 72–83

'The chains take over computer retailing', *Business Week*, December 7, 1983, pp 70–83

Joel Dreyfus, 'More power to the PC chains', *Fortune*, May 14, 1984, pp 83–8

'Sales are up – but dealers are shutting down', *Business Week*, January 13, 1986, pp 20–21

Geoff Lewis, 'Personal computers: just another commodity', *Business Week*, March 10, 1986, p 57

Kevin Higgins, 'Computer industry adopts leaner, market-driven distribution system', *Marketing News*, April 11, 1986, pp 5, 12

'The computer slump', *Business Week* cover story, June 24, 1985, pp 50–56

'How to sell computers today – and how not to', *Business Week*, September 2, 1985, pp 61–2

'Car dealers: trading-in the old way', *The Economist*, October 25, 1985, pp 65–6

'Car makers try the soft sell approach', *Fortune*, May 12, 1986, p 57

'Dealers: kicking carmakers' tires', *Business Week*, June 2, 1986, p 86

William Hampton, 'American super-dealers are moving into the fast lane', *Business Week*, June 16, 1986, pp 66-9

'A Giant among combos', *Progressive Grocer*, January, 1986, p 58

Bill Saporito, 'The Giant of the regional food chains', *Fortune*, November 25, 1985, pp 27-32

Julie Franz, 'Test marketing: travelling through a maze of choices', *Advertising Age* special report, February 13, 1986, pp 11-35

'Firm: consumers cool to new products', *Marketing News*, January 3, 1986, pp 1, 45

'It's Coke vs Pepsi - again', *Business Week*, August 2, 1982, pp 48-9

'New items costly to grocery chains', *The Globe and Mail*, May 30, 1984, p B8

'In-store purchase decisions growing', *Marketing News*, September 26, 1986, p 10

Richard Edel, 'Trade wars threaten future peace of marketers', *Advertising Age*, August 15, 1985, pp 18, 20

Richard Edel, 'Trade price discounts holding hostage', *Advertising Age*, February 6, 1986, pp 18, 20, 22

Felix Kessler, 'The costly coupon craze', *Fortune*, June 9, 1986, pp 65, 66

Graham Phillips, Chairman, Ogilvy & Mather, US 'Marketing in the new world of scanners', reported in O&M's in-house journal *Viewpoint*, May/June, 1986, pp 2-5

Paul Edwards, 'Sales promotion comes into its own', *Advertising Age*, July 28, 1986, p 65

B. Mitchell, 'Communicate to become retail smart', *Rydges*, October 1985, pp 22-3

Arthur Bragg, 'National account managers to the rescue', *Sales & Marketing Managment*, August 16, 1982, pp 30-34

Bill Saporito, 'Procter & Gamble's comeback plan', *Fortune*, February 4,1985, pp 24-8

Gary Geipel, 'At today's supermarket, the computer is doing it all', *Business Week*, August 11, 1986, pp 54-5

## Chapter 9: references

1 Rena Bartos, 'The facts of life: The changing consumer market-place', E.S.O.M.A.R. Conference on: 'Marketing, Advertising and Research: are there east and west?', Tokyo, Japan, 30 June–2 July, 1986, conference readings pp 245–67
2 Ronald Michman, 'The male queue at the checkout counter', *Business Horizons*, May–June, 1986, pp 51–5
3 Leo Bogart, 'What forces shape the future of advertising research?', *Journal of Advertising Research*, Feb/Mar, 1986, pp 99–104
4 William McKenna, 'In home electronic measurement of consumer behavior – the new research frontier', E.S.O.M.A.R. conference proceedings, Tokyo, 1986, pp 301–319
5 Gerald Eskin, 'Electronic single source measurement of media exposure and buying', E.S.O.M.A.R. conference, Tokyo, 1986, separate paper presented, pp 1–27
6 Laurence Gold, 'Future information technology', E.S.O.M.A.R. conference proceedings, Tokyo, 1986, pp 321–35

## *Other references*

'Marketing: the new priority', *Business Week*, November 21, 1983, pp 66–73

'Marketers zero-in on demographics', *Dun's Business Month*, October 1984, p 60

Bruce Steinberg, 'The mass market is splitting apart', *Fortune*, November 28, 1983, pp 76–82

'Snapshot of a changing America', *Time*, September 2, 1985, pp 22–4

'53rd Annual Report of the grocery industry', *Progressive Grocer*, April, 1986

Priscilla Donegan, 'The myth of the male shopper', *Progressive Grocer*, May 1986, pp 36–42

'Insurer markets to Hispanics with Spanish sales promotion materials, services, and ads', *Marketing News*, December 21, 1984, p 10

'Asian-Americans targeted by insurance firm', *Marketing News*, April 11, 1986, p 24

Anne Fisher, 'Courting the well-heeled car shopper', *Fortune*, August 5, 1985, pp 46–52

Joanne Cleaver, 'Affluent marketing: fragmentation enriches problems in reaching group', *Advertising Age*, Special Report, March 13, 1986, pp 11–23

Anthony Ramirez, 'The decline of first class', *Fortune*, May 26, 1986, p 35

Amy Dunkin, 'How cosmetics makers are touching up their strategies', *Business Week*, September 23, 1985, pp 62–4

Edward Baig, 'Low-budget banking', *Fortune*, November 25, 1985, pp 55–6

Robert Levy, 'High-times for a low-end retailer', *Dun's Business Month*, March, 1985, pp 56–8

Aimée Stern, 'Companies target big-spending teens', *Dun's Business Month*, March 1985, pp 48–50

'Marketers should target the 51st state: the college market', *Marketing News*, February 28, 1986, p 28

Raymond Serafin, 'Pontiac's ad efforts sport collegiate look for spring', *Advertising Age*, March 31, 1986, p 80

Patricia Winters, 'Prince tries pasta for gourmet market; a product for 'aspiring yuppies''', *Advertising Age*, February 24, 1986, p 80

Geoffrey Colvin, 'What the baby-boomers will buy next', *Fortune*, October 15, 1984, pp 18–24

'The upwardly mobile downhill slide', *Time*, January 23, 1984, p 39

Richard Phalon, 'Out of breath', *Forbes*, October 22, 1984, pp 39–40

John Rossant and Pamela Ellis-Simons, 'Yuppies uncork a boom in fine French wine', *Business Week*, May 20, 1985, pp 42–4

Jack Kelderman, 'Financial woes for baby boomers', *Automotive News*, December 30, 1985, p 11

'Growing pains at 40', *Time*, May 19, pp 34–42

'Sun, fun and sales meetings', *Time*, July 14, 1986, p 43

Peter Petre, 'Marketers mine for gold in the old', *Fortune*, March 31, 1986, pp 48–54

Joan Berger, 'The new old: where the economic action is', *Business Week*, November 25, 1985, pp 50–54

Margaret Mironowicz, 'Wild to see the world', *The Globe and Mail*, May 18, 1984, p 19

Verne Gay and Paul Edwards, 'Chevy woos women', *Advertising Age*, September 9, 1985, pp 1, 130

'The lather wars have shampoo makers hunting for niches', *Business Week*, January 9, 1984, p 124

Brian Lowry, 'Nike pushes upscale women's wear', *Advertising Age*, January 27, 1986, p 6

Jaclyn Fierman, 'High-fashion names knock themselves off', *Fortune*, June 10, 1985, p 45

'TV: networks fighting changes in viewership', *Advertising Age*, November 29, 1984, p 14

Richard Edel, 'Advertisers switch buying functions', *Advertising Age*, November 21, 1985, pp 43–44

Aimée Stern, 'Test marketing enters a new era', *Dun's Business Month*, 1985, pp 86–90

Barbara Buell, 'Big brother gets a job in market research', *Business Week*, April 8, 1985, pp 48–9

'ARF panel projects future role of media research', *Advertising Age*, March 24, 1986, p 114

Felix Kessler, 'High-tech shocks in ad research', *Fortune*, July 7, 1986, pp 38–40

Jack Honomichl, 'Tracking Nielsen's ERIM development', *Advertising Age*, November 14, 1985, pp 16, 17, 39–41

Christine Dugas, 'A harder sell for Madison Avenue', *Business Week*, August 26, 1985, pp 18–19

Verne Gay, 'P&G cuts new media pie', *Advertising Age*, December 3, 1984, pp 1, 92

'New? Improved? The brand name merger', *Business Week*, October 21, 1985, pp 74–76

'Advertising's bigger than ever', *The Economist*, March 9, 1985, pp 78–9

'Marketing's new look', *Business Week*, January 26, 1987, pp 48–53. See also: Thomas Moore, 'Different Folks, different strokes', *Fortune*, September 16, 1985, pp 61–62

'Ads in year 2000: agency executives forecast their appearance and delivery', *Marketing News*, December 21, 1984, pp 1, 10

## Chapter 10: references

1 Thomas Bonoma, *The Marketing Edge*, The Free Press, New York, 1985
2 R.C. Bennett and R.G. Cooper, 'The misuse of marketing: an American tragedy', *Business Horizons*, November–December, 1981, pp 51–60
3 D. Schultz and R. Dewar, 'Retailers in control: the impact of retail trade concentration', *Journal of Consumer Marketing*, vol. 1, no. 2, 1983, pp 81–9
4 Tom Peters and Nancy Austin, *A Passion for Excellence*, Collins, London, 1985
5 Theodore Levitt, *The Marketing Imagination*, The Free Press, New York, 1983
6 Sir Michael Edwardes, *Back from the Brink*, Collins, London, 1983

*Other references*

'Marketing: the new priority', *Business Week*, November 21, 1983, pp 66–73

'Promotion aimed at upscale targets is long-term task', *Marketing News*, June 6, 1986, p 27

Barry Feig, 'Products need share of heart', *Advertising Age*, January 27, 1986, pp 18, 20

Rena Bartos, 'Marketers must cater to women's independence', *Marketing News*, June 6, 1986, p 14

Anthony Curtis, 'The man who made it happen', *Motor*, June 2, 1983, pp 41, 43

'An industrial invalid revives', *Time*, February 6, 1984

David Fairlamb, 'Comeback of a class car', *Dun's Business Month*, November, 1985, pp 64–6

'It's a fresh start for Europe', *Business Week*, February 17, 1986, pp 18–27

Michael Dale, 'How we rebuilt Jaguar in the US', *Fortune*, April 28, 1986, pp 90–94

Maggie McComas, 'Cutting costs without killing the business', *Fortune*, October 13, 1986, pp 68–76

Peter Dron, 'Jaguar USA: gloom to glory', *Motor*, June 2, 1983, pp 56–7

'Jaguar: success by evolution', *NZ Motor World*, August/September, 1986, pp 59–60

'A big leap for Jaguar', *The Economist*, October 11, 1986, pp 64–5

P. Dormer and J. Thackara, 'Design and the age of quality', *Design*, July, 1984, pp 32–5

'Will you go Yugo for only $3,990?', *Dun's Business Month*, December, 1985, p 49

'Warning: without quality, Yugo down', *Advertising Age*, May 19, 1986, p 8

'Seven wary views from the top', *Fortune*, February 2, 1987, pp 48–53, and Peter Nulty, 'How managers will survive', pp 39–41, both in *Fortune* special report. 'The Economy in the 1990s', pp 16–53

## Chapter 11: References

1. Thomas Bonoma, *The Marketing Edge*, The Free Press, New York, 1985
2 Theodore Levitt, *The Marketing Imagination*, The Free Press, New York, 1983

3 Barbara Jackson, 'Build customer relationships that last', *Harvard Business Review*, November–December, 1985, pp 120–128
4 M. Lele and U. Karmarker, 'Good product support is good marketing', *Harvard Business Review*, November–December, 1983, pp 124–132

## Other references

'There are two kinds of supermarkets: the quick and the dead', *Business Week*, August 11, 1986, pp 52–3

Jaclyn Fierman, 'How Gallo crushes the competition', *Fortune*, September 1 1986, pp 26–33

'Curcio: a new age of innovation', *Dun's Business Month*, November, 1985, pp 53–4

'Pul-eeze! Will somebody help me?', *Time* cover story, February 2, 1987, pp 42–51

'Making service a potent marketing tool', *Business Week*, June 11, 1984, pp 164–170

Carol Loomis 'IBM's big blues: a legend tries to remake itself', *Fortune*, January 19, 1987, pp 34–41

'Fort Howard: new marketing muscle from Maryland Cup', *Business Week*, July 18, 1983, p 118

'Maryland Cup sells more than just paper cups', *Business Week*, June 26, 1978, pp 104: B-1, G-1

Peter Petre, 'How to keep customers happy customers', *Fortune*, September 2, 1985, pp 42–8

John Stackhouse, 'Micro giant joins hunt for the best office team', *The Bulletin*, April 22, 1986, pp 50, 52

'Compaq expanding', *The Economist*, April 27, 1985, pp 80, 83

Jo Ellen Davis, 'Will Compaq be dethroned as king of the compatibles?', *Business Week*, July 28, 1986, p 53

Brian O'Reilly, 'Compaq's grip on IBM's slippery tail', *Fortune*, February 18, 1985, pp 44–48

Mark Ivy, 'Compaq must try harder to stay No. 2', *Business Week*, May 13, 1985, pp 56–7

'Now the battling airlines try mass marketing', *Business Week*, April 28, 1980, p 104

Peter Nulty, 'A champ of cheap airlines', *Fortune*, March 22, 1982, pp 127–134

'Fare games: flying has never been cheaper', *Time* cover story, January 13, 1986, pp 30–38

George Russell, 'Air pocket in the revolution', *Time*, July 7, 1986, pp 42–44

'The fall of People and the rise of the oligarchs', *The Economist*, June 28, 1986, pp 63–64

'Hard times for the people at People', *Fortune*, August 4, 1986, pp 10–11

'Unfriendly skies', *Time*, September 1, 1986, pp 24–5

Jeremy Main, 'The US air travel mess', July 7, 1986, pp 32–7

## Conclusion: references

'Apple computer: machinations', *The Economist*, March 17, 1987, pp 72–4

Verne Gay, 'P&G made record cuts in prime-time spending', *Advertising Age*, February 23, 1987, pp 3, 92

Nancy Giges, 'Coke's NBC buy launches brand's "new feeling" ads', *Advertising Age*, March 2, 1987, pp 2, 70

'And now for Chrysler's next big turnaround...', *Business Week*, March 23, 1987, pp 30–31. See also: Raymond Sorafin, 'Global route: AMC buy puts Chrysler on road again to Europe', *Advertising Age*, March 16, 1987, pp 3, 86; 'American Motors: "Jeep, Jeep"', *The Economist*, March 14, 1987, pp 68–9; Brian Moynahan, 'Iacocca zooms into overdrive', *The Sunday Times*, March 15, 1987, p 73

'General Motors: what went wrong', *Business Week*, March 16, 1987, pp 45–51

Bro Uttal, 'Speeding new items to market', *Fortune*, March 2, 1987, pp 54–7

# Index